Critical Studies Series

NINETEENTH-CENTURY AMERICAN POETRY

NINETEENTH-CENTURY AMERICAN POETRY

edited by
A. Robert Lee

VISION
and
BARNES & NOBLE

Vision Press Limited
Fulham Wharf
Townmead Road
London SW6 2SB

and

Barnes & Noble Books
81 Adams Drive
Totowa, NJ 07512

ISBN (UK) 0 85478 375 X
ISBN (US) 0 389 20377 7

Printed and bound in Great Britain by
Unwin Brothers Ltd.,
Old Woking, Surrey.
Phototypeset by Galleon Photosetting,
Ipswich, Suffolk.
MCMLXXXV

Contents

Introduction

by A. ROBERT LEE

It seems a matter of indifference what, & how, & how much, you write, if you write poetry. Poetry makes its own pertinence and a single stanza outweighs a book of prose. One stanza is complete. But one sentence of prose is not.
—Ralph Waldo Emerson, *Journal*, 28 November 1839

I heard that you ask'd for something to prove this puzzle
    the New World,
And to define America, her athletic Democracy,
Therefore I send you my poems that you may behold in
    them what you wanted.
               —Walt Whitman, 'To Foreign Lands'

I reckon—when I count at all—
First—Poets—Then the Sun—
Then Summer—Then the Heaven of God—
And then—the List is done—

But, looking back—the First so seems
To comprehend the Whole—
The Others look a needless Show—
So I write—Poets—All—

Their Summer—last a Solid Year—
They can afford a Sun
The East—would deem extravagant—
And if the Further Heaven—

Be Beautiful as they prepare
For Those who worship Them—
It is too difficult a Grace—
To justify the Dream—

               —Emily Dickinson

'Poetry makes its own pertinence'—like all good aphorists Emerson distils and makes strikingly memorable a general truth. He also reminds us of the poet in himself who wrote not only verse like 'Each and All' or 'The Snow-Storm' and his great Transcendentalist essays but the lifelong working Journals. Further, this particular aphorism speaks with the most direct relevance to *American* poetry, both the tradition at large and the two essential voices of its nineteenth-century phase who offer the departure points for this new collection of essays, Walt Whitman and Emily Dickinson. If we acknowledge, and it is hard not to, that almost by cultural and historic birthright American poetry—and indeed all the best and liveliest of American writing—has been 'modernist', concerned in Ezra Pound's lustrous phrase to 'make it new', then how the American poem has sought to establish its own 'pertinence' becomes of even greater importance than otherwise. As so often, Emerson offers a pivotal insight.

To seek possession simultaneously of their own singular identity and of a larger, self-consciously aware 'American' identity, has long been the complex fate of most American poets. Whitman and Dickinson could hardly better testify to that fate. On first view Whitman manifestly puts himself forward as the declamatory, outward-inclined bard of America's 'athletic democracy', Walt as the nation's custodial 'definer' and 'unpuzzler'. By seeming contrast, Emily Dickinson, for all that she acknowledged herself to 'see—New Englandly', customarily is thought the poet of privacy *in extremis*, 'comprehending the whole' as her poem says by exploration of the deepest inward realms of spirit. Unchallengeably different they are, as different as their Long Island and Amherst origins, or their verse-forms, or even their strange sexual destinies. Yet in their very difference they also serve to complement one another, both pledged to 'make their own pertinence', both at the same time ineluctably American. They also give us American poetry at its first, best strength.

Each of the essays which appear in this collection to one degree or another acknowledges this double tension in American poetry, its inward and outward inclination. Furthermore, it takes no very long acquaintance to see that the matter turns several ways at once: Whitman, for instance, speaks infinitely more privately than often allowed, Dickinson more 'publicly'. Behind Whitman's expansive manner, as expressed, say, in 'Song of Myself' and other exhortatory poems in *Leaves of Grass*, lies the more inaccessible figure, whose private hesitations and reticences we can glimpse in his love-poetry and letters. Emily Dickinson, too, by writing privately in public (given that of her nearly 2,000 poems only a handful saw print in her lifetime), shows that by education and sheer curiosity she did understand the world—its human feelings at least—in a way which refers infinitely beyond New England and the narrow Massachusetts and Puritan stock from which she derived. For both of them 'pertinence', the manner in which their poetry establishes its own voicing and subject, becomes a way of handling the complex equations of Self and Americanness, the private and the public.

Beyond these two it is tempting to say, with no mincing of words, that nineteenth-century poetry constitutes a minor accomplishment. One would have to add, however, that American poetry, chronologically and otherwise, does not run in tandem with English poetry. Its Romantic phase comes later, as does its major phase, that of the generation of Wallace Stevens, William Carlos Williams, Hart Crane, Robert Frost, T. S. Eliot and Ezra Pound. Yet we also recognize something quintessentially nineteenth-century in Whitman and Dickinson, less that they write as contemporaries of Tennyson and Browning than that they share the urge of fellow-writers of the American Renaissance—that vital efflorescence of letters and thought heralded in Emerson's *Nature* (1836) and 'The American Scholar' (1837) and which counts among its company alongside Whitman and Dickinson the likes of Melville, Hawthorne, Thoreau and Poe—to establish new literary forms and idiom as fit modes of expression for a new 'Americanness' of experience.

Though, too, we read them as poets who have come into their own, settled reputations, we do so anachronistically. They hardly were so in their own lifetimes. Throughout the different incarnations of *Leaves of Grass*, from its first pseudonymous appearance in 1855 to the famous Death-bed edition of 1891–92, Whitman had essentially a cultist following, those who saw in him the sexual prophet, the mystic, or the supposed Pre-Raphaelite fellow-spirit admired by the Rossettis and others. Only as more and more the full implication of his vision and innovations of poetic language and measure has won recognition has he been seen for the splendid poet he was. He still, to be sure, does not always win assent. There are readers who will forever find him clangorous, too urgent and 'inclusive', the defects listed by D. H. Lawrence in *Studies in Classic American Literature* (1923). Emily Dickinson, as noted, we read as a posthumous voice, whose crystalline, dramatic and dash-laden poems we recognize as much for their visual design as their compacted intensities of meaning. We also read both of them through subsequent tradition, Whitman as the begetter of a poetic line which includes Carl Sandburg, Hart Crane, William Carlos Williams and latterly Charles Olson and Allen Ginsberg, Dickinson as the begetter of a 'confessional' line, often New Englandish in temper as in Robert Lowell, and which notably includes other American women, Sylvia Plath and Anne Sexton pre-eminently.

But if not Whitman and Dickinson, who when not looking across the Atlantic to 'Our Old Home' did nineteenth-century Americans read? Essentially, we would have to say, the so-called Fireside or Schoolroom poets, those public mannerist voices of whom Henry Wadsworth Longfellow was first and foremost. He, and his coevals, James Greenleaf Whittier, James Russell Lowell, Oliver Wendell Holmes and William Cullen Bryant, served as America's overwhelming sense of what it was to be a poet—makers of homely, public-minded, ceremonial verse. Most of them, for all their stupendous popularity, we now look back upon in wonderment and askant. Yet we may be in danger of turning too far the other way, for theirs is a poetry which still has its redemptions, minor though they may be. They also obscure poets who only latterly we have begun to disinter. Edgar Allan Poe has always had his 'Gothic' reputation, and the French through Mallarmé and others have long kept his claims as a poet in view. But to the English-speaking world it has been as the author of 'The Fall of the House of Usher', or the Dupin detective and horror stories, that he has enjoyed his essential reputation. Behind him and the others also lies the Melville who wrote poetry, a statement in itself which can still slightly astound. Yet it was in the sad inglorious aftermath of *Moby-Dick* and his other major fiction that Melville took to poetry, the author of four volumes and a vast miscellany of other verse. Even more obscurely, of late we have begun to encounter the names of Jones Very and Frederick Goddard Tuckerman, introspective New Englanders both, yet whose vision we have come to understand as unexpectedly interesting. There remains, too, the name with which this Introduction began, Ralph Waldo Emerson, the oracular statesman of Transcendentalism, yet a poet richly in his own right, a worthy versifier whom no account of nineteenth-century poetic tradition can ignore.

With these kinds of considerations in mind, each of the essays offered in this volume addresses itself to the names above. Eric Mottram first of all takes on Whitman the visionary philosopher-poet, the prophetic 'life' figure who sees in America not just a new geo-political reality but a new order of human possibility. Mark Kinkead-Weekes, from a complementary perspective, explores the quieter, more lyric Whitman, the author of poems as sure of imaginative touch as 'When lilacs last in the dooryard bloom'd', 'Out of the cradle endlessly rocking' and 'Crossing Brooklyn Ferry'. In his account of Emily Dickinson, Jim Philip situates her both as heir to ancestral New England and Puritan tradition and as a mind taking cognizance of its own powers and directions, knowledge as in itself startling imaginative drama.

Robert von Hallberg approaches Poe as an instance of the American poet-critic, a Poe who in *Eureka* and essays like 'The Philosophy of Composition' and 'The Poetic Principle' offers himself as a major theorist—especially about poetry as *'The Rhythmical Creation of Beauty'*, anti-moralistic and a pioneer of the case for 'autonomous' art. Brian Harding sees Emerson's poetry as also something of the upshot of theory, the view that art can emulate Nature by being at once static and dynamic, at once design and life. My own case for Melville's poetry is first to establish that there *is* a case and then to see on its own terms the kind of poetry to be encountered, whether in *Battle-Pieces*, his Civil War verse, or *Clarel*, his massive quest-epic after Belief, or in the shorter, privately printed collections which with the exception of *Billy Budd* mark the close of his career. James Justus takes another look at the Fireside group, beginning from

11

Bryant and including Longfellow, Whittier, Lowell and Holmes, an endeavour to establish the kind of poetry they were writing and the public response they sought to elicit. David Seed examines the worlds of two other quintessential New England poets, Jones Very and Frederick Tuckerman, both very much discoveries of recent vintage, the one that strangest of paradoxes a Puritan mystic, the other a quasi-Emersonian Nature poet though without Emerson's endemic hopefulness. In the concluding essay Graham Clarke turns to the 'imaging' of American landscape in the allied arts of nineteenth-century poetry and painting, the shifting interplay of fact, image and myth in how the nation chose to envisage its own physical being.

It was Emerson, in a well-known passage from 'The Poet', who wrote:

> Our log rollings, our stumps and their politics, our fisheries, our Negroes and Indians, our boats and our repudiations, the wrath of rogues and the pusillanimity of honest men, the northern trade, the southern planting, the western clearing, Oregon and Texas, are yet unsung. Yet America is a poem in our eyes, and it will not wait long for metres.

It was he, too, who spoke keenly of writing and acting in 'the first-person singular'. Both inclinations say a great deal about being an American poet, especially in an era in which the nation fresh from Independence sought writerly affirmation of its own recent becoming. To Whitman it fell to act on Emerson's cues the one way, to Emily Dickinson another. Around them, whether in the poetry of the Southern-raised Poe, the genteel Fireside poets, the 'hidden' Melville, Very and Tuckerman, or Emerson himself, and to a lesser extent Thoreau, there emerged yet other routes and idioms. If they amount to the lesser vein, they still form an inherent part of American poetic tradition and deserve our attention. This collection pays them, and the greater presences of Whitman and Dickinson, fresh due.

It is again a pleasure to record my debt to the American Council of Learned Societies, and especially its Director, Richard Downar, for a year's Research Fellowship, which enabled me to get the design of this book sketched out and each essay commissioned.

1

Law and the Open Road: Whitman's 'America'

by ERIC MOTTRAM

Within the impositions of competitiveness and civil war, possessive individualism and the interlocking systems of class, racial and financial power in the United States, Whitman's creative energy is directed as much as it can be towards keeping the options of freedom open. Therefore he engages those main issues of inheritance, myth and law by which the State controls human lives as subject. That is, he invites any reader repeatedly to resist the immobilities of fixed structures of ends to means which any state-controllers require. He offers 'America' as a unifying term of the world, a form of healing of division after civil war (the history of the world and the immediacies of the so-called United States), and a condition of health. Within that term he would include, unlike one persistent Romantic timidity, the city and machine technology. 'America' is a non-destructive, non-exploitive programme for human living. It is, of course, threatened by the historic rigidities of the West which the United States incorporated. When his openness is invaded, particularly during and after the War Between the States, Whitman may become shrilly affirmative, sentimentally reiterative, and jingoistic. His nerve understandably fails him. But generally he meets Thoreau's sense of necessary friction with the State, and Melville's and Hawthorne's wariness of all powerful individuals who use class, law and professional permissions against the heart and

13

the people. But beyond their genius, he includes a unique sense of the body's desire, its freedom, which cuts through all consciousness of freedom, and is the source which may heal schizophrenic conflicts. He becomes, therefore, the great predecessor of those Americans—Henry Miller, Allen Ginsberg, Jack Kerouac, Charles Olson, Robert Duncan included—

> who know how to leave, to scramble the codes, to cause flows to circulate, to traverse the desert of the body without organs. They overcome limits, they shatter the wall, the capitalist barrier. And of course they fail to complete the process, they never cease failing to do so. The neurotic impasse again closes.

Their work 'itself constitutes a successful psychoanalysis, a sublime "transference" with exemplary collective virtualities'.[1] It refuses the oedipal impositions which fetter the coded American and offers an opening—an open road, an open field, a resistance to closure.

Whitman's poems repeatedly generate from positions between what Sartre calls praxis and the practico-inert. Freedom is 'the irreducibility of the cultural order to the natural order' ('Question de méthode', Preface to *Critique de la raison dialectique* (1960)). In *L'Etre et le Néant*, Sartre distinguishes between non-conscious reality or being-in-itself and human consciousness or being-for-itself, and the possible creative interaction, of resistance and enjoyment between them. We choose and decide (praxis) within the material environment and the body. In Olson's celebrated opening to 'The Kingfishers', 'What does not change/ is the will to change.'[2] What then causes the will not to change is the State exemplified by Sartre as 'societies of repetition' which are pre-historic or non-historic, demanding the establishment of exact equilibrium based on rituals of inheritance, myth and law. No law or mechanism exists for totally defining and determining change; no prior scheme or cause of interpretation of process. Freedom is men and women responsible for what they do and the possibility of living creatively and non-exploitively. What then of those who wish to remain pre-historic or tribal? What of the desire for stability and immobility? Whitman's 'Song of Myself' extends a detailed invitation to mobility, to learn 'how to leave'—but not in a state of absolute security that there is in fact any one there to take it and act upon it. The 'you' moves to 'we' in a state of two, but the 'I' is uncertain. 'I' says *come* but feels bound to conclude: 'I stop somewhere waiting for you.'[3] Opportunities the poem's persona, the 'I', offers for freedom of movement, of the body's desires, of the mind's consciousness, and of participation in what the editors of the Comprehensive Reader's Edition sensibly call the 'legacy of great natural force, untranslatable but found everywhere—in the sky or under foot', can be refused, and are. This uncertainty is a necessary gap in Whitman's work—or, rather, an agitation out of which the necessity for poetic composition grows with extraordinary fertility. He believes it explicitly to be the human part of the constant 'procreant urge of the world' (CRE, 31), but uncertainty of reception for this affirmation, or even, at some points in his career, its accuracy, painfully checks exuberant confidence. The Civil War wrecked not only his health but his earliest faith in an open society.

Whitman's writing therefore flourishes at the centre of those modern discussions of law and freedom which are taken up so primarily by the American Renaissance. Severely put, it is a matter of De Sade as he is placed by Georges Bataille citing a letter from the Marquis of 29 January 1782—a prior critique, as it were, of Bentham's hedonistic calculus:

> You want the whole universe to be virtuous and you do not feel that everything would perish in an instant if there were nothing but virtues on earth. . . . You do not understand that, since vice must exist, it is as unjust of you to punish it as it would be to poke fun at a blind man. . . . Enjoy yourself, my friend, enjoy yourself and do not pass judgment. . . . leave to nature the care of moving you as she pleases and to eternity that of punishing you.[4]

Writing on Jean Genet, Bataille makes this further commentary on the De Sade issues:

> it seems to me that on the whole the question of Good and Evil revolves around one main theme—what Sade calls irregularity . . . the basis of sexual excitement. The law (the rule) is a good one, it is Good itself (Good, the means by which the being ensures its existence), but a value, Evil, depends on the

possibility of breaking the rule. Infraction is frightening—like death: and yet it is attractive, as though the being wanted to survive out of weakness, as though exuberance inspired that contempt for death which is necessary once the rule has been broken. These principles are bound up with human life.[5]

Whitman desires to incorporate death within exuberance, to break down the either/or divisiveness, without challenge from Poe's 'imp of the perverse': 'a *mobile* without motive' which is irrational 'force' against reason.[6] But Poe's challenge comes from a solitary man within Poe's constant sense that communication is primarily disastrous. As Bataille writes—and he is using images which are constant in Whitman: communication on an open road and the sense of fullness in unregulated life—

> only one path leads from the rejection of servitude to the free limitations of sovereign humour: this path, which Sartre does not mention [i.e. in his study of Genet], is the path of communication. It is only if liberty, the transgression of laws and sovereign consumption are envisaged in their true form that the foundations of a moral code are revealed for those people who are not entirely regulated by necessity and who do not want to renounce the fulness which they have glimpsed.[7]

At the end of the Civil War Whitman wrote in affirmation of the communication still possible between two men as the unit of the nation, of the necessity of his mobility and challenge, still hoping for response in what he calls, in both its social and sexual forms, 'adhesiveness' (CRE, 322). The poem reads as a summary of his courageous belief in human possibilities of making a state out of love without determinism and possessiveness:

> As I lay with your head in my lap camerado,
> The confession I made I resume, what I said to you and the
>   open air I resume,
> I know I am restless and make others so,
> I know my words are weapons full of danger, full of death,
> For I confront peace, security, and all settled laws, to
>   unsettle them
> I am more resolute because all have denied me than I could
>   ever have been had they accepted me,
> I heed not and have never heeded either experience,
>   cautions, majorities, nor ridicule,

And the threat of what is call'd hell is little or nothing to me;
Dear camerado! I confess I have urged you onward with me,
    and still urge you, without the least idea what is our
    destination,
Or whether we shall be victorious, or utterly quell'd and
    defeated.

The calm of these long expert measures, as they spread before the eye for the voice's breath to take up, just contain the sense of the scene as a temporary but enriched stillness possible in the vortex of conflicts, a moment of relief from the schizoid society. Instinctual need has been transformed to a conscious art in which any reader may recognize his own necessity. But the issue with regard to the State is survival itself, the urgency only the more concentrated by the self-ravaged nation between 1860 and the date of the poem, 1865–66. Whitman generally comprehends his full context—in the words of Jean Baudrillard:

> . . . needs—such as they are—can no longer be defined adequately in terms of the naturalist-idealist thesis—as innate, instinctive power, spontaneous craving, anthropological potentiality. Rather, they are better defined as a *function* induced (in the individual) by the internal logic of the system.[8]

Part of the urgency appears, too, in a poem written five years earlier, at the beginning of the war, 'Myself and Mine' (CRE, 236–38). It begins:

> Myself and mine gymnastic ever,
> To stand the cold or heat, to take good aim with a gun, to sail
>   a boat, to manage horses, to beget superb children,
> To speak readily and clearly, to feel at home among
>   common people,
> And to hold our own in terrible positions on land and
>   sea. . . .

This is not a matter of embroidery or the making of ornaments but the chiselling 'with free stroke the heads and limbs of plenteous supreme Gods, that the States may realize them walking and talking'. But these are exemplary in the general way of art; they do not stand for dominating precept:

> Let me have my own way,
> Let others promulge laws, I will make no account of the laws,

17

> Let others praise eminent men and hold up peace, I hold up
> agitation and conflict,
> I praise no eminent man, I rebuke to his face the one that was
> thought most worthy. . . .

The exemplary man conceals secret guilt, needs to chatter, blab 'by rote'—'years, pages, languages, reminiscences'—in a state of imposition in order to complete people in the State:

> Let others finish specimens, I never finish specimens,
> I start them by exhaustless laws as Nature does, fresh and
> modern continually.

> I give nothing as duties,
> What others give as duties I give as living impulses,
> (Shall I give the heart's action as a duty?)

The poet arouses 'unanswerable questions', fundamentally concerned with communication—expressly with the core of adhesiveness, that 'touch' which people in power cannot tolerate, unless it is the touch or the torturer, the executioner, the slaver:

> Who are they I see and touch, and what about them?
> What about these likes of myself that draw me so close by
> tender directions and indirections?

> I call to the world to distrust the accounts of my friends, but
> listen to my enemies, as I myself do,
> I charge you forever reject those who would expound me,
> for I cannot expound myself,
> I charge that there be no theory or school founded out of me,
> I charge you to leave all free, as I have left all free.

> After me, vista?

The present, though, is not an emptiness to be arbitrarily filled with the egos of the happy few in agreement: 'Every hour the semen of centuries, and still of centuries' should impregnate the present, and 'touch' occurs in history. Therefore it is the history of human beings and societies which must impress us. Their time is short but the poem ends in endlessness under the existential imprint of time and therefore death: 'I must follow up these continual lessons of the air, water, earth,/ I perceive I

18

have no time to lose.' We may remember here the admonition that those ignorant of the past are doomed to repeat it. Whitman's 'Great Are the Myths' (1855–60) (CRE, 585–88) is a poetic discourse on the issue of inheritance that might regulate from myth and law, and the nature of resistance to the possibility of their impositional fixity rather than their potentiality to release full life for the open road. Myths, nations and 'their poets, women, sages, rulers, warriors, and priests' are accepted, looking back. But so are liberty and equality—the crafts and helmsmen of nations are 'the muscle of life and death', 'perfect science'. Today is 'great' and 'beautiful' as the past was: 'It is good to live in this age—there never was any better.' The poet cannot refuse the past; it is a human construct in which, therefore, all of us are involved—we, in those of the past, made it. The word 'great' applied to all of history means both size and monumentality. If it means value, that is because it is a sign of the human process, and that is part of Earth process; the Earth 'goes as far onward from this, as this from the time when it lay in covering waters and gases, before man had appeared.' Truth is process, the changes—with which man is 'in love'; they 'never leave each other'. These commonplaces—even platitudes—of process are qualified by 'love', and people in love do not exploit each other. Love is a responsibility within process. 'Truth in man is no dictum, it is vital as eyesight'—like Melville in *Moby-Dick* the poet recognizes that truth is process and is to be discovered: 'I scale mountains, or dive in the sea after you.' Or in the terms of Olson's 'Maximus, at Tyre and at Boston', 'we are only/ as we find out we are.'[9] Laws have been made and become 'landmarks', but this, too, is part of the discovery of what social justice could be. And justice is linked to love. Dictum causes war. Justice is a paradox because it is 'immutable' but not dogma:

> Great is Justice!
> Justice is not settled by legislators and laws—it is in the Soul,
> It cannot be varied by statutes, any more than love, pride,
>   the attraction of gravity can,
> It is immutable—it does not depend on majorities—
>   majorities or what not come at last before the same
>   passionless and exact tribunal.

The retracing, accumulative, self-adjusting structure of the poem—this extracting paraphrase spoils it—dramatizes the Whitman problematic: how to leave the road open and to fully engage love, and yet use history as opening in process. It is characteristic that he finds democratic beliefs threatened by the fear of majority rule as control by ignorant force in the people. The poem takes its place with *Coriolanus* and *Culture and Anarchy*, with the scorn of voting in *Walden*, and Lawrence's essay 'Democracy'. Whitman even reverts to a placing of Carlylean beliefs in greatness on the judge as hero—'the grand natural lawyers and perfect judges', visionary men of what Wittgenstein warns against—*Übersichlichkeit*, 'they over see all eras, states, administrations.' These are not the everyday judges in the courts, therefore, but a combination of philosopher, historian and theoretical lawyer who stands at the point of equilibrium in process. 'Great' is used to admire both 'Goodness' and 'Wickedness', since both 'the eternal equilibrium of things is great, and the eternal overthrow of things is great.' The paradox of process is that these forces have equal 'purport' in 'reality'. Whitman allows absorption in the scope and size of process to demonstrate angelic consciousness apart rather than human participatory moral action. Once 'paradox' is accepted as descriptive value, permission is given to any person who seizes power under the conditions of greatness—the familiar corruption of the worship of the heroic vitalist,[10] the natural hero, the Dionysian force that embodies process or cosmic energy or some such myth. And it *is* myth, as Whitman's opening lines acknowledge. To appreciate the aesthetics of process a person must stand so far back that he becomes angelic and commits a form of hubris. This is the far side of theory and a kind of nostalgia for law from which Whitman has to move dialectically towards participatory humanity, his sense of openness. The visionary may claim to see all but he may not judge it from closed precept. As William Empson reminds us so accurately in *The Structure of Complex Words*,[11] the 'all-user' is an absolutist and reverts to the sense of allness 'whenever there is any serious emotional pressure'. That Empson is primarily criticizing Milton here is not limiting but very much to the point. We are considering epicists: 'That his feelings were crying out against his

20

appalling theology in favour of freedom, happiness and the pursuit of truth was I think not obvious to him. . . .' Melville's exasperated comment to Hawthorne on Goethe's 'Live in the all' is also to the point (he was probably remembering Carlyle's translation of Goethe's *'im Ganzes . . . zu leben'* as 'to live . . . in the whole', as the editors of the letters point out).[12] 'All' supresses 'separate identity' by spreading it into the planets and the plants; but toothache is not suppressed by being told to live in it. Melville acknowledges that the Whitman feelings can be experienced but checks it to a particular condition only:

> You must have often felt it, lying on the grass on a warm summer's day. Your legs seem to send out shoots into the earth. Your hair feels like leaves upon your head. This is the *all feeling*. But what plays the mischief with the truth is that men will insist upon the universal application of a temporary feeling or opinion.

Whitman, however, certainly knew how to retreat from the excitements of omnipresence. In 'Visages' (CRE, 597) he pierces through the title surfaces to 'the accepted hells beneath'. Things are as they are. Such relativist realism leads to an acceptance of one's place in a non-hierarchical All. But the poem ends: 'Of criminals—To me, any judge, or any juror, is equally criminal—and any reputable person is also—and the President is also.' Such levelling is familiar anarchism in nineteenth-century American opinion, and is reinforced— against the hefty power of lawyers, both then and now, and foreseen by De Tocqueville—by an untitled poem (CRE, 608–9—'Calamus-5' in the 1860 *Leaves of Grass*):

> States!
> Were you looking to be held together by the lawyers?
> By an agreement on a paper? Or by arms?
>
> Away!
> I arrive, bringing these, beyond all the forces of courts and
>   arms,
> These! to hold you together as firmly as the earth itself is
>   held together.
>
> The old breath of life, ever new,
> Here! I pass it by contact to you, America. . . .

The poem then celebrates 'adhesiveness'; contact, affection and love 'shall solve every one of the problems of freedom'. Defensive nationalism will arise from unity based on emotions deeper than written law. The last sentences of the 1855 preface to *Leaves of Grass* had stated (CRE, 729):

> An individual is as superb as a nation when he has the qualities which make a superb nation. The soul of the largest and wealthiest and proudest nation may well go half-way to meet that of its poets. The signs are effectual. There is no fear of mistake. If the one is true the other is true. The proof of a poet is that his country absorbs him as affectionately as he has absorbed it.

Now, five years later, Whitman proposes all Americans as 'masters of the world under a new power', scorning 'all the remainder of the world': 'The dependence of Liberty shall be lovers,/ The continuance of Equality shall be comrades.' 'Partners' and 'lovers' will produce an ecstatic and 'indissoluble' continent in a state of democracy: 'I will make the most splendid race the sun ever yet shone upon,/ I will divine magnetic lands.' In this way some of the reasons why the French Revolution turned to tyranny may be avoided, and those threats to America stated in 'Democratic Vistas'— where 'vista' includes a less than ecstatic vision of his nation (1867–71). The 'procreant urge' towards a new society remains the aim but, as always in Whitman, beneath the enthusiastic celebration thrust painful urgencies of doubt— before the Civil War as well as later:

> Intense and loving comradeship, the personal and passionate attachment of man to man—which, hard to define, underlies the lessons and ideals of the profound saviours of every land and age, and which seems to promise, when thoroughly develop'd, cultivated and recognized in manners and literature, the most substantial hope and safety of the future of these States, will then be fully express'd. . . . It is to the development, identification, and general prevalence of that fervid comradeship, (the adhesive love, at least rivaling the amative love hitherto possessing imaginative literature, if not going beyond it,) that I look for the counterbalance and offset of our materialistic and vulgar American democracy, and for the spiritualization thereof. Many will say it is a dream, and will

22

not follow my inferences: but I confidently expect a time when there will be seen, running like a half-hid warp through all the myriad audible and visible worldly interests of America, threads of manly friendship, fond and loving, pure and sweet, strong and lifelong, carried to degrees hitherto unknown—not only giving tone to individual character, and making it unprecedentedly emotional, muscular, heroic, and redefined, but having the deepest relations to general politics. I say democracy infers such loving comradeship, as its most inevitable twin or counterpart, without which it will be incomplete, in vain, and incapable of perpetuating itself.[13]

To resist this statement as mere 'dream' is today even more absurdly inaccurate than it would have been in the post-Civil War years. In fact, the counter-culture declarations and protests of the 1960s and 1970s in America frequently showed Whitman coming into his own as a cultural resource for Americans opposing America from their dream of a true America. His urgency at its most poetically controlled and emotionally forcible appears in 'Respondez!', initially entitled 'Poem of the Propositions of Nakedness' in 1856—a tract which certain Americans still required in those recent decades of criticism. It appeared in all editions of *Leaves of Grass* until 1876 (CRE, 591). Four crucial lines were added after the Civil War. Line 2, after the opening cry of 'Reply! Reply!' reads: 'The war is completed—the price is paid—the title is settled beyond recall. . . .' Then the address to the nation—not simply, under customary democratic sentimentalities, an attack on leaders, but presented to everyone: 'Let no one evade!' The scathing, almost Swiftian propositions move out from the edge where faith is broken:

> Let murderers, bigots, fools, unclean persons, offer new
>   propositions!
> Let the old propositions be postponed!
>
> Let the faces and theories be turn'd inside out! let meanings
>   be freely criminal, as well as the results! . . .
>
> Let men and women be mock'd with bodies and mock'd
>   with Souls!
> Let the love that waits in them, wait! let it die, or pass
>   still-born to other spheres!

> Let the sympathy that waits in every man, wait! or let it
>   also pass, a dwarf, to other spheres!

Where in the exuberant confidences and potentialities of 'Song
of Myself' (1855) Whitman had sung his Emersonian self-
reliant challenges—'Do I contradict myself?/ Very well
then. . . . I contradict myself;/ I am large. . . . I contain
multitudes'[14]—now he excoriates the divisiveness of a hypo-
critical nation which infuriates him. His counter-frictional
optimism has reversed:

> Let contradictions prevail! let one thing contradict another!
>   and let one line of my poems contradict another!
> Let the people sprawl with yearning, aimless hands! let their
>   tongues be broken! let their eyes be discourag'd! let
>   none descend into their hearts with the fresh
>   lusciousness of love!

Then lines 17–19, added after the wartime and post-war
corruption in 'These States', are followed by a further assault
on the idea and practice of 'America'; the poetic structure
remains highly controlled in pointed juxtapositions which
build into a critical demolition of 'the theory of America':

> (Stifled, O days! O lands! in every public and private
>   corruption!
> Smother'd in thievery, impotence, shamelessness, mountain-
>   high;
> Brazen effrontery, scheming, rolling like ocean's waves
>   around and upon you. . . .

'Management, caste, comparison' create internal exile one
man from another. 'Inalienable right' becomes the right to
'tyrannize'. The culture of 'teachers, artists, moralists,
lawyers' is 'ashes'. Human beings exist in the 'perfect equality'
of animals. The *socius* has become a chaos of national
hypocrisy, the end of the creative and open: 'Let us all,
without missing one, be exposed in public, naked, monthly, at
the peril of our lives! let our bodies be freely handled and
examined by whoever chooses!/ Let nothing but copies at
second hand be permitted to exist upon the earth!' (The image
from the slave market is apposite since slaves are treated as

24

duplicates, objectified into degraded numbers.) Law and punishment are meaningless—'let judges and criminals be transposed' and slaves and masters, reformers and idiots, be exchanged. Like Melville's Pitch, in *The Confidence-Man*, men 'sleep armed' since 'none believe in good will'. The city, in Blakean terms, has become a chartered danger zone of mutual exploitation, the scene of commerce, prostitution, and the end of happiness: 'What real happiness have you had one single hour through your life?'.

So the 'you' invited into confident touch contact in 'Song of Myself' is suspect. Whitman proposed radical reinforcement of national cultural anticipation of endless opening space as limitless resource. But now he recognizes, as Melville does in *Moby-Dick*, that American space is there to be conquered. Happiness is the pursuit of conquest. 'Vista' was to have meant space which did not have to be conquered or even necessarily permanently occupied. What Camus calls '*cette lutte entre midi et minuit*' could be lived out without mutual rape and the rape of the earth. But where Camus could write in 1957, 'there is no reason for being surprised that such a society chose as its religion a moral code of formal principles and that it inscribes the words "liberty" and "equality" on its prisons as well as its temples of finance',[15] Whitman had to be surprised. The interior theme of his poetry is the violation or threat of violation of the human body and its necessary environment of desire and mutuality.

He created his Walt persona in order to appear as a poet at work within society, not aloof or academic or genteel or fashionable, but committed—exemplary without being establishment. After the Civil War, as a healer of divided culture, he has to envisage not only recovery but expansion of power. America as democracy itself must conquer the world's space as 'the great histrion', the master extension of Columbus (CRE, 417). A celebration of industrial and commercial power demonstrated in the American Institute's fortieth annual exhibition in 1871 extends into 'Passage to India' of the same year and 'Prayer to Columbus' of 1874, celebrating 'a worship new' (CRE, 412), a global Americanism.

Whitman's positions within and without or beyond the nation generate the movement of his poetry between acceptance and disappointed assault. 'The theory of America' and its practice is never static, in the first instance because of that very proposition stated at the beginning of the opening poem of the 1871 *Leaves of Grass* (CRE, 1): 'One's-Self I sing, a simple separate person,/ Yet utter the word Democratic, the word En-Masse.' The affirmation contains the hesitation, 'sing' and 'separate person' confronting 'utter' and 'En-Masse'. 'You', 'I' and 'We' have to be continually substantiated, praised and criticized. This is a major part of Whitman's uniqueness, and the hero-poet's stance. The prescriptions of Carlyle belie their confidently emphatic prosody.

When Carlyle died in 1881 Whitman memorialized him as 'a representative author', a literary predicator of 'our stormy era, its fierce paradoxes, its din, and its struggling parturition periods',[16] whose 'final value' is his 'launching into the self-complacent atmosphere of our days a rasping, questioning, dislocating agitation and shock'. He had reviewed six volumes of Carlyle—whose opinions, of course, fertilized Emerson, Melville and many other American nineteenth-century figures—in 1846, and that exuberant rhetoric entered Whitman's poetry, along with the cadencing of *bel canto* and the Bible—a syntax for the personal, persuasive voice, the tone of proclamation, and the self-conscious utterance of prophecy. He read in *On Heroes, Hero-Worship and the Heroic in History* that the poet is a member of those Great Men on whom society primarily depends:

> It is an inexplicably complex controversial-calculation between the world and him! He will read the world and its laws; the world with its laws will be there to read. . . . *Vates* means both Prophet and Poet. . . . they have penetrated both of them into the sacred mystery of the Universe; what Goethe calls 'the open secret'. . . . That divine mystery, which lies everywhere in all Beings . . . of which all Appearance, from the starry sky to the grass of the field, but especially the Appearance of Man and his work, is but the *vesture*, though all others were but toying with it.

The prophet reveals 'what we are to do', the poet 'of what we are in love', but these functions 'cannot be disjoined'. Metre in the language of revelation and love is music:

A *musical* thought is one spoken by a mind that has penetrated into the inmost heart of the thing; detected the inmost mystery of it, namely the *melody* that lies hidden in it; the inward harmony of coherence which is its soul, whereby it exists, and has a right to be, here in this world. All inmost things, we may say, are melodious; naturally utter themselves in Song. The meaning of Song goes deep. . . . All deep things are Song. . . . [it] is the Heroic in Speech.

This programme Whitman took into the generatives of *Leaves of Grass*. Process is the harmonious 'all' context of the heroic poet. The open secret is 'circulation', 'mutual communication', 'the one vital Force' within all things. The body of man and the body of nature are one and not to be restricted:

There is but one Temple in the universe and that is the Body of Man. Nothing is holier than that high form. Bending before men is a reverence done to this Revelation in the Flesh. . . .

Whitman's 1881 Carlyle essay still uses 'prophet' in the latter's sense—in Whitman's words, 'one whose mind bubbles up and pours forth as a fountain, from inner, divine spontaneities revealing God'. But Carlyle's 'scornful analysis of democracy' must be now scrutinized more carefully if it is to be used; his lack of faith in the people in *Shooting Niagara* is to be countered from Hegel's principles. Carlyle 'seems to have been haunted in the play of his mental action by . . . the spectre of world-destruction' whereas Hegel affirms 'the whole earth' and human history to 'the assemblist' as

endless process of Creative thought, which, amid numberless apparent failures and contradictions, is held together by central and never-broken unity. . . . radiations of one consistent and eternal purpose; the whole mass of everything steadily, unerringly tending and flowing toward the permanent *utile* and *morale*, as rivers to oceans. As life is the whole law and incessant effort of the visible universe, and death only the other or invisible side of the same, so the *utile*, so truth, so health are continuous-immutable laws of the moral universe, and vice and disease, with all their perturbations, are but transient, even if ever so prevalent expressions.

Politics is part of the process, and democracy 'may rule as outrageously and do as great harm as oligarchy or despotism—

though far less likely to do so'. Evil, the 'violation' of these relations, 'the cruel and unjust', 'the unnatural', is not 'permitted' but is 'in a certain sense, (like shade and light,) inevitable in the divine scheme'. Hegel's principles are in fact 'an essential and crowning justification of New World democracy in the creative realms of time and space', in America's *vastness, multiplicity* and *vitality*.

One function of poetry, therefore, is to promote health in democracy, to reduce the pressures of violation, to provide complete confidence, even in the nature of death. In 'The Sleepers' (1855) the naked swimmer, in the blood-stained sea, shipwreck, the criminal, the diseased and the dead are part of flow and unity, the over-all beauty: 'Not the womb yields the babe in its time more surely than I shall be yielded from you in my time.'[17] Hegelian process is rarely presented as abstract philosophy in the poetry. The magnificence of 'Song of Myself' radiates from a conviction and a dramatic vitality presented through precise detail within a prosodic rhetoric of celebration and invitation. Lived and imagined life are brought together in a paean to the generative which must include death if space is to remain potential and airy. The poet speaks for himself and in doing so speaks, he believes, for 'you'. Robert Creeley witnesses that Whitman taught him 'that the common *is* personal, intensely so, in that having no one thus to invest it, the sea becomes a curious mixture of water and table salt and the sky the chemical formula of air'.[18] Edward Dahlberg locates Whitman in a similar ecological area and shows him challenging naturalism, the main nervous nineteenth-century condition concomitant with Darwinism and social Darwinism:

> Whitman's hymn to man is the very opposite of the naturalist's nausea. To the naturalist man is an accursed and evil smell; he peers into the subterranean pores, valves and orifices of the hair, the nails, the teeth, the mouth, looking for the satanic and sybaritic malodour. The naturalistic novel is the allegory of human ordure. . . . [*Leaves of Grass*] is the vindication of man's fragrant bowels, perspiration and skin.[19]

And the control of process multiplicity in Whitman's poems presented Hopkins, Claudel and Perse with models for their need to sustain the long poem. His ability to maintain pace and level over large prosodic spaces without deterioration provided Ginsberg with an antecedent for a poem as fine as 'Kaddish'. Emerson, of course, immediately sensed 'wit & wisdom', 'great power' that 'makes us happy', 'free & brave thought', 'joy' and 'courage of treatment' in the first *Leaves of Grass*. Those qualities have never diminished. Whitman's American neglect stretches dully from the Boston ban, through the panic objections of Whittier and Oliver Wendell Holmes, to those Christian aristocratic ironists called Fugitives. The roots are always the same: fear of Whitman's presentation of erotic and political desire, and a mistaken opinion as to what prosody should be.

Whitman remains a resource to us partly for the reasons contained in what Thomas Jefferson once wrote to Edwin T. Martin: 'There is not a sprig of grass that shoots uninterestingly to me.'[20] For the poem grass is instance of the common—'all flesh is grass' perhaps afforded another instigation. He opposes puritan body horror, human dualism supposedly redeemed by separated soul from body, and then punishing both. No scarlet letter appears in *Leaves of Grass*. No body is resurrected in some élitist hereafter; body and desire are to be enjoyed here and now, explicitly and erotically in 'Spontaneous Me' (1856), 'I Sing the Body Electric' (1856), and 'Song of Myself', where 'I have said that the soul is not more than the body,/ And I have said that the body is not more than the soul' (CRE, 86) is like the end of Keats's 'Grecian Urn', an aphoristic summary of what has been dramatized in instances, not an abstract dogma. 'Press close bare-bosom'd night— press close magnetic nourishing night'—'Winds whose soft-tickling genitals rub against me it shall be you!'—'Something I cannot see puts upward libidinous prongs,/ Seas of bright juice suffuse heaven'—'Mine is no callous shell,/ I have instant conductors all over me whether I pass or stop. . . . I merely stir, press, feel with my fingers, and am happy,/ To touch my person to some one else's is about as much as I can stand'—these lead to Section 28 of 'Song of Myself', a grand celebration of erotic touch, a basis for brother- and sister-hood generatives, bravely amused at the self's hesitances and openly passionate:

Is this then a touch? quivering me to a new identity,
Flames and ether making a rush for my veins,
Treacherous tip of me reaching and crowding to help them,
My flesh and blood playing out lightning to strike what is
      hardly different from myself,
On all sides prurient provokers stiffening my limbs,
Straining the udder of my heart for its withheld drip,
Behaving licentious towards me, taking no denial,
Depriving me of my best for a purpose,
Unbuttoning my clothes, holding me by the bare waist,
Deluding my confusion with the calm of the sunlight and
      pasture-fields,
Immodestly sliding the fellow-senses away,
They bribed to swap off with touch and go and graze at the
      edges of me,
No consideration, no regard for my draining strength or my
      anger. . . .

You villain touch! What are you doing? my breath is tight
      in its throat,
Unclench your floodgates, you are too much for me. . . .

Nor does touch proceed into the manipulations of possessive
individualism, as Poe repeatedly imagined it would:

I am the teacher of athletes,
He that by me spreads a wider breast than my own proves
      the width of my own,
He most honours my style who learns under it to destroy
      the teacher.
The boy I love, the same becomes a man not through
      derived power, but in his own right. . . .

The aim is to counter the separations enforced by divisive
hierarchy in law, religion, between the sexes, within the same
sex, and in narrowing political compulsions. In Camus's words:
'Liberty alone draws men from their isolation; but slavery
dominates a crowd of solitudes. And art, by virtue of that free
essence . . . unites where tyranny separates.'[21] Whitman shows
our ecological need to sense life empathically and present it in
fresh language: 'I find I incorporate gneiss, coal, long-threaded
moss, fruits, grains, esculent roots,/ And am stucco'd with
quadrupeds and birds all over. . . .' In his notebooks this
becomes a form of *practical* transcendentalism (CRE, 58):

> The soul or spirit transmits itself into all matter—into rocks, and can live the life of a rock—into the sea, and can feel itself the sea—into the oak, or other tree—into an animal, and feel itself a horse, a fish, or bird—into the earth—into the motions of the suns and stars.

Evolution is therefore not separation but part of process relationship in what Henry Adams, an admirer of Whitman, calls 'the multiverse'. Section 33 of 'Song of Myself' incorporates, further, the things we make—balloons, steamships—with the more obviously ecological: Niagara Falls, eating, voices singing at a camp-meeting, people in hospital, the dead in their coffins, the planet Earth 'speeding through space, speeding through heaven and the stars'. Verbalization as a form of localization and grasp is too limiting (Section 50): 'There is in me—I do not know what it is. . . . it is without a name—it is a word unsaid,/ It is not in my dictionary, utterance, symbol./ Something it swings on more than the earth I swing on,/ To it the creation is the friend whose embracing awakens me.' This astonishing perception marks the radiant core of Whitman's confidence without closure—confirmed in Section 25: 'Speech is the twin of my vision, it is unequal to measure itself,/ It provokes me forever, it says sarcastically,/ Walt you contain enough, why don't you let it out then? . . . Writing and talk do not prove me.' The Reichian armoured character is as thoroughly melted as possible: 'To be any form, what is that?' (Section 27). The history of gods is examined (Section 41) for its historical and not necessarily its present 'work' as 'the rough deific sketches to fill out better in myself'. The romantic anti-city convention is thrown out—'this is the city and I am one of the citizens' (Section 42)—as it is in 'Crossing Brooklyn Ferry' (1856): 'Ah, what can ever be more stately and admirable to me than mast-hemm'd Manhattan?' (CRE, 163). 'The robust soul' can use everything in history, nature and the present: the total process, athletically, for 'the bold swimmer' (Section 46), the 'untranslatable man' (Section 52), 'the new man' of whom Whitman writes in *Specimen Days* (Section 22), with his 'world of erudition, both moral and physical' not undermined by Darwin, because the persistent search for origins, 'human and other', takes its place 'as a segment of the circle, the cluster. . . . readjusting and

31

differentiating much, yet leaving the divine secrets just as inexplicable and unreachable as before—maybe more so.' America can 'fully absorb and appreciate' past and present science into 'the commonalty of humanity' with its 'new moulds, current forms'. For Whitman this is the practical programme for the poet that Emerson describes in 'Nature' (1836):

> The solid seeming block of matter has been pervaded and dissolved by a thought. . . . this feeble human being has penetrated the vast masses of nature with an informing soul, and recognized itself in their harmony. . . . seized the law. . . . He perceives that his law is still paramount, if still he have elemental power, if his word is sterling yet in nature, it is not conscious power, it is not inferior but superior to his will. It is instinct.

Looking ahead to a poet deeply read in Whitman, it is this position Wallace Stevens proposes in 'Asides on an Oboe': 'The impossible possible philosopher's man,/ The man who has had time to think enough,/ The central man, the human globe, responsive. . . .' Stevens's well-heeled aristocratic vitalism could be afforded within the American ethic. Whitman, on the contrary, explicitly steps out of it at the outset of 'Song of Myself' to gain time and energy to live centrally: 'I loafe and invite my soul.' Quality is not given but gained, but not gained through the Protestant ethic of labour as the source of value and the accumulation of both goods and virtue. Identity and quality are mobile, where the Emersonian and Carlylean poet-hero tends to be immovably centred. Whitman's central man has taken up René Char's advice: 'Uproot him from his native land. Replant him in soil presumed harmonious with the future, allowing for an incomplete success. Make him touch progress sensorially.'[24] Whitman's persona travels 'holding the universe with all its parts as one—as sailing in a ship'—but certainly not the hierarchies of Melville's ship-societies as federations under power. As late as 1888, he wrote in 'A Backward Glance O'er Travel'd Roads' that *'Leaves of Grass* and its theory [are] experimental—as, in the deepest sense, I consider our American republic to be, with its theory.' The reasons are clear: *'Leaves of Grass* is avowedly the song of

Sex and Amativeness, and even Animality'; and he quotes Taine: 'all original art is self-regulated. . . . it carries its own counterpoise, and does not receive it from elsewhere—lives on its own blood.'[25]

The poet of the 1855 preface is therefore no leisure-time artiste providing genteel pastime for a leisure class but a disturber of the assumed peace and immobility the leisured rely upon: 'He drags the dead out of their coffins and stands them again on their feet. . . . he says to the past, Rise and walk before me that I may realize you. He leaves the lesson. . . . he places himself where the future becomes present' (CRE, 716). This poet does not wait; he intervenes and invites inter-vention, 'the Female equally with the Male'. This is 'the modern man' (CRE, 1). For this reason, too, his poetry is politically processual:

> The Americans of all nations at any time upon the earth have probably the fullest poetical nature. The United States them-selves are essentially the greatest poem. . . . Here at last is something in the doings of man that corresponds with the broadest doings of the day and night. . . . a teeming nation of nations. . . . [whose genius] is not best or most in its executives or legislatures, nor in its ambassadors or authors or colleges or churches or parlours, nor even in its newspapers or inventors . . . but always most in the common people.

The American inherits and invents; he is not simply a rebel or some new Adam in a pseudo-new Eden (implying perpetual God-governance); he is an American and a poet 'by dis-covery', as is his presence on the continent and in the world (CRE, 710). The variety of American scope is the modern itself: 'the theme is creative and has vista'; 'the power to destroy or remould is freely used by him but never the power of attack.' The poet stands on the edge of discovery and creates at the interface of contributory past and open future. Whitman criticizes the false independence of capitalist America in terms similar to those in *Walden*, published the year before the first *Leaves of Grass*: 'the independence of meagre financial self-sufficiency', 'abandonment . . . to the toss and pallor or years of moneymaking . . . stifling deceit and underhand dodgings', 'the great fraud upon modern civiliza-tion and forethought', 'the wiles practiced by people upon themselves' (CRE, 723–24). Therefore poetry cannot be, as it is for the cautious liberal Arnold, beloved of the academic world of Trilling and the like, a 'consolation and stay', something 'to interpret life for us, to console us, to sustain us' *in present conditions*.[26] On the contrary (CRE, 727):

> A great poem is no finish to a man or woman but rather a beginning. . . . When the poet takes he takes with firm sure grip into live regions previously unattained. . . . Thenceforward is no rest. . . . they see the space and ineffable sheen that turn the old spots and lights into dead vacuums. . . . [the elder and the younger poet] launch off fearlessly together till the new world fits an orbit for itself and looks unabashed on the lesser orbits of the stars and sweeps through the ceaseless rings and shall never be quiet again.

The quest myth (tightening us in a sentence from origin to destination) is dislocated into an open road—back into the past, forward into the future. Whitman is therefore largely free from nostalgia for a lost centre; he is certainly free of the 'lost leader', even in his Lincoln poems where the paternalistic patriotic does intervene as a populist possibility. But he does need some concept of original human self, and some kind of process of meaning for the word *law*. He risks a closure around a concept in these two necessities. Mostly, self in vista is not nostalgia for security but rather a delight in novelty in the sense that Whitehead uses in *Process and Reality* to make the generative into a principle within process[27]:

> 'Creativity' is the principle of novelty. . . . 'creativity' introduces novelty into the content of the many, which are the universe disjunctly. . . . The ultimate metaphysical principle is the advance from disjunction to conjunction, creating a novel entity other than the entities given in disjunction. . . . Thus the 'production' of novel togetherness is the ultimate notion embodied in the term 'concrescence'. . . . [These notions] are inexplicable either in terms of higher universals or in terms of the components participating in concrescence. . . . The sole appeal is to intuition.

The man of intuition is projected in the child at the beginning of the 1855 poem later entitled 'Poem of the Child that Went Forth, and Always Goes Forth, Forever and

Forever'. The child moves out, encounters objects in an open journey towards the processual concrescence (CRE, 364–66):

> And the fish suspending themselves so curiously below
>   there, and the beautiful curious liquid,
> And the water-plants with their graceful flat heads, all
>   became part of him. . . .
>
> The streets themselves and the facades of houses, and goods
>   in the windows,
> Vehicles, teams, the heavy-plank'd wharves, the huge
>   crossing at the ferries. . . .
>
> The horizon's edge, the flying sea-crow, the fragrance of salt
>   marsh and shore mud. . . .

And, as Section 3 of 'Song of Myself' says: 'I do not talk of the beginning or the end./ There was never any more inception than there is now. . . . Urge and urge and urge,/ Always the procreant urge of the world./ Out of the dimness opposite equals advance, always substance and increase, always sex. . . .' Whitehead's intuition is Whitman's 'mystery' and his phenomenology of receptivity, and that much can be said because he had carefully read Greek and German philosophers—as he says in 'The Base of All Metaphysics' (1871) (CRE, 121). But it is love and sexuality that take human life forward, not philosophic systems and their tyrannic European contexts; as the poet proclaims in 'Song of the Open Road' (1856), his 'good fortune' is himself; he whimpers and postpones no more under compliances; 'strong and content I travel the open road' (CRE, 149). The large range of words of mobility in the eight lines of Section 8 expose the interior of his action—efflux, pervades, flows, charged, fluid, attaching, sprout, continually, exudes, distill'd, heaves—and builds towards the Whitman invitation: a voyage on the wild pathless sea of the Earth, 'with power, liberty . . . health, defiance, gaiety, self-esteem, curiosity'.

Then appears that nervousness which can be found in Jefferson, Melville, Hawthorne and Thoreau—the need to be sure that those who accept the invitation to 'the trial' are Jefferson's 'nature's aristocrats':

Allons! yet take warning!
He traveling with me needs the best blood, thews,
    endurance, . . .

Only those may come who come in sweet and determin'd
    bodies,
No diseas'd person, no rum drinker or venereal taint is
    permitted here.

'The great Companions . . . on the road' (Section 12) are both
solitary and social in their health and ability to risk. At the end
of the trial-voyage there will reach a proper old age, 'calm,
expanded, broad with the haughty breadth of the universe . . .
flowing free with the delicious near-by freedom of death'. The
self integrates and disintegrates on 'many roads' for 'many
traveling souls'. 'Progress' is not a pre-figured, pre-mapped
state, and 'goal' is no successful inclusive conclusion: 'Have
past struggles succeeded?/ What has succeeded? yourself?
your nation, Nature?' (Section 14). The self has to be de-
centred, and its ties with the State slipped, if novelty in process
is to be tried—'loos'd of limits and imaginary lines. . . . my
own master total and absolute,/ Listening to others, and
considering well what they say,/ Pausing, searching, receiving,
contemplating,/ Gently, but with undeniable will, divesting
myself of the holds that would hold me.' The child who goes
forth is never that 'growing boy' upon whom 'shades of the
prison-house begin to close' by natural, inevitable conse-
quence of being born.

The boy's losses in 'Out of the Cradle Endlessly Rocking'
(1859, revised 1860 and 1867) are to be overcome by the poet's
converting of threats to creativity—loss of confidence, grief
and death. The adult meets the child he was within the
processual voyage, but recognizes an identification with a
migrant bird mourning a lost mate and understands it as part
of his condition—'unsatisfied love', to be the 'singer solitary',
to 'fuse the song of my dusky demon and brother' (CRE, 251).
The result has to be as 'Me Imperturbe' (1860) puts it:
'self-balanced for contingencies,/ To confront night, storms,
hunger, ridicule, accidents, rebuffs, as the trees and animals
do' (CRE, 11). His personal sexuality and the Civil War could
not, however, be entirely taken up in the open-road confidence,

and Whitman would have been less than human if they had been.

Briefly, open sexuality, the 'atmosphere of perfect health' of the 1876 preface, were affirmed under severe illness and the memory of experience as a wound-dresser to Union soldiers. Blake's 'image of an American revolution whose demand for freedom would evolve long obscured poetic, sexual, and visionary powers'[28] arises only when Orc, revolutionary man, fails many times before Albion is resurrected in Jerusalem. But it is hard to live that faith without it weakening. In 'Hospital Visits' Whitman writes: 'There is something in personal love, caresses, and the magnetic flood of sympathy and friendship that does in its way, more good than all the medicine in the world.' He found a valuable level between masculine involvement and impersonal nursing, but the strains of 600 visits to hospitals among 'from eighty thousand to one hundred thousand of the wounded and sick, as sustainer of spirit and body in some slight degree, in the time of need',[29] ruined his health; Matthew Brady's photograph of 1862 shows a white-bearded old man of 43.

'Hours Continuing Long . . .' (1860) shows a more sexual confidence undermined. The root is a shameful sexual suffering when the lover sees his man content without him: 'Hours of torment—I wonder if other men have the like, out of the like feelings?' (CRE, 596). *Drum Taps* (1865) shows a certain rebirth from disillusion to a recognition of his own erotic facts, an understanding of the use of his love in a socially acceptable wartime employment, and a call for a renewal of all union. But the 1870 notebook contains painful self-analysis of 'weakness', 'humiliation' and resistance to desires: 'Depress the adhesive nature./ It is in excess—making life a torment./ All this diseased, feverish disproportionate adhesiveness.' In one extraordinary poem, 'Spirit Whose Work Is Done', dated under the title 'Washington—1865' (CRE, 324), he invites the spirit of conflict itself to become the spirit of creative impulse in hopes of renewing all energies:

> Ere departing fade from my eyes your forests of bayonets . . .
> Spirit of hours I knew, all hectic red one day, but pale as
>   death next day,

Touch my mouth ere you depart, press my lips close,
Leave the pulses of your rage—bequeath them to me—fill
    me with currents convulsive,
Let them scorch and blister out of my chants when you are
    gone,
Let them identify you to the future in these songs.

But a major part of Whitman's poetic faith and energy
would be placed at the disposal of national healing, national
expansion, propositions edging into apparently imperialist
closure. The greatest poet is 'a seer . . . he is not one of the
chorus', he wrote in the 1855 preface. In 'Long, Too Long
America' (1865) the seer has a new responsibility to address
America (CRE, 311):

Traveling roads all even and peaceful you learn'd from joys
    and prosperity only,
But now, ah now, to learn from crises of anguish, advancing,
    grappling with direst fate and recoiling not,
And now to conceive and show the world what your
    children en-masse really are. . . .

'Pioneers! O Pioneers' (1865) loudly articulates healing
nationalism through the tradition of westward expansion, the
New World taking up the cosmic burden of the Old, conquering
wilderness, inaugurating a new era. The open energy terms of
1855 are shriller now and more abstract—talk of 'a newer
mightier world' and 'world of labour and the march', of
'conquering, holding, daring, venturing as we go the unknown
ways'. The core dedication is to the engineering of a continent.
The 'all' terms move west from the Pacific shoreline into Asia.
'Years of the Unperform'd' (1865), later called 'Years of the
Modern' (CRE, 489), ecstatically places American technology
in the vanguard of all nations. Liberty is reiterated in noisy and
conventional emphases of size—a 'force advancing with
irresistible power on the world's stage'. God-like man 'colonizes
the Pacific, the archipelagos,/ With the steamship, the electric
telegraph, the newspaper, the wholesale engines of war. . . . the
world-spreading factories'. The masses 'interlink all geography,
all lands' in one global 'en-masse' Euro-American power
structure. To say the least, Whitman's idealism has turned
politically careless; Melville's *Typee* (1846) could have informed
him of the fate of colonized Pacific archipelagos.

In 1860 appeared 'A Broadway Pageant' celebrating for the readers of the *New York Times* the first Japanese ambassadors to the United States. Since in fact America had coerced Japan into treaty agreements, the poem reinforces official imperialism in the name of liberty. Columbus failed to discover Cathay in the Caribbean, but now Japan comes to the U.S.A.: 'Comrade Americanos! to us, then at last the Orient comes'. Under 'Orient' Whitman includes Asians from Assyria to Japan, and Polynesians from 'the Great Sea'. Once the Frontier reached the 'Western golden shores', Liberty persists westwards:

> I chant the world on my Western sea . . .
> I chant the new empire grander than any before, as in a
>   vision it comes to me,
> I chant America the mistress, I chant a great supremacy,
> I chant projected a thousand blooming cities in time on
>   those groups of sea-islands . . .
> My stars and stripes fluttering in the wind,
> Commerce opening. . . .

The poem then turns the eyes of 'Libertad' eastwards to where the Prince of Wales, later Edward VII, is about to visit America: 'The sign is reversing, the orb is enclosed,/ The ring is circled, the journey is done. . . .' A less militant poem appeared in 1871, 'Passage to India', in which Whitman's national and global enthusiasm is more theatrical and less prophetic of *Lebensraum*. In the 1876 preface he explains that this work gave 'freer vent and fuller expression to what, from the first, and so throughout, more or less lurks in my writings, underneath every page, every line, everywhere' (CRE, 745). He told Horace Traubel (CRE, 471) that 'there's more of me, the essential ultimate me, in that than any other poems. . . . the burden of it is evolution—the one thing escaping the other— the unfolding of cosmic purposes'. But here again, the action of 'the whole Earth' moves towards American justification, a poeticized Manifest Destiny: 'The whole Earth—this cold, impressive, voiceless Earth, shall be completely justified.' Whitman may have believed himself in 1876, but his earlier poetry had not intervened personal or national justificatory purposes to complete it. The repeated images of circularity in 'Passage to India' complete themselves in the New Empire.

In the twenty-five lines of Section 9, the voyage westwards rushes through 'mastership' of Asia, and then volleys upwards into a new frontier:

> O sun and moon an all you stars! Sirius and Jupiter!
> Passage to you!
> Passage, immediate passage! the blood burns in my
>   veins!
> Away O soul! hoist instantly the anchor!
> Cut the hawsers—haul out—shake out every sail! . . .
>
> For we are bound where mariner has not yet dar'd go,
> And we will risk the ship, ourselves and all.

Whitman's voice, pouring out from 'the seas of God', as the America-ship sails out, representing the fusion of all races, sounds only too like that of Captain Ahab who risked the *Pequod* and all hands against the illusory absolute. But there remain Whitman's heartening poems of the 'procreant urge of the world' in less ebullient voice, the still astonishing poems of erotic and ecological respect, of nation as part of adhesiveness in multiplicity without the colonizing aims of these States. In 1860, in one of his best love poems, Whitman reaches the only rest in voyage his earlier self could properly maintain (CRE, 122–23):

> When I heard at the close of the day how my name had
>   been receiv'd with plaudits in the capitol, still it was
>   not a happy night for me that follow'd
> . . . when I thought how my dear friend my lover was on
>   his way coming, O then I was happy,
> O then each breath tasted sweeter, and all that day my food
>   nourish'd me more, and the beautiful day pass'd well,
> . . . And that night while all was still I heard the waters roll
>   slowly continually up the shores,
> I heard the hissing rustle of the liquid and sands as directed
>   to me whispering to me to congratulate me,
> For the one I love most lay sleeping by me under the same
>   cover in the cool night,
> In the stillness in the autumn moonbeams his face was
>   inclined toward me,
> And his arm lay lightly around my breast—and that night I
>   was happy.

40

Law and the Open Road: Whitman's 'America'

NOTES

1. Gilles Deleuze and Félix Guattari, *Anti-Oedipus: Capitalism and Schizophrenia* (New York: Viking Press, 1977), pp. 132–34.
2. Charles Olson, *The Distances* (New York: Grove Press, 1960), p. 5.
3. H. W. Blodgett and S. Bradley (eds.), *Walt Whitman: Leaves of Grass—Comprehensive Reader's Edition* (New York: New York University Press, 1965), p. 89—the text hereinafter referred to as CRE with relevant page numbers.
4. Georges Bataille, *Literature and Evil*, trans. Alastair Hamilton (London: Calder and Boyars, 1973), p. 90.
5. Ibid., p. 159.
6. E. H. Davidson (ed.), *Selected Writings of Edgar Allan Poe* (Boston: Houghton Mifflin, 1956), p. 226.
7. Bataille, op. cit., p. 169.
8. Jean Baudrillard, *For a Critique of the Political Economy of the Sign*, trans. Charles Levin (St. Louis: Telos Press, 1981), p. 82.
9. Charles Olson, *The Maximus Poems* (New York: Jargon/Corinth Books, 1960), p. 95.
10. Eric Bentley, *A Century of Hero-Worship* (Boston: Beacon Press, 1957).
11. William Empson, *The Structure of Complex Words* (London: Chatto and Windus, 1951), pp. 101–4.
12. M. R. Davis and W. H. Gilman (eds.), *The Letters of Herman Melville* (New Haven: Yale University Press, 1960), p. 131.
13. Emory Holloway (ed.), *Walt Whitman: Complete Verse, Selected Prose and Letters* (London: Nonesuch Press, 1938), p. 710 and footnote.
14. Malcolm Cowley (ed.), *Walt Whitman: Leaves of Grass—The First (1855) Edition* (London: Secker and Warburg, 1960), p. 85.
15. Albert Camus, 'Create Dangerously', *Rebellion, Resistance and Death* (London: Hamish Hamilton, 1961), p. 179.
16. Justin Kaplan, *Walt Whitman, A Life* (New York: Bantam Books, 1982), pp. 171–74.
17. Cowley, op. cit., p. 115.
18. Robert Creeley, 'Introduction', *Whitman: Selected by Robert Creeley* (Harmondsworth: Penguin Books, 1973), p. 7.
19. Edward Dahlberg, *Can These Bones Live* (New York: New Directions, 1960), pp. 66, 68.
20. Edwin T. Martin, *Thomas Jefferson: Scientist* (New York: 1952).
21. Camus, op. cit., p. 189.
22. Holloway, op. cit., pp. 816–17.
23. Wallace Stevens, *Collected Poems* (London: Faber, 1959), pp. 250–51.
24. René Char, *Leaves of Hypnos*, trans. Cid Corman (New York: Grossman, 1973), No. 37.
25. Blodgett and Bradley, op. cit., pp. 562–63, 572–73.
26. Matthew Arnold, 'The Study of Poetry', *Essays in Criticism*, Second Series (1880).
27. A. N. Whitehead, *Process and Reality* (1927–28; New York: Free Press, 1969), p. 26.

28. Jerome Rothenberg and George Quasha, *America a Prophecy* (New York: Doubleday, 1974), p. xxx.
29. Richard M. Bucke (ed.), *Walt Whitman, The Wound Dresser* (New York: The Bodley Press, 1949), p. 44. See also: Walter Lowenfels (ed.), *The Tenderest Lover: The Erotic Poetry of Walt Whitman* (New York: Dell, 1970), and 'The Wound-Dresser' and 'A March in the Ranks Hard-Prest, and the Road Unknown', CRE, 308 and 308.

2

Walt Whitman Passes the Full-Stop by. . . .

by MARK KINKEAD-WEEKES

> No one will get at my verses who insists on viewing them as a literary performance, or attempt at such a performance, or at aiming mainly towards art or aestheticism.[1]

> Now I reverse what I said, and affirm that all depends
>   on the aesthetic or intellectual,
> And that criticism is great—and that refinement is greatest
>   of all. . . .[2]

> Do I contradict myself?
> Very well then I contradict myself,
> (I am large, I contain multitudes).[3]

There is need, of course, for opposite stresses. And there is something refreshing about the very openness of Whitman's contradictions: the gross egotism and the eager democracy, the defiances and the need to embrace everything, the pleasure in attitudinizing and the awareness of pose. The draught of fresh air that still blows through his pages comes also from his determination to have nothing to do with the merely 'literary' and to have the courage, instead, to trust his voice to take him freely and organically to original forms of utterance. The first vital challenge of his poetry is that we may have to throw away our normal critical toolkits—the equipment tends not to fit. Yet there is need also to emphasize how much of Whitman remains blab, yawp and belch. How right Pound was when he told his father that he could not read *Leaves of Grass* 'without swearing at the author almost continuously'.[4] How right D. H. Lawrence was to denounce Whitman's inability to imagine the otherness of the other, which makes so many of the embracing gestures unbearably facile.[5] Whitman's attitudinizing frequently masks unwillingness to examine what he is saying. Might it not have been better if he had 'let it all out' less and discriminated more?— since letting it out can as easily be a sign of flatulence as of liberty. I must also confess to being rather weary of hearing so much from critics about Whitman's *attitudes*, which strike me on the whole as sadly flabby.

Perhaps as a consequence of this concern with Whitman's attitudes, there has been insufficient effort to establish what it is that makes Whitman a great and revolutionary *poet*, an extraordinary user of words and discoverer of form, though in far fewer poems than is generally admitted. For myself, and on the Alexandrian library test, I think that 'Song of Myself' could be allowed to perish with excessive grief, provided that 'When lilacs last in the dooryard bloom'd', 'Out of the cradle endlessly rocking', and 'Crossing Brooklyn Ferry' were preserved; and it is only a little teasing to suggest that we can get at what makes these his major poems far more surely by looking at Whitman's syntax than at his sentiments.

The real significance of many of Whitman's attitudes is their disconcerting implications for the making of poems. The one point that several critics do seem to raise about the poetics of 'Song of Myself' is the insistence not only on organic form but also on democratic syntax. The voice not only has to be free to take its way wholly independent of preconceived formal organization and careless of structure, finding its own; but, also, nothing that it says can be intrinsically any more important than any other thing. So, continuously, half-lines may equally celebrate opposites; and, more significantly, the syntax has to be radically co-ordinative rather than sub-ordinative. This reaches a democratic extreme in those passages where each line has become an independent as well as an equal unit.

I believe a leaf of grass is no less than the journey-work of
    the stars,
And the running blackberry would adorn the parlors of
    heaven,
And the tree-toad is a chef-d'oeuvre for the highest,
And the pismire is equally perfect, and a grain of sand, and
    the egg of the wren,
And a mouse is miracle enough to stagger sextillions of
    infidels,
And the cow crunching with depress'd head surpasses any
    statue,
And the narrowest hinge in my hand puts to scorn all
    machinery. . . .[6]

But it is not merely that the lines are equal, so that the
syntactical relation between them can only be 'and'; it follows
also that the order of the lines cannot be important. In fact I
have misquoted: the first line is where Whitman put it, but not
one of the others is in its textual place in relation to those that
precede and follow. Yet few readers will have noticed because
there is really nothing *to* notice. One can play the same game
with the sections of the work to some extent, though not so
much. They do fall into groups thematically like an extempore
sermon, but different critics give equally plausible classifica-
tions, all of which are very approximate. The sections are often
'poems' on their own, and one can play ducks and drakes a
good deal with their ordering before one makes any real
difference. This has its bearing of course on the theme of the
poem and its revolutionary and experimental nature; but the
trouble is that the organic and democratic impulses, carried to
such lengths, tend to produce flabby formlessness in the work
as a whole. There is no need for the poet to question whether
any bit of it is doing any work, and the Song becomes an
anthology, of distinctly uneven quality, where the good is often
neutralized by being cocooned within the flabby. Similarly the
more democratic one's syntax, the more likely one is to
produce catalogues in which there is little real imaginative life,
for in art (whatever may be true politically—and it is very
naïve to conflate different kinds of activity) quality depends on
exploratory discrimination.

How above all is such a poem to end? It cannot *conclude*,

45

with any sort of climax or finality, without playing its premises false. In one sense of course Whitman went on writing it through the various editions from 1855–92, so that it kept on being the song of himself. In another sense he kept passing the full-stop by, so that the poem goes on far too long. Even so there had to be some sort of ending, however arbitrary, and the solution is a neat one, achieving a final relation of the poet and the reader that is yet not concluded. 'I stop somewhere waiting for you': the poem thus openly proclaims that its formal ending is merely arbitrary; but this is also its deeper thematic point about time and the human life which the poem projects into the future, where Walt is still alive, not so much under our boots as on the page as we read, kept going by that present participle. There is a 'point' but no full-stop.

Only, the poetry carries little imaginative conviction because its statements so often remain assertions rather than creations which can command the suspension of disbelief. The tone of the last line is clever and jokey, with a fine full ring, and a nice ambiguity about *our* deaths as well as our gift of renewed life to the poem and the poet, but one is not inclined to take it very seriously. There is, however, in that continuous present participle, an indication of how radically Whitman may be committed to writing in not merely the present tense, but the continuous-present, projected forward beyond the apparent 'end'. This seems to me a major feature of his best work, and a very significant one. I propose now to consider seriously the ways in which the three major poems achieve form, and discipline, and conviction, in banishing the full-stop and making the poem a grammar of eternal life, achieving a triumph over the threat of death and finality in the *poetry*, the structure of the poetic language, not merely 'what it says'.

'When lilacs last in the dooryard bloom'd' (1865–66, 1871) is probably the most accessible of the three, because Whitman achieves a primary order and organization (which 'Song of Myself' so notably lacked) through the structural imagery of the lilac, associated with on-going life, the star that is associated with the death of Lincoln, and the song of the hermit thrush—and we are quite familiar with that kind of organization. It is therefore no accident that in a representa-tive collection of essays on Whitman this is the only poem of the three that gets fairly full treatment, by Charles Feidelson in 'Whitman as Symbolist'.[7] Yet in trying to discover how the poem finally brings together its different modes of apprehension we may find that symbolism is less important than syntax.

Since the poem proceeds by rewriting itself again and again, extending itself each time, but circling back into itself having taken in more, there is a sense in which the whole is already present in embryo in the first short section:

> When lilacs last in the dooryard bloom'd,
> And the great star early droop'd in the western sky in the
>   night,
> I mourn'd, and yet shall mourn with ever-returning spring.
>
> Ever-returning spring, trinity sure to me you bring,
> Lilac blooming perennial and drooping star in the west,
> And thought of him I love.

The first three lines are set firmly in the past tense, but then project an eternity of mourning into the future. Lincoln is dead. The language carries an odd suggestion that 'last' in 'Where lilacs last . . .' could mean 'for the last time', and though it clearly does not mean that, the 'ever-returning spring' merely brings a recurrent springing up of past grief. There is no present life. But the next three lines contain what the first three leave out, though they also leave out what those contain. Now the tense is the present, with not only the lilac 'bloom*ing* perennial' but the droop*ing* star's continuous presence also allied with a continuity of love. And, though we do not notice this until afterwards, the poetry has not merely juxtaposed two different modes of being and feeling but is already beginning to mediate between them, and contain them in a more inclusive medium. Already we cannot take the star as merely 'symbolic' of death or the lilac of life, one confined to the past and the other to the present and future; for the essence of what has happened is that each is beginning to participate in the mode of the other.

The next three sections then take up each of the elements we have met, and extend them. The fallen star is mourned anew, but the exclamatory mode of the grief now, which may strike one at first as objectionable apostrophe, suddenly reveals its point in its syntax. There are no verbs, hence there can be no sentences, only clauses. Nothing can be done; there can be no shaping into meaning; only cries of loss, grief, obscurity, helplessness. In contrast the verse for the lilac swells out, the growing thing *stands*, and the present participles proclaim its continuous and active life. (But is the poet's action as he breaks the sprig of lilac a death-action or a love/life-action? We shall see. . . .) In the fourth section we are given a surrogate for Whitman's poetry in the song of the hermit thrush which contains, in the present, both death and life. Growing, breaking, warbling, bleeding, have been associated with one another more firmly than before.

In Sections 5 to 9 the poem is rewritten again. Now the spring of continuous life out of winter, and the mournful cortège of death, are visually and dramatically juxtaposed. Through a spring landscape (which yet reminds us how it has sprung from death, violets from gray debris, grains of wheat ambiguously from 'shrouds') there is suddenly threaded the passing of Lincoln's coffin. Immediately the process is then reversed; the funereal pomp of the great procession passing sonorously through the land is suddenly brought up against the poet, bestowing his gift of lilac as an explicit fusion of life and love with death. It is not for that coffin only; for Whitman is determined to offer in gift and song the reminder of the burgeoning life of spring for all deaths. In Section 8, however, finality is allowed its say, in the memory of how the great star 'Concluded, dropt in the night, and was gone'. Only, it had manifestly not gone, for there it is a month later 'sailing the heaven', and the poem is conceiving a new awareness, therefore, of what the star 'must have meant'. Already, as the bird's song is taken up again in Section 9, the poet hears and understands; but he is not yet ready to give the understanding full expression, for he has not yet included enough. The process of the poem reveals itself as a cumulative delaying, which allows the potential reconciliation which has been present since the first section to keep announcing itself, but continually holds it back in order to get more into it, more resonance. The poem is prevented from developing in a straight line; above all it is prevented from coming to an end.

In that sense, already, we can see how its form is its theme; for the poem is preventing Lincoln's death from becoming final, in preventing itself from becoming finalized.

In Sections 10 to 12 the poet completes the elegiac formalities, composing an American elegy for the dead leader, decking funeral song and chamber. From east and west, sea and land, the winds are summoned to fuse with the poet's living breath, perfuming the grave. He creates American genre pictures of life for the dead man, of sunset in April, but also of the cyclical life of the sun. In singing for death he creates life through the senses. Once more in Section 13 the bird sings on. Once more, but for the last time, the poet hangs back, held by the star and the lilac.

In Section 14 the final rewriting begins by plunging us back into the past tense; and the poet is ready to announce now, in the recreated context of the approaching summer, but under the cloud of the long black funeral trail, his possession of both the 'thought' and the 'knowledge' of death. Between them, as between companions, he finally moves to hear the hermit thrush's song. The distinction between 'thought' and 'knowl-edge' requires no abstract formulation—Whitman merely expresses in a figure what the movement of his poem has been all the time. Between potential conception and actual realiza-tion, each stronger with each rewriting, the poem has moved from the beginning. And now the birdsong is permitted to voice its withheld syntactical secret; that death's rhythm is, no less than life's, *a continuous present and not a full-stop.*

> Come lovely and soothing death,
> Undulate round the world, serenely *arriving, arriving,* [my
>   italics]
> In the day, in the night, to all, to each,
> Sooner or later delicate death. . . .

Death is part of a continuous cycle, and must be celebrated along with life, even joyfully. One retorts, of course, that the lyricism is facile and sentimental, finding it simple to see death 'universally', and call it pretty names, because the eyes are closed to actual human experience. Is death 'lovely and soothing', 'delicate', 'cool-enfolding', 'soft', 'floating . . . bliss' to the dying or to the bereaved? Fortunately Whitman himself has just proclaimed that 'thought' must go hand in hand with 'knowledge'; so the conceiving of death's universal rhythm has to be fused with a realization of the 'debris' of the dead and the suffering of those who remain. Lyricism is stilled into a silent nightmare vision of a civil war battlefield. (He had of course been to the front to search for his brother and had been a volunteer army hospital nurse from 1862–64.)

> I saw battle-corpses, myriads of them,
> And the white skeletons of young men, I saw them,
> I saw the debris and debris of all the slain soldiers of the war.

Yet he will not have the reverse sentimentality either. By dying, the dead no longer feel the tragedy of the full-stop and the past tense; it is the living who carry the full weight of these.

> But I saw they were not as was thought,
> They themselves were fully at rest, they suffer'd not,
> The living remain'd and suffer'd, the mother suffer'd,
> And the wife and the child and the musing comrade suffer'd,
> And the armies that remain'd suffer'd.

This section is perhaps still too visionary; it lacks the quiet factual horror of his letter to his mother on 29 March 1864; but it saves the poem which, without it, would be as sentimental as the song of the thrush taken alone. Yet the full-stop after 'suffer'd' is as half-a-truth as the rhythm of death as continuous present. What end can the poem attain that is not sentimental or partial?

The answer is to create a poetry that encompasses all that has gone before, beginning with letting go, ending; but re-marshalls all into a unique form which can not only make the full-stop on which we have just ended only a phase to be passed by, but can also convincingly retrieve what is past and make it infinite. It works like the winding and unwinding of a spool so that neither movement is the whole, and I think my insistence on syntax justifies itself, since this is how it is done. (The 'symbols' of lilac star and bird are revealed as only the means to a marvellously creative syntactical end.) First, Whitman circumvents that full-stop by 'passing', apparently in farewell, going back through his poem from the end to the beginning, enacting a process of continual separation. He takes leave of each element in the complex whole, one by one, 'passing', 'ceasing'—yet each element as it is passed is there to us in the continuing life of present participles. But finally there is a retrieving out of the night whose achievement is even stranger; for the memory of the elements is woven together and projected in that form we refer to precisely as the infinitive.

> Yet each to keep and all, retrievements out of the night,
> The song, the wondrous chant of the gray-brown bird,
> And the tallying chant, the echo arous'd in my soul,
> With the lustrous and drooping star with the countenance
>   full of woe,
> With the holders holding my hand nearing the call of the
>   bird,
> Comrades mine and I in the midst, and their memory ever
>   to keep, for the dead I loved so well,
> For the sweetest, wisest soul of all my days and lands—and
>   this for his dear sake,
> Lilac and star and bird twined with the chant of my soul,
> There in the fragrant pines and the cedars dusk and dim.

The poem nominally 'ends' with the word 'dim' and a full-stop; but its form proclaims the opposite, centring on the infinitive 'to keep'. There is no verb—'twined' is a past-participle—because what is 'infinitive' must be neither present past nor future, but a mode secured beyond all. 'Passing . . . I leave . . . I cease . . . yet each and all *to keep* . . . *there* . . .', this is the poem's achieved grammar of eternal life. The meaning is enacted in the language, fully formed and controlled, where 'Song of Myself' orates and attitudinizes. 'Lilacs' is a revolutionary poem for which we have to find an uniquely appropriate critical approach. I know no other poem like it.

Or rather, I do: 'Out of the cradle endlessly rocking' (1859, 1881), which is indeed in some ways even better. For if one had to formulate a limiting criticism of 'Lilacs' it might well be that, for Whitman, it is still too 'symbolic'; in his terms almost too 'literary'. The three 'symbols' are appropriate and are handled tactfully, but they have a certain initial arbitrariness, a sense of being imported into the poem as machinery. Whereas the sea, the mocking bird and the child are concretely fused in an actual memory, and the eliciting of their interaction is more spontaneous and organic than the elaborate tour de force of 'Lilacs'.

Once again the poem is adumbrated in potential at the beginning, and then rewritten and extended. This time, however, instead of beginning even apparently in a 'symbolic' way, Whitman starts with a splendid oratorio interweaving the senses and the tenses in music. The first energy is a gathering movement in the language, done this time by the prepositions. From all directions, out of, over, down from, up from, out from, from under, borne hither, the various elements of the remembered scene are gathered together. The weaving is done in terms of sound (the sea rocking, the mocking-bird's shuttle); of light (the interplay of moonlight and shadow); of inner and outer space (the boy on the beach, and the inner movement of the heart responding to the notes); and of time (the man in the 'now' of the poem fusing with the boy in the past). The past is created as a repository of energies, still going on in present participles within the past tense, and capable of being tapped and brought bodily into the present, uniting with the 'words' the experience had already given rise to. The past becomes actively present and the poet aspires to unite the here with the hereafter.

> From those beginning notes of yearning and love there in
>   the mist,
> From the thousand responses of my heart never to cease,
> From the myriad thence-arous'd words,
> From the word stronger and more delicious than any,
> From such as now they start the scene revisiting,
> As a flock, twittering, rising, or overhead passing,
> Borne hither, ere all eludes me, hurriedly,
> A man, yet by these tears a little boy again,
> Throwing myself on the sand, confronting the waves,
> I, chanter of pains and joys, uniter of here and hereafter,
> Taking all hints to use them, but swiftly leaping beyond
>   them,
> A reminiscence sing.

The second section of the poem proceeds to orchestrate the memory of boy and bird—with the sea only as murmurous background—by playing the boy's language against the bird's song. Here again, watching the tenses will show the curious way in which, as they are interwoven, each is transformed into the mode of the other. The boy begins in a subtly 'imperfect' past. 'Once' secures pastness from the start, but the poetry emphasises, in the repeated 'every day', the continuous being of the nesting birds and the continuous activity of the boy 'peering, absorbing, translating'. Suddenly one realizes that there is no finite verb ('crouched' being, again, a past participle). Meanwhile the first birdsong is a tremendously confident present imperative: 'Shine! shine! shine! . . . Singing all time, minding no time,/ While we two keep together.' With the disappearance of the she-bird, however, the boy's tense hardens into the perfect; but the bird's song becomes more tentative: 'Blow! blow! blow! . . . I wait and I wait *till you blow* my mate to me' (my italics). Now however the boy's language begins to turn from the past into the present; the past tense changes back into the-present-in-the-past, done in participles; and that becomes infinitive and 'now'.

> I, with bare feet, a child, the wind wafting my hair,
> Listen'd long and long.
>
> Listen'd to keep, to sing, now translating the notes,
> Following you my brother.

Conversely, in a beautifully modulated process too long to quote, we hear the confidence in continuity ebbing away in the birdsong, revealing a greater and greater tentativeness, breaking the rhythm, getting softer and more despairing, till eventually the full impact of loss locks home in the past tense.

> Loved! loved! loved! loved! loved!
> But my mate no more, no more with me!
> We two together no more.

The two complementary processes are enacted in the language. In the birdsong we are made to *experience* how the living present cannot be held, but turns agonizingly into the past with the inescapable fact of death. Conversely, in the 'translation' we experience the opposite process as the past is made to live so vividly again that it becomes a mode of present energy. As the birdsong dies away, the language surges into continuous activity, rendered in a powerful series of present participles, and out of that concentration of energies the poet is born. The bird has become a daimon-'demon', wakening inspiration for a thousand songs, but also arousing torment. Out of the intuition of grief and death poetry starts to life, but the process is then projected into an endless future, with the realization that he will never cease perpetuating the bird, will never escape the cries of unsatisfied love, 'the sweet hell within,/ The unknown want'.

And it is in answer to the pain of that—which is *always* the present projecting the future, unable to cease or be satisfied, unable to achieve the rest of the past—that the sea (which has been murmuring in the background all the time) is at last allowed to sound through.

> Whereto answering, the sea,
> Delaying not, hurrying not,
> Whisper'd me through the night, and very plainly before
>   daybreak,
> Lisp'd to me the low and delicious word death,
> And again death, death, death, death.

I do not think that 'delicious' is as damaging as the lapse into sentimentality at the corresponding point in 'Lilacs'. For, in context, the sound and rhythm of the language in these lines *is* tranquillizing, with something of the whisper of sea on sand that all men find soothing; and not only has the pain of loss already been secured, but we have just been made to realize, also, how intolerable it would be to banish the past tense and live without death. Yet what the sea whispers is not the bird's tragic apprehension of the past as finished, any more than it is the boy's sense of an unfinishable present and future. The next lines ensure that we hear sound and sense aright, not only whisper-ing, but with the spaces between the words that show the secret meaning. The rhythm of death is, even more clearly than in 'Lilacs', a cyclic recurrence of that which gives rest again, and again, and again, like the 'shsh' of wavelets on the shore or the soothing of a mother at the cradle, but rocking endlessly:

> Hissing melodious, neither like the bird nor like my arous'd
>   child's heart,
> But edging near as privately for me rustling at my feet,
> Creeping thence steadily up to my ears and laving me softly
>   all over,
> Death, death, death, death, death.

Presumably the last line 'rocks' by a breath-pause between each 'death'. All the poet has to do, finally, is to 'fuse' birth and death in a series of paradoxes. What the weaving together of birdsong, responsive song, and sea song has achieved is a sense of how the intuition of death brings both the poet and his poetry to life, and soothes the ache of endlessness with finality, which is yet endlessly recurrent. The sea is both aged crone and sweet-smelling mother.

There is also a hidden paradox in the syntax of the ending; for the delay caused by the parenthesis, especially if the lines are read aloud, ensures that the last line echoes in the mind on its own, as well as in its grammatical relation to its predecessors.[9] One can see how this curious effect would have been spoilt if Whitman had written 'The sea whisper'd *to* me', for though the sea does whisper to him, it also in another sense whispers *him*, into poetic being, and the 'me' is not yet finite, though the poem has happened. Moreover Whitman has also invented a new tense, the past-present, for the experience is apparently in the past, a memory, yet it is equally obviously happening now, when the poem finally comes into existence—as it ends.

If one were still to carp a little, it would be because death continues to be seen in a context which takes the sting out of it, though there is less damaging sentimentality than in 'Lilacs'. (There is also, however, less to counteract it of the tragic stature of the Civil War, or indeed the death of Lincoln.) Whitman certainly never focuses on what it is like to die. Nevertheless the talk about 'delicate' or 'delicious' death is not merely a question of Whitman failing to make himself realize what death is and means with sufficient resonance. At least part of the trouble is that he is not really interested in death, but is using it notionally in order to explore the ability of poetry to connect past and future. If one were now to draw up a recipe for a poem that would be even better, even less question-begging than 'Out of the cradle', it would be one in which the poet no longer needed to talk of death in order to achieve his dance of the tenses. And, since the superiority of 'Out of the Cradle' to 'Lilacs' rests on the absence of symbolic manipulation, it should be a poem still more 'everyday', still less exotic and contrived. I am describing what I take to be Whitman's finest poem.

'Crossing Brooklyn Ferry' is a deeply democratic poem in the sense that it springs naturally and unforced from the experience of anyone who has ever crossed on a big-city ferry—a marvellously complex and convincing work built out of the very ordinary. From the beginning it is concrete and specific, set matter-of-factly in space and time: the flood tide, the sun half an hour from setting, the hundreds of people sharing the experience, the people who will cross years hence. The poem seems to grow spontaneously, unmanipulated, with no showing off of the poet, or his powers, and yet from the start there is a quiet declaration that the 'usual' may be more extraordinary and meaningful than one supposes.

The second section allows the setting and the crowds to sustain the individual poet. He and all the other individuals are alone, 'disintegrated', yet part of the 'scheme'; his actions in walking the streets and being borne on the flood are 'similitudes' of both past and future; they have happened before and will happen again; and this gives them a glory in their ordinariness for they connect him with 'certainty of others'. The tense breaks into the future, in the calm and naturally justified conviction that others *will* do and see just as he does and sees.

In the third section Whitman enacts just this in enacting the crossing. In closely observed visual detail he brings the scene alive: the gulls wheeling above in the last of the sunlight, the low sun aureoling the reflection of his head in the water, the haze on the hills, the shipping coming in from the bay, the activity in the docks, the light fading, the fires from the foundry chimneys casting flickering lights on housetops and the chasms of the streets. There seems little to say about this section except to point to the vividness, the conviction that this is just what he saw, and what one would see essentially oneself. Difference of place and date are insignificant.

So when he declares his love for Brooklyn and Manhattan, and the stately river, it is matter of fact; and we accept equally his feeling for the others crossing with him, for the affection of the whole portrayal includes them. We can even accept quite simply that imagining the future the same as his present has brought him 'near' to those who will look back on him—

ourselves—because he looked forward to them—'The time will come, though I stop here to-day and to-night.' This gives a strange yet simple feeling, for of course the time has come and Walt Whitman has stopped . . . in a sense.

But in a sense this is not so. In the fifth section the poem begins to stir and grow curiously. For it was with the body that is now dead—as he foresaw, putting himself into the past—that Walt Whitman was himself in his personal identity, 'struck from the float'. It was in his body that he was what he had called in another poem a simple separate person. And it was also through the physical imagination that he is able to enter past and future. In the sixth section he writes a self-analysis quite free from posturing and attitudinizing; simply emphasizing how it was his life in the body that gave him the ordinary experience of humanity, the evil as well as the good, the friendship and the reticence. (Perhaps Whitman's homosexuality adds a level of meaning here, but one would distort by emphasizing it, because he is stressing the common experience of all human beings.)

In the seventh section he springs a comic surprise; telling us that he has considered us seriously before we were born, and teasing us with the thought that he may be looking at us, and enjoying it, as we read. And in the eighth section, after reminding us of his evening scene in not only its beauty but its human relationship, he insists that something has happened, while we were not looking. The 'play' immortality is suddenly revealed in a truer mode.

> What is more subtle than this which ties me to the woman
>   or man that looks in my face?
> Which fuses me into you now, and pours my meaning into
>   you?
>
> We understand then do we not?
> What I promis'd without mentioning it, have you not
>   accepted?
> What the study could not teach—what the preaching could
>   not accomplish is accomplish'd, is it not?

It *is* accomplished—that annihilating of time that is immortality, that fusion of present, past and future that has been the

57

subject of all three poems, but that this one has achieved so quietly that one had not even noticed.

Away back in the third section, as Whitman subtly placed future 'crossers' in the present and himself in the past ('Just as you feel . . . so I felt'), he had made us identify with the scene as happening to us 'now'. It manifestly does happen as we read, the experience of crossing the ferry, and he is with us as we cross in his crossing. We experience from moment to moment the turning eye, and the movement of the ferry from the near side to the far side coming near, and the fading of the sun into the dark. More subtly still, within the scene itself, Whitman has provided us with common optical illusions which themselves enact, in miniature, the whole strange intersection of time that is the central experience of the poem. 'Just as you stand and lean on the rail, yet hurry with the swift current, I stood yet was hurried.' The passenger stands apparently still on the spot, but is being carried from one side of the river to the other, stands apparently steady in the present, yet is being carried momentarily from the past into the future. As he looks up the gulls seem to float motionless; but they are moving and he is moving, as the slow drift away finally shows. The reflected face in the water is even more significant. The 'centrifugal spokes of light' that aureole the face happen because the sun is shining past a moving object onto moving water; and yet the face appears to the observer on the boat to be still, whereas in fact it is moving fast. The face Whitman gazed at each split second was gone from the water the next, but another was there in its place . . . and it was still there when he wrote the poem in 1856, and revised it in 1881, and it is still there when I am reading it now, and will be there when you read it in the future. The poetry marvellously creates an experience which is pluperfect before the poem, perfect in the poem, present and manifestly happening as we read, and available in the future. Moreover we are always *crossing* Brooklyn ferry in the poem; we never get to the other side, finish it all off, say 'that's done'. Whitman has connected his past, his present, and our future in which he is clearly immortal, in the poetry.

So he has earned the right in the final section to celebrate the crossing again, and all the things he 'saw', in that continuous present tense and imperative mood that are his favourite modes of expression, because the limitation of finite time is abolished and control is assured. 'Flow on', he cries, 'flow and ebb . . . frolic on . . . drench . . . cross . . . stand up . . . throb . . . suspend here and everywhere, eternal float of solution . . . gaze . . . sound out . . . live', and so *on*. The rich vitality is urged on into continuous active life; and the imperative takes place both in his time scheme and in ours. Lastly he celebrates what enabled him to bridge present, past and future: the bodily senses which made his experience both his then and ours now, and the lastingness of the world of appearances. These are spiritual too, for it is they that have linked Walt Whitman in immortality with us. By the final paragraph, for the first time in any of the three poems, the dominant pronoun has become 'we', with an inevitability quite unforced by exhortation. 'What the study could not teach—what the preaching could not accomplish is accomplish'd, is it not?' If he was at fault so very often in confusing poetry with oratory, in this poem he has created rather than harangued. He has realized a fusion of the tenses through the senses, and in doing so has been able (of all things for Whitman!) to be subtly reticent, and to make the achievement good before proclaiming it.

NOTES

1. 'A Backward Glance O'er Travel'd Roads', penultimate paragraph. An earlier version of this essay appeared in Brian S. Lee (ed.), *An English Miscellany* (Cape Town: Oxford University Press, 1977). We are grateful for permission to use and update the essay.
2. 'Says' (*Leaves of Grass*, 1860).
3. 'Song of Myself', Section 51.
4. 3 June 1913, *The Letters of Ezra Pound*, ed. D. D. Paige (London, 1951), p. 57.
5. *Studies in Classic American Literature* (New York, 1923).
6. 'Song of Myself', Section 31.
7. *Twentieth Century Views of Whitman*, ed. Roy Harvey Pearce (Englewood Cliffs: Prentice-Hall, 1962).
8. *The Collected Writings of Walt Whitman. The Correspondence Vol. 1*, ed. E. H. Miller (New York, 1961), p. 204–5.

9.   Which I do not forget,
But fuse the song of my dusky demon and brother,
That he sang to me in the moonlight on Paumanok's gray beach,
With the thousand responsive songs at random,
My own songs awaked from that hour,
And with them the key, the word up from the waves,
The word of the sweetest song and all songs,
That strong and delicious word which, creeping to my feet,
(Or like some old crone rocking the cradle, swathed in sweet
      garments, bending aside,)
The sea whisper'd me.

3

Valley News:
Emily Dickinson at Home and Beyond

by JIM PHILIP

1

Mother has been an invalid since we came *home*, and Vinnie and I 'regulated' and Vinnie and I 'got settled' and still we keep our father's house, and mother lies upon the lounge, or sits in her easy chair. I don't know what her sickness is, for I am but a simple child, and frightened at myself. I often wish I was a grass, or a toddling daisy, whom all these problems of the dust might not terrify—.[1]

In this letter to Mrs. Holland, perhaps her most understanding friend and correspondent, Emily Dickinson comments in her own way on an event that must have been of greatest importance for her whole family. In 1855, her father, Edward Dickinson, made the decision that the profits from his successful Amherst law practice were sufficient to make possible the repurchase of the brick mansion in Main Street, known as 'The Homestead'—built by *his* father Samuel Fowler Dickinson and in which he himself had lived as a child. This 'homecoming' for him must have been a triumph, a vindication of all his past efforts, and at the same time an absolution of that erraticness and financial collapse that had beset his father in later years, and had caused the sale of the house in the first place. The

61

Dickinsons were now back where they belonged: their power re-established in Amherst itself and in the college for which from 1835 Edward Dickinson served as Treasurer and in the state of Massachusetts at large. The family had reclaimed its legacy of pre-eminence in Connecticut Valley life, the inheritance of what Richard B. Sewell calls 'the River Gods'.[2] For Emily herself, however, as her letter suggests, reclaiming the family homestead brought out an altogether more ambivalent response.

For all its symbolic value, the house is also for her the site of a daily labour of 'regulation', and in this respect, as she points out, not much has changed for herself or her sister Vinnie. More importantly, and more disturbingly, this new 'home' is also the place where her mother continues her largely inarticulate processes of 'sickness'. Care as well as exasperation underlie the daughter's words, and also, surely, the tentative diagnosis that the problem had as much to do with the soul, as she might have put it, as with the body. As she comes finally to phrase it, it is 'problems of the dust' that her mother is facing, that is to say feelings of reduction, of pointlessness, of unfulfilment. The reluctant, avoided and unstated conclusion of this passage is that 'the home', the place of such triumph, may also be the place of anxiety and dissolution, possibly even of destruction.

We have evidence, here, of some of the lived conditions out of which Emily Dickinson's writings were forged. To describe her as a genius marred by domestic enslavement would of course be extreme and false. For one thing her letters express a genuine affection for her father and pride in his achievements. To the extent that her life was one of service it was undertaken in a spirit of genuine and selfless care. Moreover it is clear that in no sense were her adolescence or early adulthood periods of isolation. Amherst was a lively community, both socially, and, through the influence of the College, intellectually. The Dickinson children played their full part in the life of the younger set, and distinguished visitors that their father's professional and political interests brought to the house must have been an added benefit. However, her letters of the 1850s do display an undeniable and increasing element of disjunction. As in the letter to Mrs. Holland there is a wariness, an urge to examine in a more complex light the defining pressures of her

life, to understand their origins, and to take full measure of their
forming, or deforming, power. There are also signs of a
burgeoning individuality, of a willingness to acknowledge and
explore aspects of herself, even though they may not fit any of
the accepted rôles or codes.

In a hesitant, probably unfinished but nevertheless revealing
poem of 1862 we find an attempt to present this opening field of
unrest.

> I put new Blossoms in the Glass—
> And throw the old—away—
> I push a petal from my Gown
> That anchored there—I weigh
> The time 'twill be till six o'clock
> I have so much to do—
> And yet—Existence—some way back—
> Stopped—struck—my ticking—through—
> We cannot put Ourself away
> As a completed Man
> Or Woman—When the Errand's done
> We came to Flesh—upon—
> There may be—Miles on Miles of Nought—
> Of Action—sicker far—
> To simulate—is stinging work—
> To cover what we are
> From Science—and from Surgery—
> Too telescopic Eyes
> To bear on us unshaded—
> For their—sake—not for Ours—[3]

These lines are remarkable for the way in which they evoke,
but also dismantle, the familiar world of domestic duty. There
is a sense of business, of absorbed 'regulation', but we should
not miss from the start of the undertones of exasperation and
even obsession. The 'new Blossoms' will soon in their turn be
'old'; there will be other detritus that will 'anchor' itself to the
clean surfaces. A confined and time-bound world is estab-
lished, so that 'I have so much to do' is already ironic, and we
are prepared for the later transformations of the same activity
into a 'ticking', and finally into 'Miles on Miles of Nought'.
Most importantly, though, this life is seen as accompanied by
another state of being, an 'Existence', a 'completion', that is at

once displaced into the past and continues to haunt the present as an unrealizable but disruptive possibility. Dickinson's dashes are a distinctive feature of her style, used often to slow the line down and to insist upon the choice, freight and relation of single words. Where they proliferate, as they do in the central lines here, they are surely a sign of an emotional charge so powerful, but so 'other' that it resists the efforts of formulation. If we read with care we can posit a deep disturbance here, of frustration, of delay, of guilt, of anger both at the self and its assumed creator. In the final lines there is the related but painful recognition that these occluded energies may be the real ground of our being; they are 'what we are', and the fabric of daily life is in comparison a 'simulation', a secondary and incomplete charade. The implications of this new reading of the human personality are not lost on Dickinson. To trace them out to their full extent would require a rigorous 'Science', a 'surgery', but this venture is at the same time feared because of the full horrors it might reveal.

Perhaps enough has been said to suggest the way in which this poem operates, as does the body of Dickinson's work, within a field of rich and powerful transitions. The writing is concerned here not simply with household frustration, but with larger disruptions of which this is the immediate symptom. What is really being challenged is that whole network of theological assumptions which had underpinned New England life from its Puritan origins, and which had survived in the Connecticut Valley in particularly strong forms: the assertion of God as an unknowable but infinite power; the subjugation of women to men; the investment of socially determined rôles and divisions with the powerful aura of 'duty'; and the inhibition of passion and free inquiry through the mechanism of guilt and fear. What is glimpsed here as an alternative is that expression, exploration and embodiment of human subjectivity that, in its various forms as art and literature, as psychology, and as radical social practice, has conditioned the modern period. Dickinson's work is transitional in a fuller sense, however, in that it is often capable of reversion into the very conditions that it seeks to surpass. We can see in this poem how the new explorations are feared and resented as much as they are desired. It remains possible to read the poem as the confessions of a penitent, seeking out the erratic elements in her own nature so as to expose and eradicate them. As such it bears relation to that long tradition of Puritan meditative verse, of which Edward Taylor, a previous seventeenth-century inhabitant of the Valley, offers the most striking example.

This ambivalence of judgement, and the open and unresolved syntax in which it is embodied, should act as pointers to one essential quality of her art, that is to say the way in which she habitually eschews resolution in favour of doubt. She accepts and presents herself as an open field of contradictions. It is this quality particularly that marks out her work against that of the Transcendentalists who, in the same period but in their own ways, were seeking to overcome some of the hierarchial and repressive tendencies of Puritanism. Emily Dickinson knew Emerson's writings, and there is evidence to suggest that she drew sustenance from his message of self-reliance, exploration and experiment.[4] However, as she read his work she must have become wary of the numbing and limiting rhetoric of Transcendentalist optimism, the assertion that all divisions, either internal or external, are only apparent divisions and capable of resolution on higher grounds. In her scepticism, and her acceptance of deep splits and riddles in the nature of herself and the world, she is far closer to her 'darker', nay-saying contemporaries Hawthorne and Melville. But she was more rigorous in her pursuit of her own depths than the former, and she was less appalled, less driven to silence, by what she found there than the latter.

These qualities, then, distinguish her writing from that of her contemporaries, but they also do much to explain its procedures and its internal organization. That is why, for instance, there are so many poems, and most of them so short. Each is a single conjecture, accepting its possible supersedence, a single step in what she herself describes as 'that precarious Gait/ some call Experience'.[5] That is why, in their metrical forms, the poems so often invite regularity only to deny it. That is why, too, they rely so often on such devices as irony, paradox and ellipsis. That is why they are so deeply imbued in metaphor and analogy, the simplicity of the vehicle providing an anchor for the range and complexity of the tenors.

Moreover, as I have indicated, her 'open' syntax, ellipses and characteristic uses of the dash mark the strained and uncertain relation between language and what is felt to lie beyond it. Overall this is a case in which, to an unusual and illuminating extent, the writing is conditioned by enquiry rather than definition, by questions rather than answers. From her letters and from the limited knowledge that we have of her personal life, it is clear that Dickinson's earlier hopes were that she might live out her own processes of discovery in and through the company of others. However, as her own self-presentation became more complex, and as friends dispersed or increasingly compromised with the pressures of existing institutions and ideas, so this channel was slowly and reluctantly abandoned. Underlying her greater retirement and commitment to writing in the 1860s is the conviction that in language she might sustain that desired openness which in Amherst she could not.

Dickinson's refusal to edit, to conclude, is thus embodied throughout her work, and it is helpfully suggested in this brief poem that records both the fascinations and the disappointments of literary fiction:

> No Romance sold unto
> Could so enthrall a Man
> As the perusal of
> His individual One—
> 'Tis Fiction's to dilute to Plausibility
> Our Novel—When 'tis small enough
> To Credit—'Tisn't true![6]

This should stand as a warning not only to the novelist, but also to the critic who seeks to encapsulate within a few pages another's lengthy commitments to language, and through it, to life. However, it should be possible, within the whole field of Dickinson's recorded experience, to point to certain elements which, through repetition and through insistence, assume the nature of a generating ground. It is rather like listening closely to an extended conversation, and trying to discover within it the springs of motive.

2

One issue that should certainly concern us is that of 'pain'. There are many poems that revolve around this as their central term, and it is clear that Dickinson found it a useful one both for defining certain qualities within her own experience, and for reaching out to that of others. 'Teach me the skill/', she demands in one poem, 'that I instill the pain/ Surgeons assuage in vain'.[7] But what is this pain? In one of her most well-known poems it is embodied as 'the Hour of Lead', as an experience of paralysis, numbness:

> The Feet mechanical go round—
> Of Ground, or Air, or Ought
> A Wooden way,
> Regardless grown. . . .[8]

Robert Weisbuch neatly paraphrases this as a state in which 'all meanings, all aspirations, all duties . . . become "regard-less", indifferent.'[9] Other connected images are those of freezing, of burial, and, importantly, of falling. It is these latter which predominate in perhaps the most striking poem of all:

> I felt a Funeral, in my Brain,
> And Mourners to and fro
> Kept treading—treading—till it seemed
> That Sense was breaking through—
>
> And when they all were seated,
> A Service, like a Drum—
> Kept beating—beating—till I thought
> My mind was going numb—
>
> And then I heard them lift a Box
> And creak across my Soul
> With those same Boots of Lead, again,
> Then Space—began to toll,
>
> As all the Heavens were a Bell,
> And Being, but an Ear,
> And I, and Silence, some strange Race
> Wrecked, solitary, here—

> And then a Plank in Reason, broke
> And I dropped down, and down
> And hit a World, at every plunge,
> And Finished knowing—then—[10]

The void of lost identity, relationship, meaning and purpose could not be more vividly expressed. The brain is populated by anonymous strangers, whose activities are as ceaseless and non-sensical as they are invasive. Their function is to bury a further self that remains alive, though bereft of action, speech and company. As the metaphorical scene shifts from the church to the universe this isolation is imaged as an enormous journey across space and time in which the only contact is that of collision and rejection, impelling further movement.

3

Poems of this kind have such a vertiginous speed that we imagine their unstated conclusions can only be in breakdown and madness. But we should remember that the very writing of them implies a certain degree of control and manipulation. Moreover other texts bear witness not only to survival, but also to processes of transformation and confirmation available by no other means. Take, for instance, the following:

> The Province of the Saved
> Should be the Art—To Save
> Through skill obtained in Themselves
> The Science of the Grave
>
> No Man can understand
> But He that hath endured
> The Dissolution—in Himself—
> That Man—be qualified
>
> To qualify Despair
> To Those who failing new—
> Mistake Defeat for Death—Each time—
> Till acclimated—to—[11]

This must certainly be one of Dickinson's 'surest' poems. There is a confident announcement not only of endurance, but of passage to a fuller state, the 'Province of the Saved'.

Moreover, the confirmation is not simply one of being, but also of function and vocation. Out of these experiences there emerges a new conception of writing as 'The Science of the Grave', as a force able to confront the most terrifying of human experiences, and illuminate them in ways not possible before, a public and therapeutic task. We should not under-estimate the extent to which the poem speaks from a position of dignity and purpose beyond the confines of a limiting theology. The 'Saved' that the speaker has joined are clearly no longer those who profess a traditional faith. There is no sense here of an influx of grace granted by omnipotent force. Rather the recovery has occurred 'in Themselves'—'in Himself'. Its processes, though not fully declared or understood, are yet felt to be internal, and generated from within the negative experiences themselves. It is interesting in this context to recall Dickinson's firm refusal at several points in her life to join those communal 'Awakenings' that were a recurrent feature of church life in the Valley.[12] She sought other outcomes for her own anxieties, and poems like the present one confirm that the choice was not a fruitless one.

Both of the last poems quoted have curiously elliptical but suggestive endings. In the first the sufferer 'Finished knowing—then—', which may suggest unconsciousness, but also the gaining of a new kind of knowledge. In the second he or she is 'acclimated—to—', which implies an equally radical but spontaneous transformation. Yet another poem returns from the same ground with the conviction that something indisputable but at the same time inexplicable has occurred. The celebration of an incontrovertible 'Fact' is a rare and important event in Dickinson's writing!

> If any sink, assume that this, now standing—
> Failed like Themselves—and conscious that it rose—
> Grew by the Fact, and not the Understanding
> How weakness passed—or Force—arose—[13]

If we were to use a different terminology to describe these phenomena we would perhaps say that the fall into unmeaning has been transformed through acceptance: that, beyond despair, some new root has been found for the human personality on the ground of irrational but instinctive 'Force'.

The poems that best evoke these crucial movements are those that deploy as their central symbol the explosive power of the volcano. Thus, in Poem 175, the speaker wonders 'If this stillness is Volcanic/ In the human face/ When upon a pain Titanic/ Features keep their place—'.[14] And in Poem 601 the same image is developed with greater vividness and relational force:

> A quiet—Earthquake Style—
> Too subtle to suspect
> By natures this side Naples—
> The North cannot detect
>
> The Solemn—Torrid—Symbol
> The lips that never lie—
> Whose hissing Corals part—and shut—
> And Cities—ooze away—[15]

It would perhaps be going too far to credit Dickinson with the discovery and articulation of her own unconscious, but at the same time one cannot help noticing the similarity between the forces embodied here, and those inner dynamics as mapped by Freud and his inheritors. Indeed it is worth noting that Dickinson was interested in the dream world, and based several of her poems directly on such material.[16] What is noticeable here is the stress on eruptive power, on a potential both for decreation and creation, a condition of ultimate 'truth', and, as we shall explore later, an interesting suggestion that it is as language, as speech, that this force can penetrate to the other levels, to the 'North', of the mind. The new sense of power, purpose and sheer hilarity occasioned by the acceptance of these sources is well embodied in the following brief poem, which restates in reversed terms the theme of the fall away from meaning:

> I'm Nobody! Who are you?
> Are you—Nobody—Too?
> Then there's a pair of us?
> Don't tell! They'd advertise—you know!
>
> How dreary—to be—Somebody!
> How public—like a Frog—
> To tell one's name—the livelong June—
> To an admiring Bog![17]

Here the need for consistency, for sustained identity, for the absorption and reinforcement of established codes is joyfully undermined and mocked. Moreover, the first verse suggests the confirming paradox that, for all the loneliness of the journey into the self, it is there that the seeds of a new and more authentic sociality may be found.

4

It is also in this context that we should consider those numerous poems that deal with the elements and creatures of the natural world. These only make fullest sense when read in relation to that exploratory account of human consciousness the course of which we have been following. The outer world is placed in dialogue with the inner, its unknowable but intuited energies providing a means for acknowledging and valuing instinctive levels of the self. It is approached with curiosity, with care, sometimes with envy, but always with a sense of provoking difference. Take, for instance, this account of the air:

> Air has no Residence, no Neighbor,
> No Ear, no Door
> No Apprehension of Another
> Oh, Happy Air!
> . . . . .
> Later than Light thy Consciousness accost me
> Till it depart, persuading Mine—[18]

Here, neither term is subjected to the other. There is no pantheistic absorption of the person into the element; nor, on the other hand, is there a celebration of the mind's power to absorb all material fact into higher law. What happens rather is a process of 'accosting' and 'persuasion'—the intuited freedom and pervasiveness of the air provoking the recognition of undeniable longings within the self. A similar sense of the natural as both separation and stimulation is contained in the description of the bobolink, as

> Extrinsic to Attention
> Too intimate with Joy—
> He compliments existence
> Until allured away[19]

The bobolink is, of course, a bird, a creature that sings, and there is much evidence to suggest that Dickinson was particularly fascinated by the sounds around her, finding in them the greatest evidence for the proposition of a pervasive 'joy', and the greatest stimulus to some of her own sources of being. But humans, too, are creatures that sing, as Dickinson keenly appreciated. Even in the years of her fullest retirement, she often invited guests to perform for her at The Homestead. Sometimes she would not meet them or speak to them, but would listen from the stairs or another room and offer a poem in exchange.[20] More than once in her writings it occurs to her to speculate that her own compulsive habits of composition may have as much to do with the sounds she is able to make:

> Reportless subjects, to the Quick
> Continual addressed—
> But foreign as the Dialect
> Of Danes, unto the Rest
>
> Reportless measures, to the Ear
> Susceptive,—Stimulus—
> But like an Oriental Tale
> To others, fabulous—[21]

We should not under-estimate the radical insight of this. Poetry is the carrier of 'Reportless subjects', that is to say of instinctual energies which exceed the rational mind, which are at once too 'quick' and too 'continual' for it. They inhabit the 'Measures', that is to say the rhythmic and syllabic interactions that occur as the poem proceeds. They are received as 'stimulus', as unconsciously and speedily as they are generated, an experience that we feed on even as we struggle to comprehend it. The suggestion can fairly be made that Dickinson's explorations of the psyche here produce a speculative approach to language that equally looks forward to modern theory. This poem approaches a meta-language, but there are others that seek to embody the very processes they describe:

> Many a phrase has the English language—
> I have heard but one—
> Low as the laughter of the Cricket,
> Loud, as the Thunder's Tongue—

Murmuring, like old Caspian Choirs,
When the Tide's a'lull—
Saying itself in new inflection—
Like a Whippoorwill—

Breaking in bright Orthography
On my simple sleep—
Thundering its Prospective—
Till I stir, and weep—

Not for the Sorrow, done me—
But the push of Joy—
Say it again, Saxon!
Hush—Only to me![22]

The present reader is moved to respond with a simple
expression of pleasure and leave it at that! A detailed and
retrospective analysis would be possible of rhythmic effects
and letter sounds tracing out both internal organization and
onomatopoeic effects. A psychiatrist might want to investigate
the deep responses which are triggered: the desire for con-
tinuous libidinal expression ('I have heard but one'), the
longing for unity that can only be experienced through a new
recognition of sundering ('Not for the Sorrow, done me—/ But
the push of Joy—')? But, whatever we say, the poem fully
demonstrates Dickinson's point that something powerful
happens prior to any formulated response—that the poem is
always in that sense 'Prospective', that it is always 'saying
itself'.

5

This account of Dickinson's investigative power would not
be complete without some approach to the sexuality which
inhabits many of her poems. Of all the aspects of subjectivity
that she sought to broach, this must have been in many ways
the most difficult, prohibited by taboos from public discussion,
and experienced personally in the context of considerable
repression. Yet if interactions between the sexes were not
talked about, they were certainly around her, and in no
unworrying fashion. Something has already been suggested of

the unequal relationship between her mother and her father. She had also to witness at close quarters (they lived next door) her brother Austin's unhappy marriage to one of her own friends, and his eventual adultery.[23] Then, too, there is evidence in those intensive but perplexing letters addressed only to her 'Master' of her own unfulfilled searchings for sexual happiness.[24] As an example of the way in which these pressures find their way into her work we may take the following:

> I like to see it lap the Miles—
> And lick the Valleys up—
> And stop to feed itself at Tanks—
> And then—prodigious step
>
> Around a Pile of Mountains—
> And Supercilious peer
> In Shanties—by the sides of Roads—
> And then a Quarry pare
>
> To fit its Ribs
> And crawl between
> Complaining all the while
> In horrid—hooting stanza—
> Then chase itself down Hill—
>
> And neigh like Boanerges—
> Then—punctual as a star
> Stop—docile and omnipotent
> At its own stable door—[25]

This might seem at first like an elaborate extension of the phrase, 'iron horse'. But it is certainly more than that, and for the poem's consistent association of the train with certain notions of 'maleness' there is some supporting evidence that we should consider. It was one of Edward Dickinson's greatest dreams, eventually fulfilled, to organize a branch line that would bring the trains to Amherst.[26] The train in the poem is male first of all in its spheres of action; it belongs outside the home, it quarries rocks, it is busy, self-important and 'punctual'. More essentially, though, it is 'male' in its unstinted powers of embrace, advance and penetration. That

74

there is celebration here, and a degree of envy, cannot be doubted. However, it would be fair to say also that limitations are suggested which operate both on the social and sexual levels; there is, by implication, a narrowness, a compulsive entrapment in action, a narcissistic self-regard. If the train is 'male', then the elements that surround and support it are 'female'. In social terms there is the provision of sustenance and comfort; in physical terms the pleasurable yielding to sexual advance. On this ground also, though, the feelings are evidently mixed. To be the site of a sought-after plenty has its satisfactions, but there is also an element of enforced passivity and reception. The poem, then, emerges as a rich expression of sexual ambivalence and yearning, having its roots in unresolved anxiety, but reaching out also in understanding and even humour. We may say that the last three lines posit a miraculous and transforming moment in which each element is able to take on some of the quality of the other. This final mystery train is 'docile, and omnipotent', and it stands at the 'stable door', where the inside takes possession of the outside.

Those who insist upon this as a poem only about a train might well consider the following, in which Dickinson addresses the same issues more directly and consciously through her familiar device of the flower and the bee:

> A Bee his burnished Carriage
> Drove boldly to a Rose—
> Combinedly alighting—
> Himself—his Carriage was—
> The Rose received his visit
> With frank tranquillity
> Witholding not a Crescent
> To his Cupidity—
> Their moment consummated—
> Remained for him—to flee—
> Remained for her—of rapture
> But the humility.[27]

Here the same range of polyvalent feelings are deployed; yet the ending is one not of imagined fulfilment, but of dissatisfied query.

6

In these efforts to trace the movements of challenge and advance in Dickinson's work we have perhaps under-estimated the extent to which she is capable of reversion into more conventional modes of thinking and feeling. The whole process, conducted as it was in virtual isolation, must have been fraught with anxiety and doubt. A fuller account would have to acknowledge those poems in which she adopts the persona of the errant child, evading her own insights with an arch humour. Her writing about the natural world often collapses into an acceptably pious display of 'wonder'. And some of the poems mimic, without emotional conviction, the movement towards the acceptance of authority in family, society or church. But of the pressure and reality of the challenge there can be no doubt, and one of the strongest evidences of this lies in her novel and unsettled reactions not to life, but rather to death. Death was a frequent visitor to Amherst, and a frequent disrupter of such bonds of family and friendship as Dickinson sought to maintain. Moreover, it seems likely that, at least once, she was thus deprived of a relationship of love in which she was prepared to invest herself totally. In the poems provoked by these events the stress lies upon the emotional experience of irreplaceable loss:

> To wander—now—is my Repose—
> To rest—To rest would be
> A privilege of Hurricane
> To Memory—and Me[28]

This, in itself, might be enough to convince us of the way in which, for her, the conventional sources of consolation have proved inadequate although they are, of course, explored in other poems. Moreover, the sense of death as an abrupt ending of the rich experiment of life often produces feelings of resentment and anger, both at the process itself, and at the God who is the projected manipulator of it. He is attacked as a 'God of Flint',[29] and, in another poem, as a sadistic joker. Wondering if death is an end, she complains:

> Would not the fun
> Look too expensive!
> Would not the jest—
> Have crawled too far![30]

In other poems, however, a tentative hope is found in the conjecture that death may offer a continuation and fruition of those processes of advancing awareness that have occurred in life, that it is an arena of 'costumeless consciousness',[31] or, as she elsewhere phrases it, a place where we discover 'how Conscious Consciousness—could grow'.[32] It is important here to recall how often she uses the analogy of death to evoke those worst experiences of negation that life has offered her. Yet those moments were ultimately ones of 'survival' and transformation. Might it not be that the analogy could work the other way, that death could be a confirming experience of the same quality, though of greater intensity? Such at any rate is the hope expressed in those poems that figure the passage through death as one stage in a continuing journey:

> As if the Sea should part
> And show a further Sea—
> And that—a further—and the Three
> But a presumption be—
>
> Of periods of Seas—
> Unvisited of Shores—
> Themselves the Verge of Seas to be—
> Eternity—is Those—[33]

Such a structure has many advantages; it dignifies and celebrates human effort, while not denying a rôle for God as the possible promoter and guardian spirit of these disclosing processes. But it is all still, as her opening warns, 'as if'.

It is 17 August 1870. Thomas Wentworth Higginson is sitting in a train proceeding up the Connecticut Valley towards White River Junction. Yesterday he took time off from his busy life as Man of Letters and Causes to visit Emily Dickinson at Amherst.[34] She had first written to him eight years previously, offering some poems for his consideration, and asking, in the idiosyncratic manner to which he had grown accustomed, whether they 'breathed'.[35] He had not fully understood them, but had asked to see more. The correspondence had continued, and he was, to a certain extent, intrigued. Now he had met her, but was none the wiser, and indeed he was somewhat exhausted. What could one make of a woman who dressed in white and who offered, as an introduction, two day-lilies? And what about her words? 'Could you tell me what home is?' 'Women talk, men are silent.' 'If I feel physically as if the top of my head were taken off, I know that is poetry.' In her own way she had told him a great deal. But the news was largely lost on him.

NOTES

1. From a letter to Mrs. J. G. Holland, about 20 January 1856. See *The Letters of Emily Dickinson*, edited by Thomas H. Johnson (Cambridge, Massachusetts: Harvard University Press, 1958).
2. Richard B. Sewall, *The Life of Emily Dickinson* (London: Faber and Faber, 1976), p. 55. Throughout this essay I am indebted to Mr. Sewall's thorough and perceptive biography.
3. From Poem 443 on pages 212 and 213 of *The Complete Poems of Emily Dickinson*, edited by Thomas H. Johnson (Boston: Little, Brown and Co., 1960). All poems or extracts therefrom are taken from this edition, and will henceforth be noted by number and page number only.
4. Karl Keller has some useful comments on this and other matters in his book *The Only Kangaroo among the Beauty, Emily Dickinson and America* (Baltimore and London: The Johns Hopkins University Press, 1979).
5. Poem 875, p. 417.
6. Poem 669, p. 332.
7. Poem 177, p. 84.
8. Poem 341, p. 162.
9. See Robert Weisbuch, *Emily Dickinson's Poetry* (Chicago and London: University of Chicago Press, 1975), p. 109.
10. Poem 280, p. 128.
11. Poem 539, p. 263.
12. See Sewall, *The Life of Emily Dickinson*, p. 24 and note.
13. Poem 358, p. 170.
14. Poem 175, p. 83.
15. Poem 601, p. 295.
16. See particularly Poems 531 (p. 259), 1376 (p. 592) and 1670 (p. 682).
17. Poem 288, p. 133.
18. Poem 1060, p. 483.
19. Poem 1279, p. 559.
20. For Mabel Loomis Todd's account of such incidents, see Sewall, *The Life of Emily Dickinson*, p. 217.
21. Poem 1048, p. 478.
22. Poem 276, p. 126.
23. See Sewall, *The Life of Emily Dickinson*, pp. 170–96.

24. For the best discussion of these see Sewall, *The Life of Emily Dickinson*, pp. 512–31.
25. Poem 585, p. 286.
26. See Sewall, *The Life of Emily Dickinson*, p. 54.
27. Poem 1339, p. 579.
28. Poem 718, p. 353.
29. Poem 1076, p. 488.
30. Poem 338, p. 160.
31. Poem 1454, p. 617.
32. Poem 622, p. 307.
33. Poem 695, p. 342.
34. For a record of this incident see Sewall, *The Life of Emily Dickinson*, p. 563.
35. See *The Letters of Emily Dickinson*, p. 403.

4

Edgar Allan Poe, Poet-Critic

by ROBERT VON HALLBERG

> We are lamentably deficient not only in invention proper, but
> in that which is, more strictly, *Art*. What American, for
> instance, in penning a criticism, ever supposes himself called
> upon to present his readers with more than the exact stipulation
> of his title—to present them with a criticism and *something
> beyond*? Who thinks of making his critique a work of art in
> itself—independently of its critical opinions?[1]

Who indeed? Surely not I, and few of my colleagues aspire even
to scholarly elegance. But Poe did write criticism that can be
spoken of as not high art, but art all the same. From professors
like myself, the world does not want art, but from poets, even
when they thump out reviews, something more has come to be
expected. Poet-critics, for instance, have certainly been more
amusing than professors; sometimes they have even seemed to
joke about their own efforts, though I never understood why
they wanted to do so. It would be difficult to stipulate all the
differences between the criticism produced by scholars and that
of poet-critics, yet the distinction between these ways of writing
about literature is commonly felt by both sorts of writers. It
should be possible to indicate some of the special procedures
and objectives of poet-critics. One justification for this effort is
that American poet-critics have rather thoroughly shaken up
literary opinion in this century; another is that the lessons
academic critics might take from poet-critics have special force

now that literary criticism is a major academic industry, the most prestigious branch of which is devoted to the study of itself. More particularly, the connection between Poe's criticism and his poetry shows not only how his poems rest on general poetic principles—we always expect that from poet-critics—but, much more interestingly, how impossible it was for him to write the sort of poetry he admired most.

Poe's literary achievement seems especially hyphenated—much more so than that of other poet-critics; his place in American literary history is still a bit anomalous. He remains a popular poet, but as Eliot has remarked he is read largely by the young and untutored.[2] Sophisticated readers, like Eliot, often seem to regard his popularity as an embarrassment. And yet some poets, such as William Carlos Williams and Hart Crane, or Richard Wilbur and Daniel Hoffman, take Poe as a figure who cannot be ignored by later writers. In the history of American fiction, he seems more a pioneer of secondary genres—detective and gothic tales—than the master of a primary one. As a man of letters—poetry, fiction, and criticism—his place is secure, though as a poet he will always seem to many a mere verse-writer. More particularly, Poe can now be said to be along with Emerson one of the two earliest American poet-critics whose work continues to matter to contemporary writers. Since Poe's first literary critical effort in 1835—also the year in which Emerson began to lecture on English literature—an extraordinarily distinguished line of poet-critics has established this particular combination of talents as somehow distinctly American, and perhaps especially modern.

Insofar as Poe stands at the beginning of a line of poet-critics, this is a provisional sort of writing. These critics resist tradition in the name of independence; they attack the centre from the peripheries of the literary culture. By at least 1835, Poe wrote expressly as a Southerner, aiming his judgements against the literary centres established in Boston and New York. Once he himself had made his way to New York, in 1844, he directed his barbs against Boston. However detailed were his criticisms of Emerson for obscurity (XI, 6–7), and of Longfellow for indolence (X, 40), he never lost sight of their being established in Boston.

[Bostonians] may yet open their eyes to certain facts which have long been obvious to all the world except themselves—the facts that there exist other cities than Boston—other men of letters than Professor Longfellow. . . . The fact is, we despise them [Bostonians] and defy them (the transcendental vagabonds!) and they may all go to the devil together. (XIII, 5 & 9)

When he was invited to speak at the Boston Lyceum, he read a piece of juvenilia out of contempt for the taste of his audience (he may even have been drunk at the time), and later did what he could to publicize the gesture. How pointed was his sense of being an outsider can be guessed from the half-truth on the title-page of his first book: *Tamerlane and Other Poems, By a Bostonian*.

Henry James spoke of Poe's criticism in 1879 as 'probably the most complete and exquisite specimen of *provincialism* ever prepared for the edification of man.'[3] A half-century later, Eliot said that Poe was 'a critic of the first rank'.[4] Eliot had reason by then to know that the great American poet-critics would seem in retrospect to be mainly proud provincials: they have spoken from Hayley, Idaho; St. Louis, Missouri; Nashville, Tennessee; Gambier, Ohio; and Palo Alto, California. Poet-critics seem always to aim at independence of mind, an intelligence free of the corruptions of the centre. They have been unbeholden to publishers and reviewers and without the need to promote academic careers. One small sign of how they have insisted on their outré status is typified in Poe's unseemly habit of name-calling.

In itself, the book before us is too purely imbecile to merit an extended critique. . . . (VIII, 178–79)

The book is despicable in every respect. Such are the works which bring daily discredit upon our national literature. (VIII, 205)

Your poem is a curiosity, Mr. Jack Downing; your 'Metrical Romance' is not worth a single half sheet of the pasteboard upon which it is printed. (X, 166–67)

That any man could, at one and the same time, fancy himself a poet and string together as many pitiable inanities as we see here, on so truly suggestive a thesis as that of 'A Lady Taking the Veil,' is to our apprehension a miracle of miracles. (XII, 153)

But we doubt if the whole world of literature, poetical or prosaic, can afford a picture more utterly *disgusting* than the following. . . . (XI, 171)

Mr. Channing must be hung, that's true. (XI, 175)

What can we do but laugh outright at such phrases . . . such an ass as the author of 'Bug-Jargal?' (X, 137)

Robert Lowell said that Eliot had admitted taking particular delight in Poe's severity when it was directed against two of Eliot's own relatives.[5] Poe, altogether deliberately, set an example of impolite, even reckless criticism—'pretentious, spiteful, vulgar', James said.[6] Nearly a century later, Ezra Pound opened *Guide to Kulchur* with this promise:

> . . . I shall make a number of statements which very few men can **AFFORD** to make, for the simple reason that such taking sides might jeopard their incomes (directly) or their prestige or 'position' in one or other of the professional 'worlds'. Given my freedom, I may be a fool to use it, but I wd. be a cad not to.[7]

One American poet-critic after another has displayed independence by speaking without respect for the makers of reputation, though no one has been more acutely aware of the finer shades of renown than Poe. Built right into this kind of literary criticism is an inclination to locate principles beyond the competition of contemporary interests. The tradition of poet-critics encourages transcendental rather than historicizing criticism. Poe's attempts to speak of Ideality in particular poems is just one particularly clear instance of this practice.

Poe repeatedly expressed contempt for the literary politics of his own moment. As a provincial he did not have access to the institutions that provide recognition, and there can be no question about his ambition to achieve renown. (He was not too discreet to say in print that his criticism, in a year's time, brought the circulation of the *Southern Literary Messenger* from 700 to nearly 5,000 (XII, 85).) He criticized his own literary milieu on two principal counts. The first was its apparatus of boldly reciprocal promotion:

> The corrupt nature of our ordinary criticism has become notorious. . . . The intercourse between critic and publisher, as

it now almost universally stands, is comprised either in the paying and pocketing of blackmail, as the price of simple forbearance, or in a direct system of petty and contemptible bribery. . . . (X, 185)

Pound and Yvor Winters later made the same point about London and New York literary life: outsiders are especially sensitive to this particular corruption of criticism. But beyond the moral turpitude of his contemporaries, Poe condemned other literary critics for a lack of independent judgement. 'Few American writers', he said, '. . . have risen by merely their own intrinsic talents, and without the *a priori* aid of foreign opinion and puffery, to any exalted rank in the estimation of our countrymen' (VIII, 94).

His thoroughly American response to this state of affairs was to attempt to establish the world of letters as a meritocracy. He made a point of praising demonstrated achievement rather than capability. And he tried to encourage Americans to attend to details in the examination of literary works:

> . . . Our criticism is nevertheless in some danger—some very little danger—of falling into the pit of a most detestable species of cant—the cant of *generality*. The tendency has been given it, in the first instance, by the onward and tumultuous spirit of the age. With the increase of the thinking-material comes the desire, if not the necessity, of abandoning particulars for masses. Yet in our individual case, as a nation, we seem merely to have adopted this bias from the British Quarterly Reviews. . . . (XI, 3)

Poe was conscientious about examining details to the point of tedium; he wanted to cite evidence, like a detective, for all that he claimed about the works he examined, especially since he often criticized poets for plagiarism. The editor of the Virginia edition of Poe's collected works could not afford the space to reproduce Poe's extensive quotations. Poe can certainly seem picayune, but his motive was to free American writers from the domination of British litterateurs, and their American imitators, who cared more for their own notions and opinions than for the poems, novels and stories under review.

Like other poet-critics, Poe was extremely explicit. He did not hesitate to formulate definitions of poetry (XI, 75), drama (XIII, 112), and the novel (XI, 122)—though he suggested, too, that words cannot hem poetry in (VIII, 280–81). His most celebrated critical essay, 'The Philosophy of Composition', sets out to render explicit every detail of artistic production, for in the best poems, he seems to have believed, all details can be articulated to general principles, however humble those principles may look when they are spelled out. 'If the practice fail,' he said, 'it is because the theory is imperfect' (XI, 39). Circumstance, the chance find of an apt word or phrase, counts for nothing.

> It is my design to render it manifest that no one point in its ['The Raven' 's] composition is referrible either to accident or intuition—that the work proceeded, step by step, to its completion with the precision and rigid consequence of a mathematical problem. (XIV, 195)

In *Eureka* he claimed that what is commonly taken as intuition could certainly be explicated logically—given sufficient perspicacity and patience. He tried always to demystify literary criticism in order to free writers from those who claim to constitute an aristocracy of taste.

The melancholy that comes from this sort of criticism Poe knew all too well; his mind habitually doubles back on itself. On the one hand, he believed, in Enlightenment fashion, that '. . . the finest quality of Thought is its self-cognizance' (XVI, 204). On the other, he felt that it is a

> curse of a certain order of mind, that it can never rest satisfied with the consciousness of its ability to do a thing. Still less is it content with doing it. It must both know and show how it was done. (XVI, 40)

Behind 'The Philosophy of Composition' is that accursed sadness of self-consciousness, as though he had always to suspect himself of prefabricated poems, of mannerism. This self-destructiveness, he suggests, is an inevitable burden on poet-critics:

> To see distinctly the machinery—the wheels and pinions—of any work of Art is, unquestionably, of itself, a pleasure, but one which we are able to enjoy only just in proportion as we do *not* enjoy the legitimate effect designed by the artist:—and, in fact, it too often happens that to reflect analytically upon Art, is to

reflect after the fashion of mirrors in the temple of Smyrna, which represent the fairest images deformed. (XVI, 170)

Poet-critics, then, turn against their own kind. Poe indicated that the most appropriate recognition of great artistic achievement is restraint, or even silence, on the part of critics and explainers.[8]

Poe's constant reach for general principles usually makes him seem driven by abstract policies. He strove so to write logically—rather than tastefully—that his observations often sound woodenly consistent and categorical rather than deeply earnest or knowing; one often suspects this methodical critic of irony, especially when one recalls his belief that 'the style of the profound thinker is never closely logical' (X, 158). His criticism repeatedly turns on a simple distinction between the true and the false, as though he were speaking mainly for effect. His obsession with plagiarism is just this, though in a characteristically doubled sense, because the greatest poets, he said, are those who, so absorbed in their art, are most prone to plagiarism and least damaged by the indictment (XII, 104–6). Poe's testing of texts for true and false properties can seem crude, mechanical, and not entirely in good faith. He was indeed a categorical critic in the sense that his distinctions aim at these all-or-nothing discriminations. Seldom is he at pains to identify and somehow name a quality. Like a prosecutor, he rather pushes for conviction, which leaves him a dangerous model for other critics. Yet his bluntness has its rationale: for a critic committed, as Poe vigorously and honourably was, to tracking the literary culture, commenting on it monthly, this winnowing of the authentic from the *ersatz* is just the job at hand.

The most notorious of Poe's categorical conclusions is that a 'long poem is a paradox', since 'All high excitements are necessarily transient' (XI, 107). With that observation, a great deal of literary history recedes into darkness: Chaucer, Spenser, Shakespeare, Milton, and Wordsworth appear to have been unfortunately confused. This is Poe's point exactly. Insofar as his claim is valid, English literary history loses hegemony over

American poets. Like a lawyer, Poe marshalled rhetoric and logic, more than wisdom or truth, to gain liberty for his own poetic ambition, and that of his countrymen. The history of American poetry through the 1840s, as he certainly knew, did not suggest that American poets were likely to be remembered in the way that British poets were. The best an ambitious young American poet might do in 1830, one might have thought, would have been to strive through imitation and self-education to live up to standards set on another continent.

Poe, however, for obvious reasons, preferred to argue that some recent American short poems excel 'any transatlantic poems. After all, it is chiefly in works of what is absurdly termed "sustained effort" that we fall in any material respect behind our progenitors' (XIII, 80). These are the words of a poet whose longest poetic effort, a blank-verse drama entitled *Politian* (1835), he had the good sense not to bother to finish. The charge that American poetry was deficient in works of 'sustained effort' was put forward by critics writing for the quarterly reviews—the *North American Review* and the *Dial*. Poe framed his argument against this charge so as to attack the very idea of a quarterly review as he had three years earlier attacked the idea of a long poem. Journals, he claimed, were better suited than quarterlies to the contemporary American milieu because one sign of the times is that

> men are forced upon the curt, the condensed, the well-digested in place of the voluminous—in a word, upon journalism in lieu of dissertation. We need now the light artillery rather than the peace-makers of the intellect. I will not be sure that men at present think more profoundly than half a century ago, but beyond question they think with more rapidity, with more skill, with more tact, with more of method and less of excrescence in the thought. Besides all this, they have a vast increase in the thinking material; they have more facts, more to think about. For this reason, they are disposed to put the greatest amount of thought in the smallest compass and disperse it with the utmost attainable rapidity. (XVI, 82)

Hence short poems and magazines are faithful to the moment, which is no small advantage in the eyes of one who, like many Enlightenment writers, saw progress wherever he looked. 'The day has at length arrived', Poe thought, 'when men demand rationalities in place of conventionalities' (XII, 117). With this 'rationality' about the advantages of short poems, he tried to think his way out of a mediocre literary milieu.

Poe is often taken as an extreme exemplar of American Romanticism. Yvor Winters, William K. Wimsatt, Jr., Cleanth Brooks, and Edmund Wilson all criticize his poetry and criticism in just these terms.[9] From this view, he is interesting only as an illustrative figure, not influential as a poet or critic. If instead, however, one attends especially to his procedures as a poet-critic, he seems much less pure a Romantic; some of his principles and suppositions rather reflect what can be spoken of as Enlightenment notions.[10] One might note, for instance, his frequent efforts to derive critical judgements from firm distinctions of genre and suppositions of decorum. But the most important of Poe's Enlightenment beliefs was simply the notion that his epoch was 'emphatically the thinking age;—indeed it may very well be questioned whether mankind ever substantially thought before' (XII, 8). From this faith in the power of clear, sceptical thought came the belief that a poet or critic can begin with first principles rather than precedents and, by a train of logical propositions, arrive at truths formerly obscured by blind prejudice. More-over, one's explanations can fully prevail, because poetry, like all the world, is susceptible to clear, sceptical explanation. From the belief that general laws govern the details of literary history, it is but a short step to the notion that a critic's task is less importantly that of closely describing particular literary works than that of discovering and formulating the general laws that determine literary history. Poe's work is the first instance of a still strong tendency in American literary criticism to hold literary theory in higher regard than literary history.

This is another way of saying that however forceful Romanticism was in literary Europe of the 1830s and 1840s, American letters were still bound up with the Enlightenment ideals that brought nationhood to this former colony. Many of Poe's most distinctive literary ideas were, as he understood them, joined to national ideals. He was not an especially political poet-critic, but to overlook his nationalistic views renders his criticism and his poetry a bit peculiar. His poems and some of his criticism do now seem odd; but they are not properly regarded as incoherent, for they followed from a policy. Moreover, his strength as a model for later poet-critics has been sufficiently great that we still labour with some of his procedures without fully recognizing the policy they were once meant to implement. For instance, in order to sidestep the relative weakness of literary tradition in America, Poe argued that the power of the individual talent is supreme; the poet, for Poe and for many of our contemporaries, is above all an ingenious maker, and the lines of a poem are traces of—as we now say—strategies. Nor would Poe countenance the claim that poems cannot be fully understood independent of a context of thought, belief, or shared experience; poems were autotelic for him, as they have seemed to many modern American critics. And more than ever now, American critics give their pragmatic credence, as Poe urged, to details, especially those of stylistic analysis. Poe's reasons for this particular focus were nationalistic. Of course he hoped, as poet-critics always do, to encourage a taste for his own sort of poetry, but he also wanted to establish a distinctly American type of literary criticism—and the record indicates that he succeeded.

What Poe treasured most in terms of style is *range*, not merely of subject matter, but more particularly of tone. Although he returned to the term 'tone' repeatedly, he never claimed anything extraordinary for his sense of its meaning:

> Without pausing to define what a little reflection will enable any reader to define for himself, we may say that the chief constituent of a good style . . . is what artists have agreed to denominate *tone*. The writer who, varying this as occasion may require, well adapts it to the fluctuations of his narrative, accomplishes an important object of style. (X, 126–27)

There is a special reason why Poe would not bother to say that by tone he meant to refer, as I. A. Richards later did, to the attitude expressed by a writer; to presume a common understanding was just the point, because the measurement of range is made possible only by a prior sense of neoclassical decorum—of which attitudes are fitting to which subjects. One way of assessing a prose writer's command of tonal range is whether he or she can always seem not only various but, in diverse settings, just. The natural or easeful style—that commanded by Addison, as well as Washington Irving and Nathaniel Hawthorne—

> is but the result of writing with the understanding, or with the instinct, that the *tone*, in composition, should be that which, at any given point or upon any given topic, would be the tone of the great mass of humanity. (XIII, 147)

Fairness and civility, not novelty, are the objectives of this prose style.

Poe praises two sorts of writers very highly. First are those prose writers who give themselves so generously to their subjects that they seem to write naturally, without art—Defoe sets this standard.

> Men do not look upon it [*Robinson Crusoe*] in the light of a literary performance. . . . The powers which have wrought the wonder have been thrown into obscurity by the very stupendousness of the wonder they have wrought! We read, . . . close the book, and are quite satisfied that we could have written as well ourselves. . . . Indeed the author of Crusoe must have possessed, above all other faculties, what has been termed the faculty of *identification*. . . . Defoe is largely indebted to his subject. (VIII, 170)

Such a writer makes no compromise with the mere appurtenances of imaginative writing—with the bitter consequence, as Poe put it, that 'books thus written are not the books by which men acquire a contemporaneous reputation' (VIII, 235).

The second sort of writer he praises is best exemplified by the Irish poet Thomas Moore, whose verse does not deliberately depart from the patterns of ordinary prose usage. Moore's

> is no poetical *style* (such, for example, as the French have—a distinct style for a distinct purpose), but an easy and ordinary prose manner, *ornamented into poetry*. By means of this he is enabled to enter, with ease, into details which would baffle any other versifier of the age, and at which Lamartine would stand aghast. For anything that we see to the contrary, Moore might

solve a cubic equation in verse. . . . His facility in this respect is
truly admirable, and is, no doubt, the result of long practice after
mature deliberation. (X, 69)

The question of poetic style was rather different for Poe than
that of prose style. 'The inventive or original mind', he said,
'as frequently displays itself in novelty of *tone* as in novelty of
matter' (XI, 110). Prose writers like Addison do not aspire to
novelty of attitude; they rather rely upon a consensus about
appropriate attitudes. But poets explore surprising feelings,
and the tone of poems is often stunningly unsettling. This is
not to say that a poet's novelty of tone will be reflected in novel
phrasing or syntax. The best poetic style is, like Moore's, that
which is simply not constrained by the differences between
poetry and prose. Moore's commitment to a plain, clear style
allowed a wide range of subject matter; he concedes no
subject, no range of experience (not even cubic equations), to
essayists. (T. S. Eliot's well-known praise of the Metaphysicals'
possession of 'a mechanism of sensibility which could devour
any kind of experience' is much the same as Poe's admiration of
Moore[11].) Poe's dream was less to write about the supremely
melancholy subject, as he suggests in 'The Philosophy of
Composition', than to be able to write, like Moore, about
anything at all.

How eager and fretful Poe was to extend his own range can be
sensed in his strenuous explanation of the oddities of the
English Metaphysical poets. For understandable reasons, he
argues that Donne and Cowley were exceptionally sincere
poets:

> They used but little art in composition. Their writings sprang
> immediately from the soul—and partook intensely of the nature
> of that soul. It is not difficult to perceive the tendency of this
> glorious *abandon*. To elevate immeasurably all the energies of
> mind—but again—so to mingle to greatest possible fire, force,
> delicacy, and all good things, with the lowest possible bathos,
> baldness, and utter imbecility, as to render it not a matter of
> doubt, but of certainty, that the average results of mind in such a
> school, will be found inferior to those results in one (ceteris
> paribus) more artificial: Such, we think, is the view of the older
> English Poetry, in which a very calm examination will bear us
> out. (IX, 95–6)

The main line of English poetry is 'frank, guileless, and perfectly sincere' (IX, 94). Donne and Cowley are introduced here as the merely apparent exceptions that can nevertheless be accommodated to the general rule. The eclecticism of the Metaphysicals, their dangerously capacious range of tone, is meant to stand as evidence of their ultimate sincerity, for only poets thoroughly engaged by their subjects could skip over obvious incongruities as easily as they did. Poe strains so to resist reading the Metaphysicals ironically, because he has committed his own poetry and criticism to the belief that the best poems always express melancholy; the one kind of humour he would admit as legitimate to poetry was arch-ness—just what one senses in his most ambitious critical pronouncements (XI, 24). His interest in stylistic range was a fascination for what he must have known he thoroughly lacked as a poet.

Sincerity for Poe, as for Victorian critics, was a term of high praise; or rather, since poets are seldom said to be more or less sincere, it is a test of authenticity in poetry. Self-consciousness is the great corrupter of style:

> . . . had the mind of the poet [John G. C. Brainard] been really 'crowded with strange thoughts', and not merely *engaged in an endeavor to think*, he would have entered at once upon the thoughts themselves, without allusion to the state of his brain. His subject [Niagara Falls] would have left him no room for self. (XI, 20)

A false poet displays his or her skills in the hope that they will be mistaken for imagination. An acute critic, however, exposes those skills as wilful, predictable moves, mannerisms. The mannered writer is locked into an inflexible way of writing: 'That man is a desperate mannerist who cannot vary his style *ad infinitum* . . .' (IX, 68). Mannerism and range, as Poe properly sees them, are exact contraries. The varieties of prose usage provide a proper model for verse-writers, a hedge against mannerism, but the prose manner must, as Poe said, be *'ornamented into poetry'*.

Poe's way of thinking about poetic style involves this one central paradox: the best is a plain style, but poetry is distinguished from prose by its ornaments. His handling of this paradox had enormous impact on his own verse. Most of the aspects of figurative language that are commonly associated with ornamentation were fiercely suppressed by Poe.

> Similes (so much insisted upon by the critics of the reign of Queen Anne) are never, in our opinion, strictly in good taste, whatever may be said to the contrary, and certainly can never be made to accord with other high qualities, except when naturally arising from the subject in the way of illustration— and, when thus arising, they have seldom the merit of novelty. To be novel, they must fail in essential particulars. The higher minds will avoid their frequent use. They form no portion of the ideal, and appertain to the fancy alone. (IX, 68)

Poe knew well how often similes derive from self-consciousness and quite wrongly suggest to many readers great imaginative powers; for him, similes always reflect mere pride of technique. 'An artist', he said, 'will always contrive to weave his illustrations into the metaphorical form' (XVI, 27). Metaphor too, though, must be held in tight rein. Poe criticized Edward Bulwer severely for his 'mania of metaphor—metaphor always running into allegory' (X, 130). Pure allegory he regarded as an 'antique barbarism' (though one of his own best poems, 'The Haunted Palace', is plainly an allegory), and personi-fication as ludicrous (though his 'Stanzas [To F. S. O.]' are peppered with personifications). Metaphors should be used seldom and always kept from escalating into allegory or personification. At just those moments where modern readers have come to expect metaphor, Poe argues for literal expression: '. . . *subjects which surpass in grandeur all efforts of the human imagination are well depicted only in the simplest and least metaphorical language*' (XI, 22).

Even in poetry, Poe thought, the object of style is clarity and simplicity, certainly not impressiveness. 'What is worth think-ing', he said, 'is distinctly thought: what is distinctly thought, can and should be distinctly expressed, or should not be expressed at all' (XII, 6). Where figurative language is not conducive to clarity, it is indefensible. Even more importantly, where poetic syntax impedes immediate clarity, it must be condemned:

> Few things have greater tendency than inversion, to render verse feeble and ineffective. In most cases where a line is spoken of as

'forcible', the force may be referred to directness of expression. . . . In short as regards verbal construction, *the more prosaic* a poetical style is, the better. (XVI, 154)[12]

The poetic style Poe admired most was one stripped bare of most, but not quite all, poetic devices. Quaintnesses of phrasing were admissible occasionally, as in poems on fantastic subjects (XII, 6 & 21). But most important of all, an American poet properly ornaments his or her language into poetry through prosodic invention.

Poe placed a great burden on prosody: each foot lands with a thud. His rhymes and meters are nothing if not insistent, as though he had not heard of counterpoint or off-rhyme. As always with Poe, there are general principles involved here. '*Verse* originates', he claimed, 'in the human enjoyment of equality, fitness' (XIV, 218). The more absolute the rhymes, and emphatically regular the rhythm, the closer a poet will be to the human origins of musical language. No purpose was served, as he reckoned, by concealing prosodic art. The opening lines of a poem he placed first on a list of his best poems rhymes 'moon' and 'June' (P, 179 & 183). An earlier poem brought 'pass' and 'alas' together (P, 66). He is always pushing so hard: 'trod upon' / 'Parthenon' (P, 113); 'gala night' / 'bedight' (P, 325); 'Dian' / 'dry on' (P, 417); 'linger / 'sink her' (P, 417). Even when the rhymes are not exact, they are emphatic for the effort behind them. No one reads Poe without understanding at once why Emerson called him the jingle man.

Poe presented himself as an American inventer among prosodists. Blank verse seemed 'hackneyed' to him, as it has to many later American poets (XII, 109). 'To break the pentameter', Pound wrote, 'that was the first heave.' William Carlos Williams's indebtedness to Poe is nicely indicated by the small fact that Williams took his most dubious and idiosyncratic prosodic term, the 'variable foot', from Poe (XIV, 240). In 'The Philosophy of Composition', Poe said that his intention was above all to be original in the versification of 'The Raven'.

The extent to which [originality] . . . has been neglected, in versification, is one of the most unaccountable things in the

94

world. Admitting that there is little possible of variety in mere *rhythm* [i.e., in the choice of a normative foot], it is still clear that the possible varieties of metre and stanza are absolutely infinite—and yet, *for centuries, no man, in verse, has ever done, or ever seemed to think of doing, an original thing.* (XIV, 203)

Beyond the question of his own originality was the matter of American poetry generally: if his countrymen continued to work in blank verse, for instance, they would have to stand comparison with the masters of that line (Milton is constantly on Poe's mind, when he considers his own accomplishment). In order not to produce a merely colonial literature, American writers had to concoct forms of their own, however homemade they might appear. Why Poe thought that the need to innovate bore so exclusively on prosody is not surprising:

> That we are not a poetical people has been asserted so often and so roundly, both at home and abroad, that the slander, through mere dint of repetition, has come to be received as truth. Yet nothing can be further removed from it. The mistake is but a portion, or corollary, of the old dogma, that the calculating faculties are at war with the ideal; while, in fact, it may be demonstrated that the two divisions of mental power are never to be found in perfection apart. The *highest* order of the imaginative intellect is always preëminently mathematical; and the converse. (XI, 147–48)

Americans were compelled by necessity, rather than inclined by temperament, to master the calculating faculties, Poe argued; but given that mastery, prosody was the one part of the art of poetry where it could be made to pay off. 'Faultless versification and scrupulous attention to grammar' were the two poetic virtues Poe was constantly trying to inculcate; he would test nearly every poet, tediously, for correctness (XIV, 181). American poets needed to be correct in order to develop their own advantage over British poets, but also to avoid the condescension of their one-time colonizers.

With Poe, as with rather few other poets, one can see that his poems suffer from a particular conception of poetry. He believed that poetry is plain, clear language, but ornamented into poetry. The ornamentation of poetic language is something isolable—a rhyme, a repeated phrase—added to the plain sense. Although the poems are not simply a demonstration of his critical notions, his criticism does throw a special kind of light on the poems. In the poems and in the criticism, the same contradictions assert themselves, at the cost of the poems. For all Poe's admiration of stylistic range, Eliot was surely right to say that Poe lacks just this ability to express different sorts of feeling. Poe must have thought that poems like 'The Bells' and 'The Raven', as he explains it, express range, but they display a merely mechanical sort of variation of tone: in these poems the semantic sense of one statement varies from stanza to stanza; the obvious irony is that a misunderstanding has occurred. But two people, or a bird and a person, construing words differently is not what is properly meant by range of tone; Poe has simply concocted a mechanism for producing difference, not range.

Poe was indeed capable of writing verse that is properly spoken of as plain in style. However, the plain passages in his verse come not at all where Poe wanted to write well. Here are two passages from *Politian*, separated by only a few pages:

Lalage.   And dost thou speak of love
          To *me*, Politian?—dost thou speak of love
          To Lalage?—ah wo—ah wo is me!
          This mockery is most cruel!—most cruel indeed!
Politian. Weep not! oh, sob not thus!—thy bitter tears
          Will madden me. Oh mourn not, Lalage—

          Be comforted! I know—I know it all,
          And *still* I speak of love.
      . . . . . .
          Sweet Lalage, *I love thee—love thee—love thee*;
          Thro' good and ill—thro' weal and wo I *love thee*.
                        (P, 272)

Jacinta.   I made a change
          For the better I think—indeed I'm sure of it—
          Besides, you know it was impossible
          When such reports have been in circulation
          To stay with her now. She'd nothing of the lady
          About her—not a tittle! One would have thought

She was a peasant girl, she was so humble.
I *hate* all humble people!—and then she talked
To one with such an air of condescension.
And she had not common sense—of that I'm sure
Or would she, now—I ask you now, Jacinta,
Do you, or do you not suppose your mistress
Had common sense or understanding when
She gave you all these jewels?

(P, 276–77)

Poe's accomplishment cannot be measured by *Politian*, but my point concerns only the obvious difference between these two passages—and the point is best made with unrhymed verse. The first passage is intended to be dramatic: Politian delivers the last two lines quoted on his knees. The writing is poor because the emotions represented are bluntly named, not examined, and those names are simply repeated relentlessly in order to provide emphasis. Poe clearly thought this an important moment in the play. The later passage is less important to the dramatic action, and the writing is far superior. Jacinta, alone on stage, is not posturing as Politian and Lalage do, but rather thinking and talking in verse; the enjambments and the parenthetical syntax keep the lines moving variously toward the larger coherence of the speech. Jacinta reveals the mix of her own feelings by choosing just the right, telling phrases—'tittle' and 'common sense'. In the second passage, Poe seems to have felt less need to write remarkably, for the sake of the action, whereas in the first he is straining—by merely repeating blunt phrases—to elevate his subject. He was not an inept poet—as the second passage demonstrates—but his poems are inept just when he would have them be sublime. When he wrote without thinking about Poetry, he could write plainly, thoughtfully, and sensitively, as some of his slighter efforts, such as 'To ———' (P, 382) and 'Deep in Earth' (P, 396), show.

The great caution advanced by Poe's career as poet-critic is against the excesses of provincialism. Certainly being an outsider among men of letters enabled him to write independently, and fiercely, in ways that remain admirable. And yet his sense that he could concoct formal principles with rather little regard for literary precedents just as surely doomed his poems to remain, like Edsels, a species unto themselves. Effective advocacy of a plain style in American poetry had to wait for later poet-critics—Ezra Pound, T. S. Eliot, and Yvor Winters. At the outset of the American line of poet-critics is this extremist who took a purely intentionalist approach to writing, chiefly because the alternative could so easily have meant, in the 1830s and 1840s, subservience to British letters. This sense that the independent writer was free to write anything at all was enormously invigorating; Poe wrote about naval history, travel literature, middle eastern geography. The job of a literary critic was to educate himself and his readers in very broad terms; the work of Pound, Eliot and Charles Olson show that Poe's example has made a difference. However technical poet-critics can be, they continue to see the job of literary criticism in terms that are much broader, just in terms of subject matter, than academic critics ever dare to believe. Yet that very sense of independence is surely responsible for Poe's odd place in literary history—as a kind of tinkerer among poets.

NOTES

1. *The Complete Works of Edgar Allan Poe*, ed. James A. Harrison, 17 vols. (New York: Crowell, 1902), XIV, 74; subsequent references to this edition will be indicated simply by volume and page number. All quotations from Poe's prose are taken from this edition. All italicized passages within quotations are Poe's own.
2. T. S. Eliot, *To Criticize the Critic* (London: Faber, 1965), pp. 29–30.
3. Henry James, *Hawthorne*, ed. Tony Tanner (1879; London: St. Martin's, 1967), p. 71. And Eliot too spoke of 'a certain flavour of provinciality about his work' (*To Criticize*, p. 29). William Carlos Williams, who was seldom of a mind with Eliot, said that 'There is a flavour of provincialism that IS provincialism in the plainness of his reasoning upon elementary grammatical, syntactical and prosodic grounds' (*In the American Grain*, 1925; New York: New Directions, 1956, pp. 216–17).
4. T. S. Eliot, rev. of *Israfel* by Hervey Allen, in *The Nation and Athenaeum*, XLI (2 May 1927), 219; quoted by William K. Wimsatt, Jr., and Cleanth Brooks, *Literary Criticism: A Short History* (New York: Knopf, 1957), p. 480.

5. Robert Lowell, *History* (New York: Farrar, Straus and Giroux, 1973), p. 140.
6. James, *Hawthorne*, p. 71.
7. Ezra Pound, *Guide to Kulchur* (Norfolk, Conn.: New Directions, 1937), p. 7.
8. *The Letters of Edgar Allan Poe*, ed. John Ward Ostrom, 2 vols. (Cambridge, Mass.: Harvard Univ. Press, 1948), II, 460. See, too, *The Poems of Edgar Allan Poe*, ed. Thomas Ollive Mabbott (Cambridge, Mass; Harvard Univ. Press, 1980), p. 414; subsequent references to this volume will be abbreviated as P, followed by page number.
9. Yvor Winters, *In Defense of Reason* (New York: Swallow & William Morrow, 1947), p. 260; Wimsatt and Brooks, *Literary Criticism*, p. 479; Edmund Wilson, *The Shoes of Light* (New York: Farrar, Straus and Young, 1952), p. 187.
10. For a fuller, and quite different, account of Poe's relationship to Enlightenment thought, see Robert D. Jacobs, *Poe: Journalist and Critic* (Baton Rouge: Louisiana State University Press, 1969).
11. T. S. Eliot, *Selected Essays* (New York: Harcourt, Brace, 1950), p. 247.
12. Poe understood the corruption of inversion first-hand. He would on occasion twist a phrase around in order to get a rhyme: '. . . While from the high towers of the town/ Death looks gigantically down' (P, 200).

5

'Frolic Architecture': Music and Metamorphosis in Emerson's Poetry

by BRIAN HARDING

On 27 November 1832, Emerson entered in his journal the following resolution: 'Instead of lectures on Architecture I will make a lecture on God's architecture, one of his beautiful works, a Day. I will draw a sketch of a Winter's day.'[1] Some three years later, he drew a sketch of a winter's day in 'The Snow-Storm' and contrasted the swift architecture of the snow—accomplished in one night—with the age-long attempts of human art to mimic the 'mad wind's night-work'. The poem has often been read as an expression of the limits of man-made art,[2] though its account of the 'wild work' of the storm suggests an idea of inspiration that is both available to man and god-like in its indifference to time as measured by human criteria. The architectural analogies for poetry in 'The Snow-Storm' are not used to imply that aesthetic structures can conquer or defy time by their permanence; rather they are used to explore the idea of an art that can find meaning in the metamorphosis—in the incessant change of forms. Thus the 'frolic architecture' of this poem leads us—in related works in the 1847 edition of the *Poems*—to a fusion of the architectural-monumental idea of poetry[3] with a conception of the poem as musical and fluid. In this paradoxical fusion, Emerson expressed his profoundest thoughts on man's ability to find meaning *in* the flux of experience rather than in escape from it. 'The Snow-Storm' thus offers a most useful starting-point; it directs us to Emerson's strengths as a poet and to what can be thought as one of his most central contentions about the relationship of art to life and life to art.

A recent commentary on the poem argues persuasively that it offers—in form as in content—a demonstration of the work of the poetic imagination as Emerson conceived it; a process later described in his essay 'The Poet' as 'the passage of the world into the soul of man, to suffer there a change and reappear a new and higher fact'.[4] In his analysis, the critic shows that the language of the poem translates image into thought and north-wind into poet as it moves from the confined perception of the first part to the liberated perception of the second part. Thus we witness 'the transformation of the world (as far as the poetic eye can behold) into a panoramic work of art'.[5] Excellent though this account of the poem is, its claim that the metaphoric action occurs 'unannounced, unostentatiously, naturally' is not consistent with the poem's emphasis on the wildness of the wind and the madness of its work. Since the controlling metaphor of the poem is architectural, Emerson's insistence that the constructive function of the wind is wild, or even savage—and at the same time 'frolic'—is paradoxical. The implications of that paradox are worth exploring because the metaphor occurs often in the poems and in the prose.

Just how adeptly Emerson worked to evoke the spirit of wildness in the poem can be seen when the published version (in the *Dial* magazine, January 1841) is compared with the draft in the journals for 1834–35. In the draft, the storm 'arrived' after being 'announced by all the trumpets of the winds'. The published poem converts what had been a neutral preterite into a dramatic and vivid present:

> Announced by all the trumpets of the sky
> Arrives the snow, and driving o'er the fields,
> Seems nowhere to alight: the whited air
> Hides hills and woods, the river and the heaven
> And veils the farm-house at the garden's end.

In the draft which, as Hyatt Waggoner has said, 'seems to exist somewhere in a no man's land between poetic prose and blank verse',[6] the first sentence ends when the snow 'seems nowhere to alight' (JMN, VI, 246). The second sentence then tells of the envelopment of the landscape by the snow. In the poem, the effects of the snow-storm on the landscape are evoked in one breathless sentence, in the third line of which the original full-stop is replaced by a colon so that—finding nowhere to alight—the line rushes on in a storm of assonance— 'sky . . . arrives . . . driving . . . alight . . . whited . . . hides'— to overwhelm the reader with its wild force.[7] It is true that the sensory vividness and violence of the first part of the poem does not achieve the liberation of which the Emersonian poet was capable when he performed his god-like function. The effect of the storm on human life is at first constricting: it blocks the lane, prevents the traveller, the courier and the farmer from going about their business and confines the human actors on the scene to their 'radiant fireplace' thus making them mere 'house-mates'. In the first part of the poem, the storm shocks and disrupts the human world of practical activity. In the second part of the poem, the poetic liberation will occur as a shock to the imaginative habits and conventions of men.

The conceit on which the second part of the poem is constructed begins as an unremarkable and even commonplace metaphor (snow-heaps are buildings) and is then elaborated in ways that call into question our ideas of time and of the permanence of art. The snow-flakes become tiles from an unseen quarry; with them the storm, a 'fierce artificer' in its disregard for standards of aesthetic decorum, builds forms that are 'bastions' round trees, stakes and doors. Thus the most obviously evanescent of natural objects (flakes of snow) are imaginatively transformed into materials for solid and durable structures whose purpose is defence (we might suppose) against the onslaughts of time itself. As a consequence, our attention is called to the transience of all those shapes and forms by means of which we make ourselves at home in the phenomenal world. Further, this 'savage' architect in his wild work mocks our ideas of value by hanging 'Parian wreathes' on such unworthy objects as hen-coops and dog-kennels. Not only is this artist indifferent to 'number and proportion', he also flaunts all common-sense judgements by using ephemeral and worthless snow to suggest (or rather to *be*) the lasting and valuable Parian marble. Thus the transformation of the world into a work of art that occurs here is posited upon the belief not only—in the words of the lecture 'Poetry and Imagination'—that 'Nature itself is a vast trope, and all particular natures are tropes', but also that 'the thoughts of God pause but for a moment in any form' for they move 'as the bird alights on the bough, then plunges into the air again' (W, VIII, 15). In the lecture Emerson stated that 'The act of imagination is ever attended by pure delight. It infuses a certain volatility and intoxication into all Nature' (W, VIII, 18). In the poem, he described the architecture of the storm as 'frolic'—a word that implies both playfulness and (from its German root *'fröhlich'*) joy. Human architecture shares qualities with God's architecture—the implication is—when the imagination of man participates in the metamorphosis, rejecting common-sense criteria and accepting the incessant change of forms.

In *Poems* (1847) Emerson included 'The House', which has received less critical attention than 'The Snow-Storm' though it is closely related to the more famous poem in theme. The muse in 'The House' comes closer to the human artist of 'The Snow-Storm' than to the fierce artificer of snow-masonry, for she not only excels other architects in her craft but also takes meticulous care in the selection of materials for her building. Choosing slowly and warily, she searches the forests of many lands in order to find the 'immortal pine' and the 'cedar incorruptible' with which to construct her house of art. The other material to be used will be the 'famous adamant' that has to be quarried from the rock to provide 'each eternal block' of the edifice. Thus the slowness and thoroughness of the building process is matched by the power of the work to endure; it will be immortal, incorruptible, eternal. David Porter regards the central metaphor in 'The House' as one of a number of examples in which 'the architectural-monumental icon . . . anchors a cluster of anxieties over this primary need beneath all the emblems: the necessity of making the flux of experience intelligible'. In Porter's view, Emerson's architectural metaphors signify his belief that 'flux must have a steady principle.' More radically, Porter argues that the poet's constant aim to find an essential stasis within movement dictated the basic structure of his poems, giving them a resistless drive to moral progression and intellectual closure at the expense of complex life.[8] In 'The House', however, the architectural metaphor is complicated by a puzzling—yet crucial—allusion to music and dance:

> She lays her beams in music,
>   In music every one,
> To the cadence of the whirling world
>   Which dances round the sun—

The poem *does* claim immortality for the house of the muse— the beams laid in music will survive war and other disasters and will 'outlive the newest stars'—but if Emerson sought a 'steady principle' in the flux of experience, then he sought it in the flow of music and the movement of the dance (here, the dance of the planets) rather than in the monumental solidity of buildings. In associating his architectural metaphors with music, Emerson was attempting to formulate a paradoxical notion of a principle or law which is itself part of the metamorphic process.[9]

That Emerson is a poet of paradoxes can hardly remain in doubt after Hyatt Waggoner's study of the poems.[10] One paradoxical statement that deserves particular notice occurs in the journals on 28 June 1839. In it, Emerson writes of rhyme that 'builds out into Chaos and Old Night a splendid architecture to bridge the impassable, & call aloud on all the children of morning that the Creation is recommencing' (JMN, VII, 219). Such rhyme, he went on to say, 'should not suggest restraint but contrariwise the wildest freedom'. A few days earlier, he had recorded some reflections on music of such importance to him that he would use them more than once in his published works:

> With the very first note of the flute or horn or the first strain of a song, we leave the world of common sense & launch at once into the eternal sea of ideas & emotions. We pour contempt on the prose you so magnify yet the sturdiest Philistine is silent. The like allowance is the prescriptive right of Poetry. You shall not speak truth in Prose,—you may in Verse. (JMN, VII, 217–18)

When he used this passage in the lecture now known as 'The Poet' (1841), Emerson added that 'every note is an insult to all the common sense that has been droning in our ears all day' (EL, III, 359).[11] Several years later, he used almost the same phrases when he recorded some thoughts on music, though he gave added force to his ideas by stating that when 'the sun shines, the worlds roll to music . . . the poet replaces all this cowardly self-denial and God-denial of the literary class, with the one blazing assurance that to one poetic success the world will surrender on its knees.'[12] When successful, the poet pierces the 'brass heavens of Boston & Christendom' and lets in 'one beam of the pure Eternity which instantly burns up this whole universe of shadows & chimaeras in which we dwell' (JMN, IX, 204). The wildness of the poetry, in Emerson's theory, was inevitable when the truths sought attempted to 'bridge the impassable'—to use accents of eternity in a world of time.

For all Emerson's interest in the subject, his poem 'Music' was not published in his lifetime and appears only in the Appendix to the Centenary Edition of the poems, with Edward Emerson's note explaining that he obtained Cabot's permission to include it 'among the minor poems' in spite of Dr. Holmes's objections.[13] Though certainly not a great poem, it is an interesting one and complements the more famous 'Bacchus' and the more powerful 'Merlin' by showing us the poet in a receptive rôle, attending to the music that sounds through all things rather than making his own song. The music heard by the speaker in the poem is 'sky-born' and it sounds 'from all things old' as well as 'from all things young'. It peals out in cheerful song, not only from 'all that's fair' but also from 'all that's foul'. Listing the conventionally poetic topics that may be assumed to be musical—the stars, the rose, the rainbow, a woman's song, the notes of the redbreast—the speaker claims that 'something sings' also in the darkest and meanest of things and (in the phrase that offended Dr. Holmes) 'in the mud and scum of things'.

The Neo-Platonic doctrine on which 'Music' rests came to Emerson by way of Thomas Taylor's translations and commentary. Taylor's note to Proclus's *On the Theology of Plato* seems to have been a direct source for the poem, for it summarizes the belief that the world-soul resembles a musical instrument and emits a sound so that 'everything participates of this harmonical sound, in greater or less perfection, according to the dignity of its nature.' Consequently, 'while life everywhere resounds, the most abject of beings may be said to retain a faint echo of the melody produced by the mundane lyre.'[14] There are radical implications in the poem, however, that are not present in Taylor's version of Proclus, for 'Music' makes no mention of degrees of perfection or of greater or lesser participation in the world-harmony. Instead, the poem insists that 'something sings' in the darkest and meanest things and in the fair and beautiful; in terms of music, there is no difference. If the refrain 'something sings' seems vague, this is because the poet admits that the singing is a mystery. The balanced phrases and emphatic rhymes suggest the confidence that the music can be heard, but like the German Romantics whose interest in the meaning of music anticipated his own, Emerson acknowledged that the meaning could not be fully expressed in conceptual terms.[15]

Perhaps to compensate for his self-acknowledged 'want of ear' (JMN, IX, 108–9), Emerson repeatedly read and made notes on William Gardiner's *The Music of Nature* in the years 1837–43. Though that unphilosophical work is more likely to have helped Emerson appreciate orchestral music than understand the meaning of music,[16] when he came to write his lecture 'The Poet', he included quotations from Gardiner and showed a more sustained interest in the relationship between music and poetry than he would in his essay with the same title in *Essays: Second Series* (1844). More significant than any reference to Gardiner's book is the statement that the material of the true poet is

> language, the half god, language, the most spiritual of all the works of man, yet language subdued by music—an organ or engine . . . scarcely less beautiful than the world itself, a fine translation into the speech of man of breezes and waves and ripples, the form and lights of the sky, the color of clouds and leaves.

Developing this idea, Emerson argues that 'love and thought always speak in measure or music' and that 'with the elevation of the soul, the asperities and incoherence of speech disappear, and the language of truth is always pure music' (EL, III, 358).

The world imagined here and 'translated' into musical speech is obviously a world of changing forms—a world of meta- morphosis. Similarly, in 'The Method of Nature' (another lecture given in 1841) the speech of genius is said to be musical 'because it is itself a mutation of the thing it describes. It is sun and moon and wave and fire in music, as astronomy is thought and harmony in masses of matter' (W, I, 218–19). In his 1841 lectures, then, Emerson both associated musical thought with imaginative participation in the metamorphic process and suggested that musical language could intimate truths beyond the reach of conceptual thought.

Just one year earlier, Thomas Carlyle had defined musical thought in his lecture 'The Hero as Poet' as thought that penetrated to the heart of things, detecting their secret melody. The music in question was, he said, 'a kind of inarticulate unfathomable speech'.[17] There are repeated references in Carlyle's writings to the 'heavenly melody' with which men could feel at one in their prelapsarian state of unity with nature, when their lives were part of the 'Spheral Music', for—like Emerson—he adopted the nineteenth-century con- ception of the true poet as an Orpheus who could regenerate language. Though Carlyle was a purveyor of German romantic ideas concerning music from the late 1820s on, he was certainly not the only—or even the major—source of Emerson's interest in the Orphic tradition, for similar ideas were current in the works of the Swedenborgian theorists who helped Emerson formulate his ideas of language.[18] The sig- nificance of Carlyle's belief that to see deeply into things was to 'see musically' is rather that it parallels Emerson's in claiming a range of meaning beyond 'articulate speech', though the British Transcendentalist lacks Emerson's intense concern with the metamorphic implications of musical thought.

'Bacchus' (1846) is a more famous and a more confident poem than 'Music' for the celebration of the poet's powers in the second part of the poem shows them becoming increasingly capable of meliorating the human condition.[19] 'Bacchus' draws on Taylor's translation of the *Hymns of Orpheus* as well as on the *Phaedrus*,[20] so that there is nothing surprising in the lines: 'Wine which Music is,—/ Music and wine are one.' The intoxicated poet is granted an insight into the Unity, the One, that is denied to men who retain their common-sense judgements, for—as Emerson's own motto to the poem says—'The man who is his own master knocks in vain at the doors of poetry.'[21] The Dionysian abandonment of self as taught in the *Phaedrus* leads to a restoration of lost knowledge when 'Winds of remembering/ Of the ancient being blow.' When this happens, the new vision is metamorphic, for the 'solid-seeming walls of use/ Open and flow.'

In redeeming human reason from its subjection to 'Nature's lotus' the wine-music of 'Bacchus' converts sadness into joy, for it 'turns the woe of Night,/ By its own craft, to a more rich delight'. The power of the wine is derived from the fact that the vine from which it is produced has a root that 'feels the acrid juice/ Of Styx and Erebus' as well as tendrils that wave in the heavenly hills. As in 'Music', awareness of the spheral music involves the recognition of the dark and wretched aspects of experience; in 'Bacchus' the darkness is even the darkness of death. When he drinks the wine, the poet can see so far into the metamorphic process that he can talk with kings yet unborn and can intuit the evolution of grass to man, but he also converses with chaos. His self-abandonment involves a willing rejection of his safe world and his comfortable habits of thought. The 'walls of use' that lose their solidity and begin to flow are, among other things, the walls of mental habit. As in other major poems which celebrate the wine-music of the metamorphosis, the liberation of human reason is accomplished in the spirit of the wild. Edward Emerson's note to the poem refers us to the statement, in 'Poetry and Imagination', that the vine is the most geometrical of plants and the poet is a better logician than the anatomist. The logic, however, is the logic of passion, the 'noble passion' of 'wise surrender to the current of Nature'.[22]

'Woodnotes I'—first published in the *Dial* in October 1840—tells of a 'forest seer' who is so at home in nature that he can accept the idea of his own death with perfect confidence in a benevolent controlling purpose. He hears the death-crash of a perfect but aged tree as a 'hymn', so confident is he in the rightness of the natural order. With such a belief, the 'musing peasant' is able to be 'the heart of all the scene' and to live in perfect harmony with the natural world, untroubled by the knowledge of his own mortality. 'Woodnotes II' is a more complex poem, particularly in the version originally published in the *Dial* in October 1841, and it is more disturbing, for in lines later dropped from the poem (and restored only in the notes to the Centenary Edition) the pine-tree tells of a time before animal life existed on the planet and looks forward to a time when man will have vanished from the earth. As if taunting man with the relative brevity of human existence the tree states that

> Only the mountains old
> Only the waters cold,
> Only moon and star
> My coevals are.

The elements spoke to the tree in an age

> Ere Adam wived,
> Ere Adam lived,
> Ere the duck dived,
> Ere the bees hived,
> Ere the lion roared,
> Ere the eagle soared,

and they will speak to the tree again 'O'er the grave of men' of the 'time out of mind,/ Which shall come again'. The runic lines of the pine-tree are not, therefore, comforting to man. The tree invites man to listen to 'the mystic song/ Chanted when the sphere was young' but doubts if 'wise man' will hear even a part of that song. The song of the tree is, in fact, a song of 'The rushing metamorphosis/ Dissolving all that fixture is', and it has the power of the metamorphosis, for it 'Melts things that be to things that seem,/ And solid nature to a dream.' The tree, then, becomes the voice of 'the dreadful Destiny' and it tells of human life and death in telling of fate and will.

The hope offered to man is that if he will cease to talk with his 'feeble tongue' and will, instead, take his part in the song of the pine-tree (weave his rhyme with that of the tree) he will be 'no more the fool of space and time'. In the draft of the poem in the journals, the point is made more clearly: 'Talk no more with thy tongue/ And learn with me our practick song' (JMN, VIII, 505). The 'practick song' of the draft becomes the 'fatal song' of the poem—a song which 'knits the world in music strong'. Man may, therefore, participate in the music of nature. To do so is to renounce or abandon the idea of the self as fixed and static:

> All the forms are fugitive,
> But the substances survive.
> Ever fresh the broad creation,
> A divine improvisation,
> From the heart of God proceeds,
> A single will, a million deeds.

Creation is no more final than virtue is final in 'Circles'. All life is a process, nothing is fixed:

> Onward and on, the eternal Pan,
> Who layeth the world's incessant plan,
> Halteth never in one shape,
> But forever doth escape,
> Like wave or flame, into new forms
> Of gem, and air, of plants and worms.[23]

Not only does the tree include itself in the metamorphosis—'I, that to-day am a pine,/ Yesterday was a bundle of grass'—it also concludes that 'stars of eternity' and ephemeral meadow flowers are of equal value to the traveller through time. In lines later dropped, the power of music to suggest meanings beyond the limits of conceptual thought is stressed:

> I will teach the bright parable
> Older than time,
> Things undeclarable,
> Visions sublime.

What cannot be 'declared' can, it seems, be intimated through song, and the song will be, like creation itself, an 'incessant plan' and a 'divine improvisation'; it will be faithful to the process of creation rather than to any completed state. In its own version of the architectural metaphor, the pine-tree advises the listener to build a 'final tomb' to those friends who have not been able to respond to the spirit of the song.

In 'Monadnoc' (1845) there is a confusing variety of mood, yet the underlying theme is the power of music to take us beyond the spirit-matter dichotomy on which our conventional notions of the world are structured. This poem, like

'Woodnotes II', puts human life against a time-scale so vast that it dwarfs man and his values. The mountain, like the pine-tree, speaks in runic utterances that are chilling to man's sense of his own importance, for it anticipates the time when it will gaze over an empty landscape 'when forests fall, and man is gone'. In 'Monadnoc', however, we return to the optimism of the 'Prospects' chapter in *Nature* (1836), for the mountain acknowledges the power of the true poet:

> For it is on zodiacs writ,
> Adamant is soft to wit:
> And when the greater comes again
> With my secret in his brain,
> I shall pass, as glides my shadow
> Daily over hill and meadow.[24]

In the 1847 edition of the *Poems*, the fourth line quoted here read 'With my music in his brain'. The reference to music is retained in the Centenary Edition in earlier lines describing the mountain crags as beads of a rosary 'On prayer and music strung'. In both versions, the key reference to music is contained in the pun used by the mountain:

> Enchantment fixed me here
> To stand the hurts of time, until
> In mightier chant I disappear.

The song—'chant'—has magic powers of control over nature; it is then, plainly an Orphic hymn.

The power of the poet's song is stated most resoundingly in 'Merlin', a poem that evolved in the journals in 1844–45. Drawing on his knowledge of the powers attributed to the songs of the ancient Celtic bards,[25] Emerson endowed the Merlin of his poem with the power to thwart kings as well as tame wild beasts. The chords of Merlin's harp chime with violent heroic deeds in the public sphere (wars and commercial activity). They also have sway over human passion, for they 'make the wild blood start/ In its mystic springs' and they tell 'secrets of the solar track'. So powerful is the bard that his blows on the harp are no less than 'strokes of fate'. Given such power, he is able to dispense blessings to men:

111

He shall daily joy dispense
Hid in song's sweet influence.
Forms more cheerly live and go,
What time the subtle mind
Sings aloud the tune whereto
Their pulses beat,
And march their feet,
And their members are combined.

In the 1847 edition of the *Poems*, the third line quoted here read 'Things more cheerly live and go'. The emendation intensifies the meaning by shifting the focus from things in general to those 'forms' (human beings) that must live and die. The poet's music can give meaning (and joy) to men's lives in spite of their subjection to time, for if the 'subtle mind' can sing the tune to which all life is lived, then the 'forms' are no longer merely passive creatures manipulated by powers beyond their comprehension—they can participate in the music to which the whole of creation moves.

'Merlin II' is more complex and difficult than 'Merlin I'; a sombre note is sounded in its conclusion, where 'subtle rhymes, with ruin rife' are sung by 'the Sisters as they spin'. The Fates 'Build and unbuild our echoing clay' and, though they do so 'In perfect time and measure', they do not invite man's participation in their rhymes as the pine-tree did in its song of destiny in 'Woodnotes II'. The song of the Fates is heard in 'the house of life' both at morning and at evening, 'As the two twilights of the day/ Fold us music-drunken in'. Commenting on the conclusion, a recent critic writes that the poet 'fades to insignificance before the relentlessly perfect weaving of the three Fates'.[26] Though this critic does acknowledge that the intoxicating song in 'Merlin II' *may* be the wine-music of 'Bacchus', he implies that the music-drunken mortals are closer to the man-child whose cup was 'drugged' in 'The Sphinx' than to the poet drunk with 'the remembering wine'. However, the architectural metaphors of 'Merlin II' may offer a way out from this stark antithesis, for the building done by the Fates is connected—through its music—with the building done by the muse in 'The House'. For Emerson, the idea of music is always a means of coming to terms with the threats posed to human schemes of value by the passage of time. Even

112

in this apparently pessimistic poem, there is at least a suggestion that the mortal who is drunk with the music of the Fates can be more than a passive victim of nemesis. If he does not help to make the song, he may share in its meaning.

The problem of 'ruin' and of the 'unbuilding' of human clay was brought home to emerson most vividly by the death of his son Waldo in 1842. In 'Threnody'—the poetic response to that loss—the note of personal suffering is intense:

> The eager fate which carried thee
> Took the largest part of me:
> For this losing is true dying;
> This is lordly man's down-lying,
> This his slow but sure reclining,
> Star by star his world resigning.

So devastating is the loss that consolation can only be offered by a voice other than that of the bereaved poet-father in the poem. To reconcile the father to the death of so promising a son, the 'deep Heart' gives the dead child a mythic status, making of him a Christ-Orpheus figure.[27] To want to hold on to such a blessed creature is to want to resist the metamorphic process itself:

> Wilt thou freeze love's tidal flow,
> Whose streams through Nature circling go?
> Nail the wild star to its track
> On the half-climbed zodiac?

Since the account of life given by the 'deep Heart' is entirely in metamorphic terms, to attempt to halt the Flowing is to 'transfix' and deny life itself, by confining its 'onward force' in a particular human form. A prose gloss on these lines is provided by a journal entry Emerson made *before* the death of his son:

> Nature ever flows, stands never still. Motion or change is her mode of existence. The poetic eye sees in Man the Brother of the River, & in Woman the sister of the River. Their life is always transition. Hard blockheads only drive nails all the time; forever remember; which is fixing. Heroes do not fix but flow, bend forward ever & invent a resource for every moment. (JMN, VII, 539–40)

In the spring of 1842, when he began to compose what would become 'Threnody' in his journals, Emerson was not at first able to apply this principle to his own loss, for the first fragments of the poem express resentment (JMN, VIII, 453). In a later notebook entry, probably made in the spring of 1843,[28] he recorded lines that were to contribute to the concluding section of the poem:

> Not of adamant & gold
> Built he heaven stark & old
> But like a nest of reeds
> Of vernal grass & scented weeds
> Or like a fleeing tent
> A bow above the tempest bent
> Of lover's sighs & sainted tears.

(JMN, VIII, 530)

When the lines were included in 'Threnody', the account of this false heaven was changed to read 'stark and cold', while the fluid quality of the reeds was stressed: 'a nest of bending reeds'.

The architecture of heaven in 'Threnody' is hardly 'frolic architecture', but like the work of the wild spirit of the wind in 'The Snow-Storm' its meaning can only be grasped if we are prepared to do violence to our mental habits. Heaven—if it is to be conceived in metaphoric terms as a structure—must surely be adamatine, for heaven is immortality. To make heaven of bending reeds and to give it the status of—in the words of the poem—a 'traveller's fleeing tent' is to undermine our understanding of the distinction between time and eternity.

The paradoxical conception of heaven in 'Threnody' does not explicitly refer to music, though the imagery of the poem links it to 'The House'. In 'Eternity' the relationship between time, music and architecture is an explicit theme. Early in this long poem, most of which was unpublished in Emerson's lifetime or, indeed, in the Centenary Edition,[29] we learn that time acts on the material world in ways analogous to thought:

> Poet of poets
> Is Time, the distiller,
> Chemist, refiner:
> Time hath a vitriol
> Which can dissolve
> Towns into melody
> Rubbish to gold.[30]

The long-awaited poet, the 'well-tempered/ Musical man' is able to see that the movement of the planets is not meaningless, for he knows that 'Sun-dance and star blaze,/ Is emblem of love.' This Orphic poet can articulate the mysteries of the universe and of life, death and rebirth. When he sings:

> Trees hearing shall blossom,
> Rocks hearing shall tremble,
> And range themselves dreamlike
> In new compositions
> Architecture of thought.[31]

Perhaps the best comment on Emerson's architecture of thought is still George Santayana's. Noting Emerson's fascination with the perpetual motion observable in nature and deciding that this was the only reality for him, Santayana concluded that

> while the poet could justify and communicate his delight by dwelling on the forms and beauties of things in transition, the metaphysician would fain sink deeper. In his desperate attempt to seize upon the real and permanent he would fain grasp and hold fast the disembodied principle of change itself.[32]

We do not have to accept the highly charged phrase 'desperate attempt' here in order to relish the Emersonian riddle in this account of holding fast to a disembodied principle. Acknowledging the impossibility of any such holding fast, Emerson attempted to express an idea of poetry that combined (through metaphor) the apparently irreconcilable qualities of architecture and of music. The poems in which these metaphors occur are among his most difficult, for they take us to the limits of meaning, yet they are also among his most fascinating experiments in verse.

NOTES

1. *The Journals and Miscellaneous Notebooks of Ralph Waldo Emerson*, ed. William H. Gilman *et al.*, 16 Vols. to date (Cambridge, Mass.: Harvard University Press, 1960–), IV, 60. (Hereinafter cited as 'JMN'.) Carl Strauch calls attention to the relationship between this journal entry and 'The Snow-Storm' in his 'Critical and Variorum Edition of the

115

Poems of Ralph Waldo Emerson' (doctoral dissertation, Yale, 1946), Part 2, pp. 545–46.

2. See, for example, Gay Wilson Allen, *Waldo Emerson: A Biography* (New York: Viking Press, 1981), p. 479.

3. The 'architectural-monumental' theme in the poems is given careful attention in David Porter's *Emerson and Literary Change* (Cambridge, Mass.: Harvard University Press, 1978). For detailed comments on Porter's argument, see below.

4. Leonard Neufeldt, *The House of Emerson* (Lincoln, Nebraska: University of Nebraska Press, 1982), p. 149. Neufeldt quotes from Emerson's 'The Poet', *Essays: Second Series, The Complete Works of Ralph Waldo Emerson*, ed. Edward Waldo Emerson, Centenary Edition, 12 Vols. (Boston: Houghton Mifflin, 1903–4), III, 21. (Hereinafter cited as 'W'.) The sentence quoted had already formed a part of the lecture Emerson delivered in 1841, printed under the title 'The Poet' in *The Early Lectures of Ralph Waldo Emerson*, ed. Stephen Whicher, Robert Spiller, et al., 3 Vols. (Cambridge, Mass.: Harvard University Press, 1959–72), III, 349. (Hereinafter cited as 'EL'.)

5. *The House of Emerson*, p. 150.

6. *Emerson as Poet* (Princeton, New Jersey: Princeton University Press, 1974), p. 105.

7. Albert Gelpi's chapter on Emerson in his *The Tenth Muse: The Psyche of the American Poet* (Cambridge, Mass.: Harvard University Press, 1975) contains an excellent analysis of 'The Snow-Storm' to which I am indebted.

8. *Emerson and Literary Change*, pp. 57; 21.

9. In the early 1830s, the natural sciences seemed to Emerson to offer such laws. For an example of his belief that the laws of science 'dissolved' apparently solid matter, see 'Water' (EL, I, 51).

10. *Emerson as Poet*, pp. 72–4 and passim.

11. The journal passage was later used in 'Poetry and Imagination', W, VIII, 52.

12. The passage was used in 'The Scholar', W, X, 265.

13. W, IX, 512n.

14. Quoted in John S. Harrison, *The Teachers of Emerson* (1910; rpt. New York: Haskell House, 1966), 142–43.

15. For the relationship between German ideas concerning music and nineteenth-century American verse, see Charmenz Lenhart, *Musical Influence on American Poetry* (Athens, Georgia: University of Georgia Press, 1956), Chap. 4.

16. The details of Emerson's interest in Gardiner's book can be found in Strauch, 'Critical and Variorum Edition of the Poems of Ralph Waldo Emerson', Part 2, p. 558.

17. *Heroes and Hero Worship* (1841; London: Chapman and Hall, 1897), p. 83. The other Carlyle quotations are, respectively, from: 'Characteristics' (1831) and 'Novalis' (1829), *Critical and Miscellaneous Essays* (London, 1857), Vol. 3, p. 2; Vol. 2, p. 77.

18. For a succinct account of the Swedenborgian Sampson Reed's Orphism,

see R. A. Yoder, *Emerson and the Orphic Poet in America* (Berkeley: University of California Press, 1978), pp. 11–12.

19. See Bernard Paris, 'Emerson's "Bacchus",' *Modern Language Quarterly* 23 (June 1962), 150.

20. See Barbara H. Carson, 'Orpheus in New England: Alcott, Emerson, and Thoreau' (doctoral dissertation, Johns Hopkins, 1968), p. 131.

21. The motto is quoted by Edward Emerson, W, IX, 443n.

22. W, IX, 445n.

23. In the *Dial* II (October 1841), 213, the line reads 'Of gems, and air, and plants, and worms'. The line was emended in the *Poems* (1847).

24. In 'The Humanity of Science' (1836), EL, II, 29, Emerson had written that 'the adamant streams' before the law.

25. See Nelson Adkins, 'Emerson and the Bardic Tradition', *P.M.L.A.* 63 (1948), 662–67, and Kenneth W. Cameron, 'The Potent Song in Emerson's Merlin Poems', *Philological Quarterly* 32 (1953), 22–8.

26. R. A. Yoder, *Emerson and the Orphic Poet in America*, p. 146.

27. Michael Cowan, 'The Loving Proteus: Metamorphosis in Emerson's Poetry', *American Transcendental Quarterly* 25 (Winter 1975), 11–22, stresses the transformation of the lost son into a Christ figure. Richard Tuerk, 'Mythic Patterns of Reconciliation in Emerson's "Threnody"', *Emerson Society Quarterly* (1981, Third Quarter), 27 (3), 181–88, emphasizes the Orphic rôle.

28. The editors date the journal entry tentatively. See JMN, VIII, 530n.

29. The poem is printed in Strauch, 'Critical and Variorum Edition of the Poems of Ralph Waldo Emerson', Part 2, pp. 383–93. Strauch dates the poem between 17 November and 14 December 1849.

30. Strauch, p. 384.

31. Strauch, p. 392.

32. *Santayana on America*, quoted in Joel Porte, *Representative Man: Ralph Waldo Emerson in His Time* (New York: Oxford University Press, 1979), pp. 23–4.

6

'Eminently adapted for unpopularity'? Melville's Poetry

by A. ROBERT LEE

1

> Whitman, Dickinson, and Melville seem to me the best poets
> of the nineteenth century here in America. Melville's poetry has
> been grotesquely underestimated, but of course it is only in the
> last four or five years that it has been much read; in the long
> run, in spite of the awkwardness and amateurishness of so
> much of it, it will surely be well thought of. . . .

So, in *Poetry And The Age* (1953), Randall Jarrell cautiously took
stock, praise generously intended though not without its saving
disclaimers.[1] Three decades on, and despite Melville's generally
assured place in the American literary canon—at least on the
evidence of the standard criticism and textbooks and the
appearance of the definitive Collected Writings begun in 1968
under the Northwestern-Newberry imprint[2]—Jarrell's fond
hopes for the poetry can hardly be said to have much advanced.
If slightly better known, the few key poems at any rate which
find their way into the anthologies, Melville's poetry remains
largely in parentheses, a kind of awkwardly also-present
literary second family. Where mentioned at all, it tends still to
be thought the slightly 'left-handed' work of a major
nineteenth-century story-maker whose best efforts from the

start lay in his powerful sea and journey fictions.³ The poetry might provide fare for the determined specialist or conversely the unsuspecting browser. But to believe it of an interest with the prose likelier than not has been to invite stark incredulity.

Even those undaunted by its assumed marginality and who press for an upward revaluation of Melville as poet, resemble Jarrell in hedging their bets. Melville showed, in select instances, that his poetry could exhibit great inventive flair. How indeed could the author of, among other things, so consequential a portfolio of fiction as *Typee* (1846), *Moby-Dick* (1851), the adroit and frequently unsettling *Putnam's* and *Harper's* short stories of 1853–56 of which five became the *Piazza Tales* (1856), *The Confidence-Man* (1857), and the post-humously issued *Billy Budd, Sailor* (1888–91), have written otherwise? But terms like 'awkward' and 'amateur' remain on hand to temper any undue larger claim. Thus, as high as Melville's reputation may otherwise have soared, whether as the only begetter of *Moby-Dick* and of the fiction before and after, or as the belatedly acknowledged near-Keatsian letter-writer, or even as the author of several fascinating travel-journals and the essay-writer and lyceum lecturer,⁴ to find his name bracketed for his poetry with those of Whitman and Dickinson still startles considerably. That would be to display the enthusiast's over-emphasis, altogether too special an act of pleading.

Our unfamiliarity with thinking Melville a poet also has to do with the nature of his dramatic rehabilitation during the 1920s under the pioneer scholarship of Raymond Weaver, Lewis Mumford, and their British co-advocates, D. H. Lawrence and John Freeman.⁵ For if the American Renaissance called for in his own time pre-eminently by Emerson in *Nature* (1836), 'The American Scholar' (1837) and 'The Poet' (1844), indeed did yield a mid-nineteenth-century cultural Great Awakening, Melville's place within it, alongside Emerson himself, Whitman, Thoreau, Hawthorne and the as then 'hidden' Emily Dickinson, derived almost wholly from his fiction.⁶ As the mariner-turned-teller, and against every likelihood, Melville had transformed his ship and South Seas adventuring into sumptuous narrative, and nowhere more dynamically than in his agreed centre-piece, *Moby-Dick*. In this New England 'voyage-out' after whale-oil, along ancestral Atlantic and Pacific sea-lanes, indisputably, it was argued, American story-telling had come of age. For out of whaling's 'ballast' Melville had fashioned nothing less than a New World Epic, a canvas as broad as that of the *Iliad*, or the *Odyssey*, or *Don Quixote*, and quite as exhilarating in its appeal to the archetypes of seafaring Quest and Man pitched against Other. Further, by its 'careful disorderliness', the inter-locking different tiers to its design, *Moby-Dick* had secreted within itself a yet deeper parable about Truth's enigmas and contrary manifestations and encodings. Under the terms of Melville's story, to quest after the White Whale and oil in general meant a quest after 'light'—both as capitalist energy-source and 'illumination' of the world. As Jarrell was further to point out, the basis for thinking Melville a poet accordingly lay in his prose, a great ocean-bred, mythicizing imagination able to combine personally known mariner life with startling visionary powers.

Moby-Dick thus in place as the cornerstone of this new-found reputation, the resort to the rest of the fiction for added confirmation followed quickly. Not only his 'whale-book', 'broiled' in hell-fire and 'wicked' as his effusive letters of 1851–52 to Hawthorne describe it,[7] but Melville's entire body of fiction was to be thought cannier and more consciously angled than hitherto had been anywhere near sufficiently recognized. Behind the lively surfaces of adventure lay an adept in the manipulation of voice, a skilled, ironic ventriloquist whose ambiguities and control of viewpoint got richly knottier as his career unfolded. To come on to Melville's poetry has meant, by and large, to meet it out of this latter-day, increasingly subtler, reappraisal of his fiction.

First, *Typee* and *Omoo* (1847), initial ventures both and by appearance 'straight' two-part sailor Autobiography embellished with Gaugin-like local colour, rightly are now acknowledged to have dissimulated at every turn. For all that Melville speaks of proffering only 'the unvarnished facts', his outward show of South Seas picaresque came laden with equivocation. Each successive capture and escape masks keener probings: Atlantic as against Pacific civilization; the power-play of colonizer over colonized; Yankee up-tightness as against 'native' sexual ease; and open-seas sailor freebooting as against the fixed Totem and Taboo structures of the Marquesas, Honolulu and Hawaii. From the outset Melville pitched his story-telling doubly, early 'fiction of fact' busy in writerly sleight-of-hand.

Mardi (1849), too, his Book of Dreams and Voyage Thither as he called it, however overwrought and predictably derided in its own time, with patient study can be seen as concealing more coherent 'lower layers' than its general unabating literariness of manner gave grounds to suppose.[8] As much as it otherwise flounders, it served both as a dummy run for *Moby-Dick* and a first shy at the 'ontological heroics' he would later, and more persuasively, make into his special hallmark.[9] *Mardi*, it was, also, which opened up his own mind to him, behind all its décor and circuitous island myth-making a most essential testing-ground for his vocation as writer. In their turn, *Redburn* (1849) and *White-Jacket* (1850), ruefully as he dubbed them 'two *jobs*, which I have done for money',[10] he again seamed with implications anything but available on a first reading. Both, for instance, offer 'realist' shipboard stories, authentic in sea incident and argot. But both also tell other stories: identity secured only after constant threat and the discard of the jackets worn by the two protagonists; the nature of survival within the closed crew-world first of an Atlantic merchant-ship and then a returning American frigate; and in *Redburn* Liverpool portrayed as a Victorian City of Dreadful Night and in *White-Jacket* the ship as emblematic of a yet more threatening man-of-war universe. Melville thereby transforms sea-going into a species of confession, psycho-drama which explores each narrator's awakening turns of consciousness. Further, distinctive in their own right as are all five of these books, taken together they came to be seen as paving the way for the mythopoeic complexity of *Moby-Dick*, whale-hunting made over into a great linear metaphor of the pursuit after First and Last Meanings and a Book of Revelation as Melville conceived it which in daring and ocean sweep of detail served decisive notice of his 'poetic' genius.

From there the re-evaluation has been equally busy: *Pierre* (1852) as a displaced, labyrinthine biography of Melville's creative inner workings; the *Piazza* and other stories— especially 'Bartleby, the Scrivener' (1853), 'The Encantadas'

(1854) and 'Benito Cereno' (1855)—as carefully enciphered sketches about alienation and a still larger metaphysics of loss; *The Confidence-Man* as his most riddling fictional 'manshow' and 'masquerade', an ensnaring All Fools Day Mississippi river journey which envisages humankind as prey to almost every manner of ruling illusion; and, finally, *Billy Budd, Sailor*, 'inside narrative', which in the triangulation of Billy, Vere and Claggart enacts Melville's last vision of Traduced Innocence, a dream-like, Orphic parable about 'welkin-eyed' male beauty sacrificed to envious, accusing hate and murderous legal punishment. Given all the attention this unexampled body of fiction attracted, it hardly surprises that the poetry suffered eclipse. Nor have matters been helped by the fact that in repute at least it is a poetry shot through with forbidding ellipses and unpleasing irregularities of diction and rhythm. Unfortunately, also, even in an age of computerized textual scholarship, great portions of it remain in need of proper editing, a task one hopes in due course to be put to rights by the Northwestern-Newberry edition.

Lately, to be sure, Melville's poetry-writing phase has begun to awaken a new kind of interest. Was it he, or us, like Hawthorne's character Wakefield, who dropped out? Have we all along been misleading ourselves into thinking that when, in December 1866, and under straightened circumstances, Melville became Inspector of Customs (No. 75) for the Port of New York, he simply embarked upon some resentful Poundian withdrawal from the word as might befit the creator of the Mute who boards the *Fidèle* or the eloquent but eventually wordless Bartleby or Babo? In part, probably, this also reflects our contemporary interest in writers who seem to retreat into silence like Ezra Pound after the *Cantos*, and latterly J. D. Salinger, or seem oddly to go 'missing' like B. Traven, and in our own time, Thomas Pynchon. In actual fact, Melville went neither silent nor missing. But such has been his legend. An American Melville conference held in 1984, at least, symptomatically has canvased the post-1860s Melville, and the poetry above all, as the great remaining challenge. How best, then, to confront the four principal volumes—*Battle-Pieces and Aspects of the War* (1866), *Clarel, a Poem and Pilgrimage in the Holy Land* (1876), *John Marr and Other Sailors* (1888) and *Timoleon*

(1891)[11]—without to the one side over-playing the critical hand, or to the other, contributing to the myth of the poetry as mere addendum to the fiction? This essay suggests one course of action to lie in the yet better understanding of the *kind* of poetry Melville wrote, verse as he alleged it designed to 'ponder' the vexing cross-ply and manifold a-symmetries of human experience itself.

He had few illusions about the likely prospects for such a poetry—by his own admission 'difficult' and unmellifluous—as he disclosed in a letter to his British admirer, James Billson, written in 1884 about the monumental *Clarel*:

> 'Clarel,' published by George P. Putnam's Sons, New York— a metrical affair, a pilgrimage or what not, of several thousand lines, eminently adapted for unpopularity.—The notification to you here is ambidexter, as it were: it may intimidate or allure.[12]

Rare it may have been, but Melville's poetry *has* managed to exert an allure for certain hardy souls, notably Walter E. Bezanson whose Hendricks House edition of *Clarel* in 1960 remains a high watermark in Melville scholarship, Robert Penn Warren and, latterly, William Bysshe Stein.[13] Theirs, to be sure, has been the minority report. But their arguments about the poetry, as a body of work which develops even further Melville's quest for usable, tested Truth, and his continuing penchant for contraries and ambiguity, has been of the utmost use. They have also laid down much of the pathfinding into his poetry's tactics, the identifying disjunctions of word-play and metric. In addition, they remind us that as early as *Mardi*, in 1849, in the *persona* of the Shelley-like Yoomy, Melville had taken to displaying his poetic wares.

2

The poetry in the context of the fiction makes for one kind of departure-point. The unadorned, literal circumstances of his life make for another, given as the evidence suggests that Melville took to poetry as a matter of greatest personal need and seriousness. In the aftermath of *Moby-Dick*, the magazine fiction and *The Confidence-Man*, a combination of public inattention and misunderstanding had driven him into brooding privacy. His would-be career as a lyceum lecturer had earned him neither income nor success. And to make any kind of living he had been obliged, in 1863, to sell 'Arrowhead', his Pittsfield farm, and to become a lowly Customs official for nearly two unrelieved decades until, in 1885, a bequest to his wife eased his way into retirement. Something of his larger attitude to the ways of the world can also be inferred from *The Confidence-Man*, for all the energy of its satiric appetite, a genuinely cool, 'distanced' vision of Illusion great and small. From the time of writing *Moby-Dick* onwards, too, he had good reason to think his neuralgia and eye trouble a re-play of the afflictions which had led to his father's death in 1832, and for which Judge Shaw, his eminent Massachusetts father-in-law, had generously funded a trip to the Holy Land in 1857 out of which in due course would emerge *Clarel*.

These interwoven worries about health, cash and family beset him throughout the whole of his later years, capped by the tragic and premature deaths of his sons, Malcolm and Stanwix, respectively in 1867 and 1886. Yet in *Battle-Pieces* against an array of odds which includes the public's general rejection of his work, he set himself the challenge of composing his own complex 'In Memoriam' to the Civil War, deservedly to be seen from a later perspective as a companion-piece to Whitman's better-known *Drum-Taps* (1865). *Clarel*, similarly, little though it has won him a readership, even more emphatically marks Melville's refusal to be ignored into silence. By its very ambition and deliberate siting at the crucible of Judaeo-Christianity, it again demonstrates Melville's undiminished resolve to face Truth in all its multi-facetedness, a great Testament to the nineteenth-century crisis of faith yet also another Melvilleian journey-narrative which circles and re-circles around the impossibility of Absolutes in a world of Relatives. Both these works, prodigious effort at the very least, when taken with the still later verse, also serve as proof—for Melville himself if no one else—that as he went about his wearying, obscure Customs rounds his imagination could still flourish, however ill-favoured he had become publicly.

Yet whatever the persistence of his inner vitality of spirit, the general toll on Melville was nonetheless considerable. One important testimony belongs to Julian Hawthorne who visited Melville in his Manhattan home in Spring, 1883, when researching material for a biography of his father, the Nathaniel Hawthorne described by Melville in 'Hawthorne and his Mosses' thirty or so years earlier in the *Literary World* for August 1850, as having dropped 'germinous seeds in my soul' and to whom the poem 'Monody' offers so touching a final tribute. To Julian Hawthorne Melville looked 'sombre, nervous' and 'a pale wraith of what he had been'.[14] Then, too, excepting *Billy Budd*, which itself most likely began life as a ballad, Melville's poetry bequeaths his only literary-creative activity across the thirty-four years between *The Confidence-Man* and his death in 1891. His poems thereby truly do signify the last part of the legacy to be settled, almost a Bartlebyesque dead-letter legacy in fact whose belated unravelling would readily have appealed to Melville's own, dark, intractable sense of the contrariness of all things.

Certainly, his wife Elizabeth, loyal as she generally always tried to be, sensed that the poetry signalled some unusual change of direction. In March 1875, as Melville turned his attention even more to the final draft of *Clarel* ('this dreadful *incubus* of a book' as she would come to call it), she confided warily to her step-mother in Boston: 'Herman is . . . pretty busy—pray do not mention to *any one* that he is writing poetry—you know how such things spread.' Whether said out of protective concern for Melville's physical well-being, or for their marriage itself, or in a moment of passing irritation, she could hardly have anticipated how painfully well history would act on her call to discretion. It remains unlikely, even now, that Melville's poetry will win any very wide readership, but whatever its complications of theme or metric it emerged from a mind assuredly as complex in grain as any in the American tradition. That, if nothing else, amounts to a summons across time and circumstance from Melville's age to our own. But his poems make many other claims. They above all continue utterly his unslackening pursuit after Truth—the eye-bloodying 'diving' he describes in a letter to Evert Duyckinck when amid the throes of *Moby-Dick*[15]—the same Truth, too, he alleged in 'Hawthorne and his Mosses' to be 'forced to fly like a scared white doe in the woodlands' and which 'reveals herself' 'only by cunning glimpses', 'covertly' and 'by snatches'. They also express Melville's attempt to shape an utterly distinct idiom, one by no means easy or companionable, but discernibly his own. In these, and other related respects, Melville's poetry continues to issue a challenge worthy of our more attentive response.

3

When ocean-clouds over inland hills
    Sweep storming in the late autumn brown,
And horror the sodden valley fills,
    And the spire falls crashing in the town,
I muse upon my country's ills—

In this stanza, from 'Misgivings', one of the opening poems in *Battle-Pieces*, Melville establishes the note which will reverberate throughout the whole sequence. For all the detail of reference—to the leading Union and Confederate *dramatis personae*, to battles fought and lost, to the soldiery and campaigns of both sides—these are poems of retrospection which in depicting the 'horror' and 'crashing spire' of the American Civil War do so both as simulated time-present and as events painingly weighed and 'mused upon' even as they settle into the past of History. In his brief prefatory Note, Melville gives an additional clue to the feelings which lie behind his war-verse:

> The aspects which the strife as memory assumes are as manifold as are the moods of involuntary meditation—moods variable, and at times widely at variance. Yielding, instinctively, one after another, to feelings not inspired from any one source exclusively, I seem, in most of these verses, to have but placed a harp in a window, and noted the contrasted airs which wayward winds have played upon the strings.

'Strife as memory', 'moods variable', 'contrasted airs'— Melville's careful phrases offer the essential directional gloss for *Battle-Pieces*. They underscore the poems as forms of commemoration, the outcome of 'involuntary meditation', and point to Melville's double sense of the Civil War as fissure both historic and personal, at once outward and deeply inward. Across a considerable body of verse, seventy-five poems or so of varying length and preoccupation, Melville writes out of the same, inverse, elegiac mood, an engrained conviction of humankind's fatal inclination to be at cross-purposes and marringly divided. Hence, in 'Misgivings', he can imagine War, Nature and Poet as subject to a single, collusive power of Conflict whose writ holds everywhere:

> With shouts the torrents down the gorges go,
> And storms are formed behind the storms we feel:
> The hemlock shakes in the rafter, the oak in the driving keel.

This warning turbulence of 'storm' and 'tempest' then leads on to an almost Yeatsian sequence of antimonies: War as against Peace; Death as against Life; and America as 'the world's fairest hope' obliged to pay grievously for 'man's foulest crime' of slavery. The dark resignation which lies behind 'Misgivings' and the accompanying other poems in *Battle-Pieces*, Melville amplifies yet further in 'The Conflict of Convictions', especially its concluding lines:

> YEA AND NAY—
> EACH HATH HIS SAY;
> BUT GOD HE KEEPS THE MIDDLE WAY.
> NONE WAS BY
> WHEN HE SPREAD THE SKY;
> WISDOM IS VAIN, AND PROPHESY.

Warring opposites presided over by silent, unknowable deity—thus, in synopsis, we are to comprehend the 'philosophy' at work in his poems. The terms belong to a familiar Melvilleian realm of unresolvable enigma and dialectic.

The interaction of War as ancestral schism, present history and the poet's own self-divisive meditation is again, and most dramatically, perceptible in the two poems which begin and close *Battle-Pieces*, *'The Portent'* and 'A Meditation'. In the former, suitably italicized and not a little eerie, the emphasis falls upon *'Weird John Brown'*, *'slowly swaying'*. Brown's hanging in 1859 as reprisal for the Harpers Ferry raid he envisages as the anticipatory knell of the war. *'Weird'*, obsessive, yet the widely assumed Christly martyr of Abolition, Brown struck Melville as embodying yet another paradox: the Cause which, however laudable its original aims, in becoming absolute

127

becomes thereby murderous. In his '*hidden*' purposes and '*anguish*' Brown thus acts as the '*meteor of war*', the harbinger of an intransigence of spirit whose effects will leave nothing and none untouched as the War takes its inexorable course. This same intransigence, for Melville, implicates both North and South, Abolitionist and Pro-Slaver, Slave victim and Slave master, and even, he implies, History itself, especially if understood as a contradictory lattice of counter-absolutes and oppressions. It is the '*sway*' of Brown's hanged body on the gallows—slow, creaking, timelike—which for Melville signals the grim, deathly rhythm of the Civil War and at the same time gives him his poetic measure for each successive 'meditation' in *Battle-Pieces*.

If Melville has us enter *Battle-Pieces* through the iconic, contrary figure of John Brown—assassin and martyr—he concludes in 'A Meditation' with other, matching paradoxes:

> O, now that brave men yield the sword,
>   Mine be the manful soldier-view;
> By how much more they boldly warred,
>   By so much more is mercy due;
> When Vicksburg fell, and the moody files marched out,
> Silent the victors stood, scorning to raise a shout.

In part, Melville is making a plea for reconciliation, an end to 'civil strife' as he calls it, and the Northern insistence on the South as 'sinner'. In his explanatory Preface to the poem, he writes that 'A Meditation' is to be attributed to a Northerner who has attended two funerals, 'THOSE OF A NATIONAL AND CONFEDERATE OFFICER (BROTHERS), HIS KINSMEN WHO HAD DIED FROM THE EFFECTS OF WOUNDS RECEIVED IN THE CLOSING BATTLES'. Death met after Appommatox and the end of the war makes its own inverse, ironic comment, as does the implied Cain/ Abel, Jacob/Esau parallel. But Melville's poem seeks to say yet more. It suggests the 'manful soldier-view' to be no longer the conquering 'shout' but the comprehending fellow-silence. 'Moody files', ostensibly a reference to the defeated Confederate ranks, calls up equally all the others who have 'filed' through the war: kin, mourners, the widowed and bereaved as much as the soldier and officer. Their suffering locates in small the larger, historic fissure of the War itself, the Union North against the Confederate South, the Blue against the Grey, and the countering anthems of 'The Battle Hymn of the Republic' as against 'Dixie'. In arguing reconciliation, Melville implicitly reminds his American readership of the War of Independence, a time of shared resistance to a common enemy, however much there too men have suffered divided loyalties and feeling. In 'A Meditation' Melville entertains scant hope that the Conflict of Convictions in the human condition can ever finally be resolved. But he does plead for a remembrance of common American humanity, a mutual conclusion to soldierly death and the wounding excitations of battle. Past wrongs like slavery he insists can be learned from, and now put to rights. 'A Meditation' may not achieve the fine lyric grace of Walt Whitman's 'When lilacs last in the dooryard bloom'd', but it derives from the same healing instinct, a calming stay against War as the brutest form of human division.

Virtually every other poem in *Battle-Pieces* draws upon similar 'meditation', Melville's troubled contemplation of the War as both the national House Divided and a source of divided feeling within himself. This applies to his poems of battle ('The March into Virginia', 'The Battle for the Mississippi', or 'The Fall of Richmond'), or the poems which assume a yet more philosophic cast ('The Stone Fleet', 'On the Slain Collegians' or 'America'), or those which make up the inset sequence he calls 'Verses Inscriptive and Memorial'. In these, and his other poems, the 'meditative' focus can be of many kinds. It can be the recollection of one-time great whaling and commercial ships, the fastest sail of their day, now scuttled in Charleston harbour as a bulwark against Federal naval attack. The irony lies that in passing from ocean-going craft into underwater monuments, in the event the scuttling has served no real purpose:

> And all for nought. The waters pass—
> Currents will have their way;
> Nature is nobody's ally; 'tis well;
> The harbor's bettered—will stay.
> A failure and complete,
> Was your old Stone Fleet.
>
> ('The Stone Fleet')

Or the focus can be a young officer prematurely aged into lonely 'Indian aloofness' by the war and the rigours of battle and command:

> A still rigidity and pale—
>> An Indian aloofness lones his brow;
> He has lived a thousand years
> Compressed in battle's pains and prayers,
>> Marches and watches slow.
>
> ('The College Colonel')

or two 'right' Causes brought into deadly conflict and now remembered as 'elegy':

> What could they else—North or South?
> Each went forth with blessings given
> By priests and mothers in the name of Heaven;
>> And honor in all was chief.
> Warred one for Right, and one for Wrong—
> So put it; but they both were young—
> Each grape to his cluster clung,
> All their elegies are sung.
>
> ('On the Slain Collegians')

or the 'mad', 'blind', behind-the-back murder of Lincoln:

> But they killed him in his kindness
> In their madness and their blindness,
> And they killed him from behind.
>
> ('The Martyr')

or Stonewall Jackson as at once Foe and Comrade:

> Justly his fame we outlaw; so
> We drop a tear on the bold Virginian's bier,
>> Because no wreath we owe.
>
> ('Stonewall Jackson')

or success at sea as also a loss and a dramatic prompting to thoughts of mortality:

> But seldom the laurel wreath is seen
>> Unmixed with pensive pansies dark;
> There's a light and shadow on every man
>> Who at last attains his lifted mark—
>> Nursing through night the ethereal spark.
> Elate he can never be;

He feels that spirits which glad had hailed his worth,
  Sleep in oblivion.—The shark
Glides white through the phosphorus sea.
                    ('Commemorative of a Naval Victory')

Similar, contrary 'meditation' marks out the principal narrative poems in *Battle-Pieces*. Three, in particular, invite inspection. In 'Donelson', a twenty-page re-creation of one of the key early Civil War sieges, Melville adeptly designs his poem to enact each rise and fall of rumour, the alternating reports of Victory and Defeat. Spoken in different voices, and punctuated with imagined orders-of-the-day and 'news from the front', it shows action under arms as an intricate, contradictory process of actual fighting, elated false hopes, setbacks, fear, even prattle, and the deepening perception that war can never be a final triumph. Through his depiction of each conflicting dispatch and alternation of myth with truth, Melville as always insinuates his sad, 'meditated' belief in the need to be done with all war:

> Ah God! may Time with happy haste
> Bring wail and triumph to a waste,
>   And war be done;
> The battle flag-staff fall athwart
> The curs'd ravine, and wither; naught
> Be left of trench or gun;
> The bastion, let it ebb away,
> Washed with the river bed; and Day
>   In vain seek Donelson.

In 'The Scout Towards Aldie', another story-poem full and particular in detail, Melville marvellously establishes the strange, almost fantastical aura associated with John Singleton Mosby, the legendary Grey Ghost of the Confederacy. At once a murderous literal guerilla threat to the Union soldiers, yet a mythy, spectral figure, Mosby in Melville's handling becomes the very personification of Death-in-Life, half-historical and half-imaginary, one in the litany of types who appear in the poetry of *Battle-Pieces*—John Brown, Ulysses Grant, Stonewall Jackson, Phil Sheridan and Abraham Lincoln. Mosby's credo, cryptic and avenging, reads like some Old Testament law: ''Tis Mosby's homily—*Man must die.*' Similarly in 'Lee in the Capitol', Melville turns a specific personage and historical 'event'—the bringing to the bench of the Confederacy's commander-in-chief—into deeper, parabular drama. Lee as field-soldier is one thing. But Melville sees in the surrender a form of cathartic ritual, an occasion to find in ceremony a means to healing and contemplation. The poem accordingly circles outward from Lee himself and the formalities in Washington to Time itself, Time as a great spiralling counter-motion infinitely more complex than mere linearity and in whose whorls and turnings is to be glimpsed crucial—and tragic—lessons: 'Historic reveries their lessons lent,/ The Past her shadow through the Future sent.'

Melville's poems in *Battle-Pieces* rarely seek to resolve their typical inversions and oppositions; rather they calibrate and then hover over the knot of tensions which have been the war. The idiom can go wrong, to be sure, bordering at worst on doggerel and infelicities of word and rhyme. But, equally, it can triumph, a striking command of likeness-in-difference and difference-in-likeness expressed as oxymoron and litotes and so deployed as to double both back and in on itself. Given the range of divisions dramatized by the Civil War, what literal reconciliation there may be Melville calls for in his magnificent, generous Supplement, one of the great Civil War addresses and easily fit company for the oratory of Lincoln in the North or the legal prose of the Confederacy's Vice-President, Alexander Stephens. Melville envisages North and South re-bonded through the shared knowledge of suffering:

> The mourners who in this summer bear flowers to the mounds of the Virginian and Georgian dead are, in their domestic bereavement and proud affection, as sacred in the eye of Heaven as those who go with similar offerings of tender grief and love into the cemeteries of our Northern Martyrs.

Melville indicates, too, in 'A Utilitarian View of the Monitor's Fight' that War—and especially for him the 'double' disaster of self-inflicted Civil War—requires an appropriate poetic:

> Plain be the phrase, yet apt the verse
> More ponderous than nimble;
> For once grimed War here laid aside

132

> His Orient pomp, 'twould ill befit
>   Overmuch to ply
> The rhyme's barbaric cymbal.

Whether, overall, Melville's Civil War poetry falls into a 'ponderousness' he did not quite intend, it is hard not to sympathize with his general wish to deprive war of its glamour, the supposed dash and headiness of the call to arms he designates 'Orient pomp'. His poems serve as memories of the war, much of the actual detail gleaned from the newspapers and the *Rebellion Record*. Even so, the history is rich in allusion, from Fort Sumpter to the Appomattox farm-house, on and away from the battle-field, from the fear of night-riots in New York City to the March into Atlanta, on land and at sea. Melville, though a non-participant, shows few illusions about war's displacing violence, its shocks and cost to the nerve. These, indeed, he often tries to dramatize in the poetry's diction, even to unfortunate effect like '*Dust to dust, and blood for blood—/ Passion and pangs!*' in 'The Armies of the Wilderness', and in his attempted half-rhymes and shifts and varyings of lineation. Yet the note throughout *Battle-Pieces* insistently is one of retrospect, an inwardly deliberated and memorial re-telling of recently endured trauma. In 'Ball's Bluff. A Reverie', for instance, he sees departing 'Young Soldiers marching lustily/ Unto the wars'. His mind turns uneasily on their departure, a 'musing' at one with the contemplative tenor of *Battle-Pieces* as a whole:

> Weeks passed; and at my window, leaving bed,
>   By night I mused, of easeful sleep bereft,
> On those brave boys (Ah War! thy theft);
>   Some marching feet
> Found pause at last by cliffs Potomac cleft;
>   Wakeful I mused, while in the street
> Far footfalls died away till none were left.

In using a term like 'ponderous', Melville no doubt was seeking to imply a more root etymological meaning, that of 'pondering' as meditation: 'Ball's Bluff. A Reverie', therefore, becomes utterly symptomatic. Its title alone calls up dream, the 'reverie' of 'far footfalls' and young soldiers 'thieved' of their lives. It seeks its resonance in the shared reference-back, the Civil War as a 'past' which arouses wakeful 'musing' in poet and reader alike. A comparison which understandably offers itself is with Stephen Crane's later Civil War classic, *The Red Badge of Courage* (1895). But in that narrative, for all its painterly and visually 'still' use of detail, the momentum lies in the forward thrust of the story, its dynamic of action—quite the opposite of Melville's measure in *Battle-Pieces*.

That *Battle-Pieces* has more and more come to be invoked in the context of Whitman's *Drum-Taps* marks an encouraging advance. Though unarguably a lesser achievement than *Drum-Taps* it also helps to challenge the implication behind Daniel Aaron's entitling of his well-known study of the Civil War as *The Unwritten War*.[16] And not only *Battle-Pieces* but a small legacy of other American war-verse can be added to the account, notably William Cullen Bryant's 'The Death of Slavery', James Russell Lowell's 'Ode Recited at the Harvard Commemoration', John Greenleaf Whittier's 'Anniversary Poem' and 'Barbara Frietchie', and even Oliver Wendell Holmes's assiduously mannered 'For The Commemoration Services'. But rarely have these, or Whitman's or Melville's verse, won comparison with, say, the poetry of Wilfred Owen, Isaac Rosenberg and the First World War generation, or with Yeats's Easter Rising poems, or at a yet further remove, with Garcia Lorca's Spanish Civil War writing. Which may indeed be right and a check to false or exaggerated attempts at revaluation. But it ought not to close the account. For in the case of *Battle-Pieces*, the designed 'meditation' of Melville's poems—not to say their troubled, intelligent humanity—amounts to considerable fare. At the very least they can, without embarrassment, offer grounds for comparisons not customarily attempted.

4

It would be hard *not* to approach *Clarel* undauntedly: a 4-part, American-Victorian 'philosophic' verse-narrative, over 18,000 lines in length and involving a plethora of figures major and minor all tied into the Pilgrimage of the title-character, and unmistakeably from the outset a challenge as poetry both to eye and ear. Matters are not helped, either, by our general modern lack of interest in, or at least unfamiliarity with and at its worst dislike of, truly long poems. Poetry like *Gawain and The Green Knight*, *The Faerie Queen*, *Paradise Lost*, *The Prelude* or *In Memoriam* offers a selective roster of what tends to get read, though how much that happens as a result of genuine preference as against school and university set-book requirement would be hard to say. And nearer to Melville's own era is there in truth a non-specialist taste for, say, Blake's Prophetic Books, the other long poems of Tennyson and his co-Victorians Browning and Morris, or Hardy's *The Dynasts*, or on the other side of the Atlantic the deeply American tradition of the Long Poem as inaugurated by Whitman's *Leaves of Grass* and which takes in, among others, the work of Sandburg, Williams, Stevens, Frost, Pound, Eliot and moderns like Olson, Ginsberg and Zukovsky?

In form and impact, *Clarel* resembles nothing so much as George Eliot's *The Spanish Gypsy*, another sizeable and largely unread verse-composition by a major writer whose reputation rests firmly upon achievements in fiction. It may well be, too, that Edgar Allan Poe's celebrated objection in 'The Philosophy of Composition' (1846) to the very notion of length in poetry—that 'extremeness of length' which destroys 'the vastly important element, totality, or unity, of effect'—has been vindicated, and has explained at least in part why long poems have rarely won an enthusiastic following. But however daunting its length, theme, or scale of ambition and canvas, like Melville's other verse *Clarel* deserves its hearing. If nothing else, it offers a major, arguably flawed and over-entangled, act of mind, yet further confirmation in the expansive vein of *Moby-Dick* of Melville as, to use again his own terms, the irrepressible writer-*diver*.

Many of the key departure-points for *Clarel* lie in Melville's own prior writing: the 'voyage-out' format which eventuates triumphantly in *Moby-Dick*; the use of colloquium as begun in *Mardi* and honed to a fine art in the voicing of *The Confidence-Man*; the play of viewpoint which in stories like 'Benito Cereno' and 'Bartleby' becomes a drama in and of itself; the Gothicized love-story of Clarel for Ruth which harks back to the Pierre-Lucy-Isabel triangle in *Pierre*; and Melville's abiding concern with the competing avatars and mythifyings of religion first explored in *Typee* and expressed as dramatically as anywhere in 'The Whiteness of the Whale' and 'The Honor and Glory of Whaling', Chapters 42 and 82 of *Moby-Dick*. But to hand also is Melville's *Journal of a Visit to Europe and the Levant*, the diary of his 1856–57 visit to the Holy Land and an indispensable source-book for the journey-notes which over twenty years of gestation led on to *Clarel*. His shorthand jottings on confronting Constantinople, for example, epitomize his encounter with the Levant in general, even for so seasoned an Atlantic and Pacific ex-whalerman a veritable 'labyrinth' and 'din' of peoples, languages, customs and beliefs: 'You loose yourself & are bewildered & confounded with the labyrinth, the din, the barbaric confusion of the whole.'[17]

Clarel itself, a pilgrimage which contains other pilgrimages and stories-within-stories, offers equally a 'confusion' of sorts, doubt and counter-conviction pitted against Faith. Its story of Clarel, the earnest American Bible student who in company with a select band of fellow pilgrims (all 'shipwrecked men adrift', Bk. IV, vii, 1) journeys from Jerusalem across the desert to the Dead Sea and Mar Saba and back again via Bethlehem, so becomes the physical expression of spiritual journeying within. In this the poem draws inescapably upon Melville's own radical scepticism, his unwillingness ever to settle for outward appearance and his lifelong unease with received Christian orthodoxy. It is the same temper, for instance, which lies behind *Pierre* and the bleak island sketches he sardonically entitled 'The Encantadas'. And it is the element in his make-up which Hawthorne intuitively seized upon in his celebrated English Notebook entry for November 1856 after he and Melville had wandered the Lancashire shoreline:

> Melville, as he always does, began to reason of Providence and futurity, and of everything that lies beyond human ken, and informed me that he had 'pretty much made up his mind to be annihilated;' but still he will not seem to rest in that anticipation; and, I think, never rest until he gets hold of a definite belief. It is strange how he persists—and has persisted ever since I knew him, and probably long before—in wandering to and fro over these deserts, as dismal and monotonous as the sand hills amid which we were sitting. He can neither

believe, nor be comfortable in his unbelief; and he is too honest and courageous not to try to do one or the other. If he were a religious man, he would be one of the most truly religious and reverential; he has a very high and noble nature, and better worth immortality than most of us.[18]

Melville could hardly have better confirmed Hawthorne's insights than in the Epilogue to *Clarel*, a summary of sorts of the poem's great dialectical themes:

> Yea, ape and angel, strife and old debate—
> The harps of heaven and the dreary gongs of hell;
> Science the feud can only aggravate—
> No umpire she betwixt the chimes and knell;
> The running battle of the star and clod
> Shall run forever—if there be no God.
>
> (Bk. IV, xxxv, 12–17)

Each of the four Books takes up precisely this 'old debate', Belief against Unbelief, the problem of Faith in an age whose historic syntheses symptomatically for Melville had come under challenge from Darwin's evolutionist theory, Burckhardt's historiography and Niebuhr's secularized History—three touchstones from among the many he invokes in the course of *Clarel*. The 'debate', furthermore, Melville sites against a Holy Land as grimy and humanly actual as his *Journal* records, but as so often previously in his scenarios also a world half-imagined, made up of walled cities, desert spaces, and meanings locked and inextricable within each tomb and vault and rock. Thus 'Jerusalem', Book 1, the poem invokes as the historic cross-road of Judaism, Christianity and Islam, yet equally a city-labyrinth whose outward form embodies labyrinths within, truths obscured by time and custom. In turn, 'Wilderness', Book II, describes real enough deserts of sand and monastery, but also the 'deserts' of human doubt which beset Clarel and his fellow-searchers; 'Mar Saba', Book III, named after the Dead Sea town, describes both a literal outpost and an outpost of all the worn credos and certitudes challenged by the very multiplicity of peoples and faiths which seek their one unique confirmation in Palestine; and, finally, 'Bethlehem', Book IV, indeed depicts a major Holy Place of Christendom but also another of Melville's enwalled, secret cities, as enigmatic as the great stone pyramids which had so fascinated him in Egypt and which his *Journal* designates 'a terrible mixture of the cunning and the awful'.

Similarly, each of Clarel's fellow-pilgrims suggests the type behind the particular, not least Clarel himself, one more in the Ishmael line of 'voyagers-out', a 'mind earnest' and covered literally and spiritually in 'the dust of travel'. His counterparts, too, recognizably embody dual identities: Vine, Hawthorne-like, speculative, discernibly belonging to the world yet projected as personifying a form of abstract aesthetic intelligence; Derwent, the Anglican divine, well-meaning but ultimately blinkered who calls to mind Melville's prior men of good intention—the lawyer in 'Bartleby', say, or the bachelor-Yankee Amaso Delano in 'Benito Cereno'; and Rolfe, the questor in whom heart and head seem to have come more or less into balance, an exemplary Bulkington figure. Against these *Clarel* arrays its absolutists: Celio, the crippled Italian doubter who dies almost wordlessly and unbelieving; Mortmain, the Scandinavian ex-insurrectionist who has 'roved the grey places of the earth' and whose idealism has inverted into despair; Agath, the Greek mariner for whom only a disaster theory can account for human affairs; and Ungar, 'Islanded in thought', the stoic American ex-Confederate officer to whom Progress is a mockery in an age of unbelievers, a tough Pitch-like figure given to the most barbed regard for humankind. These, together with the Nathan-Agar-Ruth family, exotics like the ex-Mexican Don Hannibal, and a further plethora of pilgrims, wanderers, prophets of East and West give *Clarel* its milling human cast, just as the collapse of Faith and the Holy Land give the poem respectively its theme and its geography—terms of reference overall not for the faint-hearted but typical of Melville's continuing energy of invention.

As the pilgrimage unfolds, so too each twist and turn in the 'old debate'. Melville keeps a difficult tissue of concerns under closest pressure—centrally the Christian legacy itself—a feat which threatens constantly to ruin *Clarel* by its own entanglements but which stays just the right side of imaginative order. Whatever its original authority Godhead for Clarel and his co-searchers has become 'a haze of mystery', obscured by history and a whole arcana of competing belief and superstition.

Divine Truth or otherwise remains unknowably immured within the time-worn sand and rock armature of the Holy Land. Christ's sepulchre, for instance, a place of 'caves and crag', thus bonds supplicant and Truth into a 'lone' equation:

> What rustlings here from shadowy spaces,
> Deep vistas where the votary paces,
> Will, strangely intermitting, creep
> Like steps in Indian forest deep.
> How bird-like steals the singer's note
> Down from some rail or arch remote:
> While glimmering where kneelers be,
> Small lamps, dispersed, with glow-worm light
> Mellow the vast nave's azure night,
> And make a haze of mystery:
> The blur is spread a thousand years,
> And Calvary seen as through one's tears.
>
> (Bk. I, iii, 43–54)

The debate, boldly enough, then widens into associated other directions: the claims of each different world-religion (Bk. I, v); the 'tribes and sects' within Christianity itself (Bk. I, vi); the abiding conflict of Science with Faith—'can these two unite?' (Bk. III, v, 65); the nature of Authority in an era of coming Democracy (Bk. IV, xix–xxi); and the consequence as Rolfe sees it of mankind's inevitable instinct for dissent and transformation:

> And men
> Get tired at last of being free—
> Whether in states—in states or creeds.
> For what's the sequel? Verily,
> Laws scribbled by law-breakers, creeds
> Scrawled by freethinkers, and deeds
> Shameful and shameless.
>
> (Bk. II, xxvi, 126–32)

As the poem duly rounds to its conclusion during the Easter Week, it becomes apparent that Clarel's journey can lead to no single, Truth-affirming point of arrival. Like the 'diver' Melville himself, Clarel must plunge back into the pilgrimage, 'life's wonted stream' (Bk. IV, xxxiii, 76), ever the searcher and only in the most fleeting of glimpses the finder.

Clarel draws from the same rhetorical stock as *The Confidence-Man*, another of Melville's encircling, circular narrations. Its discursive windings and counterpoint of argument and design assume a readerly patience which on past evidence has been rare. Undoubtedly, thus, it confirms Melville the poet to be mixed fare, neither the Great Thinker nor the Great Poet exactly, but who on both counts cannot easily be discounted. His poem's 'debate' indeed does veer close to contradiction for its own sake, argument which can turn and re-turn on its own axis. Similarly, his idiom can give every hostage to fortune, often prone to *longueurs* and disfiguring contrivances of sound and measure. Yet by its very persistence of enquiry, that 'honesty' and 'courage' which aroused Hawthorne's admiration, *Clarel* beckons undeniably, however uncertain its overall effect. Whatever its weaker features, it also reminds us of some of his best, not only his local powers of phrasing but his restless, exhilarating will-to-certainty.

5

In *John Marr and Other Sailors* Melville again operates in memorial vein, past sea-going and sailor life and types recalled partly to the formula of 'Ubi sunt . . .?' and partly as 'visionary' communings and dialogues. Like the title-character John Marr, the ex-mariner now by fate marooned amid the American prairies, Melville in these poems explores the contrast between ocean release and land-bound stasis, a contrast also between youth and age, action and contemplation. The sailors in all the poems amount to Odyssean innocents, their respective ships worlds in themselves yet destined to cross the oceans in quest of still others. Marr himself, literally out to grass, in his opening soliloquy 'speaks' to former shipmates and prior berths, envisaging both his and their shared history as 'subjects of meditation', 'phantoms', 'affections in the past for which an imaginative heart passionately yearns'. His may be the tone of melancholy, but melancholy made vital by the poem's circumstantial language:

> I yearn as ye. But rafts that strain,
> Parted, shall they lock again?

140

Twined we were, entwined, then riven,
Ever to new embracements driven,
Shifting gulf-weed of the main!
And how if one here shift no more,
Lodged by the flinging surge ashore?
Nor less, as now, in eve's decline,
Your shadowy fellowship is mine.
Ye float about me, form and feature:—
Tattooings, ear-rings, love-locks curled;
Barbarians of man's simpler nature,
Unworldly servers of the world.
Yea, present all, and dear to me,
Through shades, or scouring China's sea.

Melville's specificity of detail—sea friendships as 'shifting gulf-weed', tattoos, rings and love-locks as the 'form and feature' of ocean dress-code—keeps the poem free of self-indulgence, or mere complaint. An earlier line reads *'Life is storm'*, but 'storm' not to be turned away from but understood and even embraced, for Marr the 'storm' of his most deeply engaged selfhood and implicitly for Melville behind him the 'storm' of art as it takes imaginative hold of life earlier lived at full throttle and at whatever risk.

Each of the subsequent poems explores this balance of present repose and past activeness. 'Bridegroom Dick' recalls life aboard a Federal warship, its commanders and crew, at once the man-of-war order of things years before set out in *White-Jacket* and a portrait of sailordom as a masonic, risk-seeking fraternity. They, like the narrator, are now either 'hither and thither, blown wide asunder', or domesticated and given to rueful irony. 'Tom Deadlight' offers the last testament of a dying naval petty-officer, a poem of farewell richly shot through with sailorly colloquialism. Similarly, in 'The Haglets' a doomed ship is followed by three Coleridgean sea-birds, emissaries of a coming ocean sinking. It offers a vision to be read alongside that of 'The Maldive Shark', the shark as custodian of deeps which have long consumed past comrades and ships—Melville's unsettling, death'shead image of Time and Nature as inimical to human comfort. The concluding sequence, 'Pebbles', contains one of Melville's best-known lines—'Healed of my hurt, I laud the inhuman Sea'—an epitaph of sorts to the life invoked throughout *John Marr and Other Sailors*. Despite frequent commentary to the opposite, it ought not to be taken as tranquil, late-career resignation. Rather it underlines Melville's continuing sense of dialectic, the same dark, untamed dialectic which lies within and shapes 'Billy in the Derbies', the ballad-epilogue of his last prose fiction.

If for nothing else, *Timoleon* merits attention for its half-dozen authentically strong poems, each thickly sinewed and indicative of a Melville unregenerate in his view of the world's complexity. In 'After the Pleasure Party', for instance, he tackles 'the sexual feud', a Browning-like monologue set in Italy and spoken by a woman whose life has been spent in scholarly pursuits but who under the influence of Mediterranean sun and grape and the sight of a young peasant girl weighs the cost of her past aceticism. The poem's sexual currents doubtless have an autobiographical basis—*Mardi*, *Pierre*, 'The Tartarus of Maids' and *Billy Budd* all witness to Melville's troubled sense of human sexuality—yet the general drama of the self divided and in process of fissure had fascinated him from the outset. His resort to classical allusion, Amor, Urania, Pan and others, slightly solemnizes the poem, but its depiction of 'modern' feeling, sexual release as against restraint, the senses over the head, makes for powerful self-dialogue.

The sequence 'Fruit from Travel Long Ago' also first invokes Italy, landscape which again harbours landscapes within, vistas both outward and inward. In 'Venice' he imagines the city as rising 'in reefs of palaces'. A similar yet again wholly unexpected sea-image occurs in 'In a Bye-Canal':

> I have swum—I have been
> Twixt the whale's black flukes
>   and the white shark's fin

'Pisa's Leaning Tower' for him inclines like 'a would-be suicide'. The sight of a confessional in 'In a Church in Padua' makes him think of momentarily unburdened mysteries, a place of codes and ritual to recall Ishmael's encounter with the black church in New Bedford. In 'Milan Cathedral' he envisages the great white building as an architecture whose 'synodic hierarchies' parallel nothing short of 'the host of heaven'. This doubled 'travel' moves through Greece (he terms the Parthenon 'Art's meridian') and on to Egypt. There, as depicted in 'The Great Pyramid', Melville invokes once again, as so often in *Moby-Dick* and the later fiction, the immemorial stone edifice for which he felt endless fascination ('Your masonry—and is it man's?/ More like some Cosmic artisan's'). Melville, himself the riddling 'mason' of literary riddles, could have found no apter emblem, as arcane, involuted and mysterious as the Gordian knot in 'Benito Cereno' or Bartleby's world of walls. Its enigma for Melville emblematizes the world's, whose decipherment against every danger of unhingement (see 'I and my Chimney') he took on as if under compulsion:

> Slant from your inmost lead the caves
> And labyrinths rumored. These who braves
> And penetrates (old palmers said)
> Comes out afar on deserts dread
>   And, dying, raves.

> Craftsmen, in dateless quarries dim,
> Stones formless into form did trim,
> Usurped on Nature's self with Art,
> And bade this dumb I AM to start,
>   Imposing him.

In offering something of a key to Melville's conception of art as well as 'cosmic' truth, 'The Great Pyramid' might profitably be read alongside two others from *Timoleon*. 'Monody', by general consent, does homage to Hawthorne, Melville's typical perception of like natures which have gone askew ('to be estranged in life,/ And neither in the wrong') which only Art can resolve and so heal. And it is precisely, too, the tension of opposites which he seizes upon in 'Art', the challenge to make imaginative order of Life's unorder without doing injustice to the nature of either:

> In placid hours well-pleased we dream
> Of many a brave unbodied scheme.
> But form to lend, pulsed life create,
> What unlike things must meet and mate:
> A flame to melt—a wind to freeze,
> Sad patience—joyous energies;

143

Humility—yet pride and scorn;
Instinct and study; love and hate;
Audacity—reverence. These must mate,
And fuse with Jacob's mystic heart,
To wrestle with the angel—Art.

Melville's wrestle with Art, poetic art at any rate, led to notable inadequacies and outright failures. But, as he told James Billson in connection with *Clarel*, it can also allure. The full measure of his poetry's achievement has still only begun to emerge, and a poetry for itself and not as lesser companion-pieces to the fiction. Melville's own rueful estimate of its chances—'eminently adapted for unpopularity'—might have been generally prophetic. But we are no longer under obligation to let matters so stand.

NOTES

1. Randall Jarrell, *Poetry and the Age* (New York: Knopf, 1953). Even in the highly influential study by Roy Harvey Pearce, *The Continuity of American Poetry* (Princeton University Press, 1961) Melville as poet is completely ignored.

2. *The Writings of Herman Melville*, ed. Harrison Hayford, Hershel Parker and G. Thomas Tanselle (Evanston and Chicago: Northwestern University Press and The Newberry Library).

3. 'Left-handed' is Walter E. Bezanson's phrase. See Herman Melville, *Clarel: A Poem and Pilgrimage in the Holy Land*, ed. Walter E. Bezanson (New York: Hendricks House, 1966). Introduction p. ix.

4. See Merrell R. Davis and William H. Gilman (eds.), *The Letters of Herman Melville* (New Haven: Yale University Press, 1960); Eleanor Melville Metcalf (ed.), *Journal of a Visit to London and the Continent by Herman Melville, 1849–1850*; and Howard C. Horsford (ed.), *Melville's Journal of a Visit to Europe and the Levant, October 11, 1856–May 6, 1857.*

5. These are, in chronological sequence, Raymond Weaver, *Herman Melville, Mariner and Mystic* (New York: George H. Doran Company, 1923); D. H. Lawrence, *Studies in Classic American Literature* (New York: T. Seltzer, 1923); John Freeman, *Herman Melville* (London: MacMillan and Co., English Men of Letters Series, 1926); Lewis Mumford, *Herman Melville: A Study of His Life and Vision* (New York: Harcourt, Brace and Company, 1929); and Van Wyck Brooks, *The Times of Melville and Whitman* (New York: E. P. Dutton, 1947). To Raymond Weaver also goes the editorial credit for *The Works of Herman Melville*, Standard Edition, 16 Vols. (London: Constable and Company, 1922–24). Though

Van Wyck Brooks's study did not appear until 1947, he had long previously urged Melville's case in essays and occasional pieces.

6. As argued in F. O. Matthiessen, *American Renaissance: Art and Expression in the Age of Emerson and Whitman* (New York: University Press, 1941).

7. *Letters* (op. cit.). See especially Melville's letters to Hawthorne for 29 June 1851 ('Shall I send you a fin of the *whale* by way of a specimen mouthful? The tail is not yet cooked—though the hell-fire in which the whole book is broiled might not unreasonably have cooked it all ere this') and for 17? November 1851 ('I have written a wicked book, and feel spotless as the lamb').

8. 'Lower layers' is Ahab's phrase in *Moby-Dick*.

9. *Letters* (op. cit.), Melville to Hawthorne, 29 June 1851.

10. *Letters* (op. cit.), Melville to Lemuel Shaw, 6 October 1849.

11. *Battle-Pieces and Aspects of the War* (New York: Harper & Brothers, 1866); *Clarel: A Poem and Pilgrimage in the Holy Land*, 2 Vols. (New York: G. P. Putnam's Sons, 1876); *John Marr and Other Sailors, with some Sea-Pieces* (New York: Theodore L. De Vinne & Co., 1888); and *Timoleon and Other Ventures in Minor Verse* (New York: Caxton Press, 1891). References to *Battle-Pieces* are to the Facsimile Edition, ed. Sidney Kaplan, Scholars's Facsimiles & Reprints (Gainsville, Florida, 1960); to *Clarel* to the Hendricks House Edition (1966); and to *John Marr and Other Sailors* and *Timoleon* to the *Collected Poems*, ed. Howard P. Vincent (Chicago: Hendricks House, 1947).

12. *Letters* (op. cit.), Melville to James Billson, 10 October 1884.

13. See Bezanson (op. cit.); Robert Penn Warren, *Selected Essays* (New York: Random House, 1958) and *Selected Poems of Herman Melville: A Reader's Edition* (New York: Random House, 1970); and William Bysshe Stein, *The Poetry of Melville's Late Years* (Albany: The State University of New York Press, 1970). Also: R. W. B. Lewis (ed.), *Herman Melville: Stories, Poems and Letters* (New York: Dell Publishing Co., 1967).

14. Jay Leyda, *The Melville Log: A Documentary Life of Herman Melville 1819–1892*, 2 Vols. (New York: Harcourt, Brace and Co., 1951), Vol. II, pp. 782–83. Leyda usefully gives a selection of these accounts by Julian Hawthorne.

15. *Letters* (op. cit.), Melville to Evert Duyckinck, 3 March 1849. Melville is discussing Emerson: 'I love all men who *dive*. Any fish can swim near the surface, but it takes a great whale to go down stairs five miles or more; & if he don't attain the bottom, why, all the lead in Galena can't fashion the plumet that will. I'm not talking of Mr. Emerson now—but of the whole corps of thought-divers, that have been diving & coming up with bloodshot eyes since the world began.'

16. Daniel Aaron, *The Unwritten War: American Writers and the Civil War* (New York: Alfred A. Knopf, 1973).

17. *Melville's Journal of a Visit to Europe and the Levant, October 11, 1856–May 5, 1857* (op. cit.), p. 82.

18. Nathaniel Hawthorne, *Journal*, November 1856. Reprinted in Leyda, *The Melville Log* (op. cit.).

7

The Fireside Poets: Hearthside Values and the Language of Care

by JAMES H. JUSTUS

When Robert Frost appeared at the inauguration of John F. Kennedy, the spectacle of poet and president together on the same platform was an anomaly widely remarked. The poet as public institution was such a rarity in the United States that the occasion stimulated a few expressions of hope that, among all the other good augured by the new administration, the general elevation of the artist might actually usher in a new era in which the republic would sanction the official veneration of the poet. A few years earlier that kind of recognition might have gone to more blatantly national poets—Stephen Vincent Benét or Archibald MacLeish—or to troubadours—Carl Sandburg or Vachel Lindsay; but by 1961 Frost was the logical choice for the honour, which meant that his individual achievement was also that of the American people. That Kennedy's gesture augured nothing but itself is irrelevant; it revived a long-felt if covert need for the nationally sanctioned poet, an institutional figure missing since the late nineteenth century.

In that century that confirmed the success of the new republic; only Emily Dickinson and Edgar Allan Poe among American poets were untouched by the ambition to identify in some public way with the aspirations and ideals of the nation.

Walt Whitman, though he was never embraced by the popular following he thought he deserved, was considerably more successful in his drive to be the Poet of America in his own lifetime than legend had it a generation ago. If Emerson seemed too high-minded and aloof for such a rôle, an occasional effort by this sometime poet reveals the stirrings of an ambition similar to that of his contemporaries in New England and New York. But it is the achievement, individually and corporately, of those versifiers known as the Fireside Poets that, for the first and only time in American history, made the poet a public treasure.

The oldest, William Cullen Bryant (1794–1878), transformed himself from a home-grown Augustan with conservative political leanings to a Wordsworthian Romantic with liberal instincts; he began his career with *The Embargo*, a Federalist satire directed at Thomas Jefferson, and ended it in the year of his death with 'Mazzini', an address dedicating a statue of the Italian hero in New York's Central Park—a gesture that joined the struggle for Italian unity with America's similar struggle during the Civil War. The youngest, James Russell Lowell (1819–91), domesticated political radicalism by both an elevated idealism and a biting sense of humour. The others, Henry Wadsworth Longfellow (1807–82), John Greenleaf Whittier (1807–92) and Oliver Wendell Holmes (1809–94), in varying ways and at varying stages in their long careers, so visibly hectored, coerced, persuaded and prodded their audiences that an envious Mark Twain allied himself to their group as 'fellow-teachers of our great public'.[1]

It is not accidental that a variant title for the Fireside Poets is the Schoolroom Poets. To designate the identity of any writer with a corporate name is necessarily to diminish his achievement, and serious readers can distinguish among the salient characteristics of Bryant and Longfellow or of Whittier and Holmes; yet by the 1880s the great impact of these talents, now relegated in most American literary histories and anthologies to the status of 'Minor Poets' or 'Others', was corporate rather than individual. Titles might be assigned properly to the names of the poets who wrote them, but school-children who dutifully memorized 'Thanatopsis' and 'A Psalm of Life' without tonal distinctions would, when they

147

grew up, also be hard-pressed to find substantive distinctions between them. As national poets, their distinctiveness tended to be parcelled out and harmonized, and the famous lines became a scrapbook assemblage in which authorship was decidedly less important than their quotability: 'The melancholy days are come, the saddest of the year'; 'And what is so rare as a day in June'; 'Ay, tear her tattered ensign down!'; ' "Shoot, if you must, this old gray head" '; 'Thou, too, sail on, O Ship of State!'

By the time Mark Twain himself died in 1910 all these teachers of the great public had been in their graves for more than fifteen years and their portraits had been enshrined on the walls of schoolrooms from Maine to California. At some point *beloved* was an encomium bestowed on each of them. Long and productive lives are of course an important factor in the record of reverence these poets left behind: when they died Lowell was 72, Longfellow was 75, Bryant was 84, and Holmes and Whittier were 85. But perhaps more important is the fact that not one was simply a poet. These men led conspicuously public lives—as editor, professor, linguist and translator, diplomat, doctor, novelist, lecturer, essayist—whose careers defined at an upper level the dominant public values of America at mid-century: an ethical idealism that for all its failure in specific instances directed the sense of national mission. The Fireside Poets attained their status as national poets because they embodied the aspirations, needs and values of a free-wheeling, activist, expansionist society to which the most appropriate response was ambition, hard work, patriotism, familial loyalty, plucky independence and a generalized piety that would bear little theological scrutiny. Many of their famous poems celebrate such values overtly: 'The Village Blacksmith', 'Maud Muller', 'To a Water-Fowl', 'The Chambered Nautilus', 'The Vision of Sir Launfal'. Others—*The Song of Hiawatha, Snow-Bound, The Biglow Papers*, 'The Deacon's Masterpiece', 'The Prairies'—are indirect.

If we accept the premise that the Fireside Poets were institutionalized as national poets because they articulated the values of their culture, it is necessary to look closely at *how* they were formulating them. The story that these poets tell is not that of the subordination of private purpose to the constituent values that the larger culture endorsed, but of the convergence of personal and public history, of private prerogative and the public weal. All courted fame, some winning more effortlessly than others. Longfellow, to whom fame came early, achieved his success without having strong ideas about politics, religion, economics, immigration, civic affairs, or (once he was done with his Harvard professorship) education. The multi-talented Holmes made his name by being opinionated about everything. But there is no real evidence that even Lowell or Whittier, who at crucial points in their careers depended upon popular support of their views, trimmed their sails to the prevailing winds of doctrine or sentiment. Like most of their readers, these public poets could be both Christian and democratic without once sacrificing a sense of themselves as natural aristocrats. Lowell and Whittier may have momentarily risked their reputations by their firm stands against slavery and war, but their most popular poems—*Snow-Bound*, 'The Courting', 'Maud Muller', 'The Vision of Sir Launfal'— are not products of zealots.

From our twentieth-century perspective in which the very terms of discourse are inconclusive violence, alienation and loss of community, we tend to view the Fireside Poets as laureates of placidity. To re-read the collected volumes of these men is to confront a world of moral earnestness, even in Holmes's wit, in which devotion to 'the right thing' seems to be the common official policy of most Americans. But the play of reasonableness, charity, and respect for the homely virtues that Franklin had cannily Americanized a generation earlier is so emphatic not because those virtues were emphatic in American life but because they were not. The 'optimistic' century of the Fireside Poets was not a world of ebullient promise, and their response to it was not the heady Emersonian sense that all things were possible. The truth is that they combine the celebration of both the placid moment and the stirring event that tests human resolve. If Longfellow's and Holmes's concern for the large-scale issues of their society— slavery, secession, war—was somewhat perfunctory, that of Whittier, Bryant and Lowell was conspicuous. And all celebrate the triumph of right when it comes. What is even more evident in their verse, however, is the crucial importance

149

of domestic harmony—not because they think of it as the linchpin of a cultivated society, which they routinely do, but because that harmony seems threatened. They sing both of domestic virtues and extraordinary heroism, of marital bliss and martial necessity, of modesty and ambition, of homely integrity and a faith in general Humanity, general Truth, general Freedom. Significantly, Longfellow's characteristic genius is to be found in his dramatic narratives, for 'The Skeleton in Armor', 'The Wreck of the Hesperus', *Evangeline*, *The Song of Hiawatha*, *The Courtship of Miles Standish*, and many of the *Tales of a Wayside Inn* stake their appeal simultaneously on the domestic and the heroic. The dignity of Lowell's and Holmes's great ceremonial odes is consistently softened by what was once thought to be tonal lapses: familiarizing locutions and anachronisms of landscape and emotion; Holmes's is the kind of sensibility that can refer to 'an epic as clever as "Paradise Lost" '. Bryant's sweeping subjects at once pose philosophical statements and situate them in contexts that are resolutely personal, even petty; and Whittier's most stirring political poems are assaults against the loss in extraordinary leaders of the common sense, judgement and right instincts that ordinary men still possess.

The moral earnestness conveyed by these poets is, surprisingly, rarely abstract; it emerges from textures that are local and specific, as if the meditative mood is as seemly in granitic Yankees as in cultivated Englishmen. The buoyant cheer of Emerson's early work is notably missing in the Fireside Poets because their vision is not that of Adam in the garden but of Adam east of Eden. Because theirs is a world of grief, pain, tribulation, these poets take all the more seriously their mission to help assuage the received condition of all fallen Adams. Heroic gestures and grand strategies in these public poets are always scaled down, manageably conceived and executed from the perspective of the fireside, which as place is both symbolic and generative. It represents the centrality of the domestic affections in the general ethical idealism of the day, an impulse that historically incorporated the home, the church and the school so effectively that the civic and religious virtues absorbed from the pew and the school-boy's bench were merely extensions of the homely virtues taught and learned beside the hearth, the mother's knee and the father's chair. But the fireside in the work of these poets also provides genial conditions for an art that would in time become yet another extension of home, church and school. The voice of January in Longfellow's 'The Poet's Calendar' says, 'My fires light up the hearths and hearts of men.'[2] As the heart of the home, the fireside is a retreat, an escape from the cares of the world outside the home, but because of its conducive stimulation of the imagination, it is an aesthetic source as well.

Edgar Poe may have anticipated the taste of a later day when he railed against the heresy of the didactic, but in his own century he was a rarity among both his fellow artists and the reading audience for whom art meant alternative forms of teaching—and meant it so intensely that to create inapplicable beauty was to slip into the heresy of the undidactic. The question that must be asked of the Fireside Poets is not 'Should poetry teach?' but 'What does Fireside Poetry teach?' From the first these men became teachers of the great public not by being sectarian or ideological. Behind the Quakerism of Whittier, the lapsed Calvinism of Bryant and the Unitarianism of the Cambridge group is an ethical idealism that blurs distinguishing doctrines, an eclecticism that could function successfully even when the mainstream Christian emphasis became vaguely deistic or pantheistic. It is a doctrine whose only article of obligation is that it serve human need; it allows religion, aesthetics, and politics alike to ratify community, individual dignity, love, patriotism and the aspiration to better the self and others. But contrary to our gradeschool memories, these were popular voices not because they shielded their readers from actuality by issuing easy appeals to idealism, but because their works fully incorporated, *prior* to those hortatory injunctions, the general experience of what it was like to live in an uncertain world fraught with injustice, anxiety, malaise and deadening routine. What is striking about this poetry, which we tend to see as an undifferentiated collection of monitory images, is a rhetoric of care that pervades and often threatens to overwhelm the very lessons for which the poetry is designed. The popular words in the Fireside lexicon are not *do, dare, hope, work, heights* or *courage* but *strife, toils, griefs, struggle, dreary* and *anguish*; and their cumulative effect suggests a world in both tone and substance far removed from the vigorously transcendentalized one of Emerson. Both as men and representative spokesmen, these poets devised several strategies for accommodating the discouraging spectacle they observed of lives never quite fulfilled and the very conditions of the despair that resulted.

The conventional urge to escape daily cares by plunging into natural settings is most obvious in Bryant, who of the Fireside Poets was closest to the later eighteenth-century poetry that made such gestures fashionable; it is also Bryant who most readily adopted the Wordsworthian contrast between the holy innocence of childhood and an imprisoning maturity with 'its sorrows, crimes, and cares'. But the frequency with which Bryant returns to 'the eating cares of earth' suggests an orientation reaching beyond poetic convention into auto-biography and the cultural life of his time. At 24 and practising law, he magnifies the dreariness of his professional life by depicting himself 'forced to drudge for the dregs of men/ And scrawl strange words with the barbarous pen', to mingle with the 'jostling crowd,/ Where the sons of strife are subtle and loud' ('Green River'). He imagines Nature shrinking from him because of 'the signet and care on my brow' ('I Cannot Forget with What Fervid Devotion'), though he returns again and again for the calming effects of Nature because he is so 'Worn with the struggle and the strife,/ And heart-sick at the wrongs of men' ('A Summer Ramble'). But as 'Thanatopsis', his most famous poem, attests, human revivification through immersion in Nature is not finally the lesson nineteenth-century readers learned from reading Bryant; they learned instead stoic endurance. Of the group Bryant, who was a Calvinist before becoming a Unitarian, is the least comforting and the most perfunctory in his Christianity. Even the analogy of 'To a Water-Fowl', more overt than in most of his poems, is, compared to Longfellow's practice, modest in its assurance that the 'Power' that guides the bird in its flight will surely 'lead my steps aright'.

Though he is often remembered for his focus on specific

natural objects—waterfowl, mosquito, gentian, bobolink—the large sweeping subject is more congenial to Bryant's temperament, as we see in 'The Past', 'Mutation' and 'The Prairies'. He is the poet who characteristically takes the long view; his dominant themes derive from a persistent meditation on mutability: the theme of the earth as universal tomb and the principle of inevitable succession. As he broods over the earth as both 'mighty nourisher and burial-place/ Of man', he returns often to the idea of perpetual creation ('A Forest Hymn') and its correlative, the rise and fall of all living things ('The Prairies'). 'The Rivulet' suggests a changeless nature presiding over children who sport along its banks, then 'pass to hoary age and die'; in 'A Walk at Sunset' Bryant meditates on the races of men 'before the red man came', only to be succeeded by 'hunter tribes' and 'warrior generations'. His most philosophic treatment of the theme, 'Among the Trees', explores the notion that consciousness is an attribute of natural objects as well as of humans: 'There dwells a nature that receives delight/ From all the gentle processes of life,/ And shrinks from loss of being.' To meditate on inevitable succession is to entertain the human experience of loss, racial and familial. The spectre of 'loss of being' haunts most poignantly the personal poems in which stoic endurance is joylessly invoked.

These poems of change are organized around a sentient centre, usually the poet himself, whose inquiring sensibility shapes the poetic structure; the poet projects himself either backward into earlier eras, where he imaginatively catalogues the chronicle of succession, or forward, beyond his own death when he is himself succeeded. Though undeveloped in 'Thanatopsis', by 1824 the device is evident in 'A Walk at Sunset' and 'The Rivulet'. It appears in 'The Prairies', 'Earth', 'To the Apennines' and 'The Fountain'; and in 'The Planting of the Apple-Tree', a poem of old age, Bryant domesticates the metaphysics of the theme. In 'Life' he projects his death and imagines his grieving child scattering flowers on his grave, but he also foresees her heart healed and her own decline: 'To younger forms of life must yield/ The place thou fill'st with beauty now.'

If a metaphysical vision of succession generates the strength of general stoic endurance, it notably stops short of Christian assurance that one's identity is continuous. In several poems Bryant speculates on his relational continuity after death with daughter, father, sister and wife. Two of them, 'Life' and 'The Future Life', significantly conclude with unresolved anxieties and unanswerable questions. Bryant's didacticism is cooler than that of any of his peers; indeed, the lessons are so oblique that *didactic* may be neither useful nor accurate to describe his work. By the time Bryant came to write 'The Flood of Years' he had apparently resolved his lifelong uncertainty about immortality, but added that the life to come would be imperfect without recognition there of loved ones; but the final thirty lines of his optimistic vision are rhetorically prefaced by a dramatizing line, 'Hear what the wise and good have said', an ambiguity that tonally cannot erase the grim apocalyptic diorama sketched so fully in the body of the poem. If 'The Flood of Years' was meant to comfort anxious readers, it came too late to affect the general aura of restraint and tepid assertions of faith that mark most of Bryant's poetry.

In both his reformist verse and his personal lyrics Lowell reflects more accurately than Bryant the general liberal faith of New England Unitarianism, with its commitment to a humanistic religion of duty. But, as in Bryant, there is little verbal evidence that his message is very hopeful. In an early poem, 'Summer Storm', Lowell can describe life's deepest 'emblem' as a 'confused noise between two silences', a naturalistic observation that is buttressed in his mature work by a relentless language of care: *lonely, dreary, restless, uneasy, leaden, weary, gloomy, strife, drear, world's blasts, striving, many blights and many tears* march across his pages as he describes the general human lot. He also invokes a familiar set of attributes to counter such grief: *holy peacefulness, holy calm, calm hope and trust, patience, rest.* More than his peers, Lowell directs his readers to honour those abstractions that may make their cares palatable and their strivings meaningful: Humanity, Freedom, Truth.

If his vision of a world hedged, boundaried, limited and threatened, in which 'Earth's stablest things are shadows', an early strategy is to posit a principle of spiritual advancement through sorrow. 'The Heritage' is structured around a contrast between the 'cares' inherited by the rich man's son and the hardy spirit of the poor boy that comes from facing competently 'every useful toil and art'. In 'On the Death of a Friend's Child' Lowell observes that 'Heaven is not mounted to on wings of dreams' but 'sorrow builds the shining ladder up,/ Whose golden rounds are our calamities.' Six years later, however, in 'After the Burial', on the death of his own child, such hopeful wisdom is rejected:

> Your logic, my friend, is perfect,
>   Your moral most drearily true;
> But, since the earth clashed on *her* coffin,
>   I keep hearing that, and not you.

A more characteristic strategy to bear up under both 'every-dayness of this work-day world' and special blows of fate is the contemplation of ideal states, possibilities in which both boredom and cares are dissolved. 'The Vision of Sir Launfal'— that is, the vision of the heroic and good—comes in response to 'our fallen and traitor lives', 'our faint hearts', 'our age's drowsy blood'. One of Lowell's persistent images is that of the green island of peace for wearied men. It appears first in an untitled sonnet of 1841 in which he praises the thought that grows like a coral atoll until it becomes 'a speck of green', a 'pleasant island in the seas'. In 'To the Past' Lowell, in the midst of 'bleak waves of our strife and care', populates 'the green Fortunate Isles' with hero-spirits who share 'Our martyrdom and toils'. In his maturity, Appledore in the Isles of Shoals geographically literalizes for Lowell the image of the enchanted isle where, away from 'bores', 'fuss and strife', 'fools' and the 'singular mess we agree to call life', he can come 'Face to face with one's Self at last'. And 'Al Fresco' is a salute to the nature surrounding his house, an 'enchanted' island that serves as a verdant analogy to 'the spirit's dwelling-place' apart from 'our vext world' in which a perfect life can be 'Far-shrined from earth's bestaining strife'.

Just as his own house is a kind of temple in which the Self can be not only faced but improved, so the fireplace within it glows as the inspiriting centre. An important poem is Lowell's 'A Winter-Evening Hymn to My Fire'. Evoking the mythic struggle to tame fire, the poet consciously makes the chimney-place the ritual home of inspiration, wisdom and energy, and unconsciously elevates the New England hearth as the true keeper of the flame. With the power to thaw the 'Arctic outskirts of the brain', the fireside dispenses 'homely faith' and comfort; it encourages the soul not to aspire but to dwell in Memory and Hope. If in this text a languorous escapism is more emphatic than the energetic process of striving, that proportion suggests the seductive way in which idealism and a belief in human progress could be innocently subverted by patrician comfort. In 'Ode to Happiness', a despondent tribute to what Lowell calls 'Nymph of the unreturning feet', the poet tries to make the best of her *absence*. The surrogates of Happiness, her sisters Peace and Tranquillity, provide troubled lives with domesticity and predictability, their 'still lives' blessed by a strip of 'household sky' and smoke rising from 'happy hearths'. Aspiration and struggle come to nothing, and increasingly Lowell doubts the substantiality of 'these shadows/ Which we call Life and History' ('Gold-Egg') and broods publicly in the Harvard Commemorative Ode on the cunning years that 'steal all from us but woe'. In 'A Familiar Epistle to a Friend' his sense of ageing is reflected in a Wordsworthian emphasis on unconvincing substitutes: 'Knowledge instead of scheming hope', 'settled scope' for worldly adventure, judgement for 'passion's headlong whirls'. And in his memorial ode for Robert Shaw, the Boston patriot killed in the Civil War, Lowell sees a grim advantage to his loss: that Shaw will not have to endure 'mid-life's doubt'.

Despite his rôles as polemicist and satirist, Lowell returns for his professional satisfaction to the claims of the fireside. In 'L'envoi: (To the Muse)' he records the vocational frustrations that an American poet faced. If the ministrations of Nature never attracted Lowell as they did Bryant, the satisfactions in the course of empire—the stuff of the daily newspaper—were not congenial either. He feels vaguely guilty that seeking the muse across the continent—'mountains, forests, open downs,/ Lakes, railroads, prairies, states, and towns'—is as difficult for him as pursuit of her in such egalitarian places as logging camps, factories, party caucuses, the exact places where Emerson was urging American authors to find their inspiration, until Lowell hears a voice reminding him that the muse 'sits at home' at the open door, by the chimney hearth. Here the 'household mirth' is modulated by the 'sweet serious undertone/ Of duty, music all her own', and thus the 'homestead's genial heart' becomes the 'stamp and warrant' of his kind of poetry. The same muse reinforces the patrician pleasures of 'Agassiz': 'long evening-ends', lingering by 'cosy chimney-nooks', the 'high companionship' of books, and the 'slippered talk of friends'.

Though Lowell himself wears many hats during his career, the idealist in him remains the sustaining source of his most characteristic work. *The Biglow Papers* is written by the same sensibility as the man who wrote 'The Vision of Sir Launfal'. And if we are tempted to think that Lowell complacently arrived at his poetic mission, we have only to read his letters and accounts of his life for evidence to the contrary, evidence that is fully apparent in those poems showing vocational worries, vexations, personal grief and metaphysical doubt. His own life also confirms the message in the image from 'On the Death of a Friend's Child', that we mount toward heaven on a ladder of calamities. Lowell's most imaginative creative moments were associated with misfortune, personal blows such as the deaths of his children and wife, professional disappointments such as his failure to be promptly appointed minister to Spain under Grant, and national tragedies such as the Civil War and Lincoln's assassination.[3]

Like Lowell, Whittier became identified with the social and political causes that formed the subject matter of many of his well-read poems, but having, unlike Lowell, no sense of humour and little wit, Whittier composed 'Ichabod' and 'Massachusetts to Virginia' under the powerful aegis of indignation and scorn. Unashamed of his rhymed propaganda, he was always modest enough to disclaim a 'rounded art'; but his priorities, devotion to freedom and human brotherhood, allowed him to boast of being superior to mere verse-makers.[4] But Whittier was a beloved poet not because of his memorable political work but because he appropriated the common lore of his region at the very time that certain habits and customs seemed threatened by vast economic changes. No other Fireside Poet wrote such 'available' verse, and not even Longfellow recreated the New England past with the charm and sentimental appeal of Whittier in his Yankee pastorals—'Maud Muller', 'The Homestead', 'Telling the Bees', 'The Barefoot Boy', 'My Playmate'. Moreover, the poignancy behind the Currier and

Ives quality of all these genre pieces celebrating rural life is the fact of loss, not merely as subject—the mourning of a lost love in 'Telling the Bees'—but as the very condition for creating poems, the sense of pastness that accounts for his pervasive melancholy at the thought of human transiency.

In 'To My Sister' Whittier's unspecified inner tensions are transposed into a public key; he justifies turning to 'an idle rhyme' inspired by childhood as relief from a 'long, harsh strife with strong-willed men', the very image of the national competitive spirit. It is in what Robert Penn Warren calls this 'refuge in assuagement' that Whittier found full release for his poetic powers.[5] Like Bryant, Whittier voices a sense of grievance at a present because it is busy, bustling, contentious. Bryant finds solace in an unpeopled nature, Whittier in recreated moments of the past. *Snow-Bound*, his masterpiece, is at once his most personal poem and the one which his name most readily summons up. The values of the fireside—family affection, closeness and cohesion—are pitted against those of the outside world—one literally chilled, 'mindless', 'blind', 'unmeaning'. Only through the effort of the creating imagination can love and wholeness win the struggle against pain and death, and the victory is only momentary. If it is a memorial piece, a nostalgic record of New England farm life precisely detailed, *Snow-Bound* is also a stark reminder of loss and the depredations of time. The fact of loss generates this work of memory, which is structured by the temporal separation of loved ones and textured by the spatial alienation of man from nature and of man from man. As the poem begins with loss, so it ends; there is no way for the poet to compensate for the basic privations that time brings except the temporary triumph of re-creation, Keats's deceiving elf of fancy, but the residue of that creative process, the poem, is a sequence of beneficent 'Flemish pictures', now available for a contemplative audience far beyond the boundaries of New England. But whatever else these 'pictures' do, they fail to define correctives for loss because, as both Whittier and his readers knew, there are none. Properly speaking, there is no lesson in *Snow-Bound*. There is, and only can be, the sad and helpless acceptance of the human experience in time.

The values of the fireside in Whittier are love, familial

affection, friendship and the sense of belonging to a particular place; and since they all belong to the world of the past, their only utility is psychological: their mournful contemplation in a present stripped of such values. The situation in Longfellow is more complex but no more cheering. If each of the Fireside Poets achieved popularity for particular poems or volumes, none except Longfellow had the kind of cumulative and sustained success that makes his reputation still a literary phenomenon.[6] One of the reasons we often hear for such a spectacular reputation is that Longfellow, among his peers, was the most overt moralizer and the most assiduous spokesman for human aspiration, the dominant spirit of the times in both its high-minded variety, Emersonian self-reliance, and its commercial vulgarization, the self-made expediency of Andrew Carnegie. Certainly most of Longfellow's poems are structured on simple analogy—observation of example followed by application—and certainly repetitive injunctions to do and dare seem to make this poet the apostle of activism. As several modern commentators have noted, however, at the heart of the more personal of Longfellow's lyrics lies a profound anxiety that belies the apparent thrust of their subjects.[7] 'Excelsior' is usually touted as the purest expression of Longfellow's optimism; but though its dramatized courage in resisting the blandishments of ordinary human life reveals this poem as a parable of heroic aspiration, the poem ends in unambiguous failure: when the values of the fireside—here identified as family cohesiveness, paternal wisdom, romantic love and folk wisdom—are one after another rejected, the individualism of an extraordinary mission can only come to grief. What is being counselled? To be faithful to our vision we must die, alienated from the human family. In 'Prometheus' the general idealism of the youth in 'Excelsior' is specified as the poetic spirit, but the price of 'noble daring' and 'Aspiration' is the agony of punishment: the 'darkened lives' of Dante, Milton and Cervantes. 'Epimetheus', a companion piece, is even more negative:

> Disenchantment! Disillusion!
>   Must each noble aspiration
> Come at last to this conclusion,
> Jarring discord, wild confusion,
>   Lassitude, renunciation?

One of the curious features of this lyric poetry is that a poet whose remarkably peaceful and comfortable life would seem to have precluded an obsession with such worry is even more repetitive than Lowell in the language of care. The humble poet whom Longfellow invokes in 'The Day is Done' has composed his melodies despite 'long days of labor' and 'nights devoid of ease', yet his modest creations will help quiet the reader's 'restless pulse of care', our 'cares that infest the day'. Longfellow's first great success, 'A Psalm of Life, is marked not by optimistic cheer but a stoicism even grimmer than Bryant's. The life that is real and earnest is to be neither enjoyed nor bewailed but simply endured; the only realistic goal is 'that each to-morrow/ Find us farther than to-day'. The example of the sublime life as model for a later generation is transitory; 'footprints on the sands of time' by their very nature are more evanescent than the corporeal being who made them. What one learns from all this— 'to labor and to wait'—is minor balm. The metaphor of life as a battlefield is accompanied by the injunction to act in the present, to be wary of the future and to be indifferent to the past; there is no promise of significant reward for labouring except the patient spirit that the activist must fall back on. 'The Light of Stars', originally published as 'A Second Psalm of Life', is no more optimistic; since the poet's inspiration comes from the 'mailèd hand' of Mars, his advice, as hopes one by one depart, is to be resolute and calm, for by such inner discipline one can learn how 'sublime' it is to 'suffer and be strong'. Unremitting toil constitutes the cheerless duty of 'The Village Blacksmith', and what attracts Longfellow to the Jews buried at Newport is that they were 'Taught in the school of patience to endure/ The life of anguish and the death of fire'. The explicit function of *Voices of the Night*—to whisper 'Be of good cheer!' to all those who doubt and fear—in its 'L'Envoi' is imagistically denied by dark and hoar forests, Pentecostal tongues of fire, funeral lamps and the vast plains 'where Death encamps!' The famous ballads—'The Wreck of the Hesperus' and 'The Skeleton in Armor'—are tales of death with lessons on the necessity of bearing up. Unsurprisingly, Longfellow in 'The Goblet of Life' celebrates fennel, bitter but necessary medicine 'for strength to bear/ Our portion of the weight of care'.

The darker implications of life in *Voices of the Night* persist through Longfellow's succeeding volumes. Indeed with old age, personal tragedies of loss and the gradual dying off of friends, the dark strain is intensified. 'The Wind Over the Chimney' is a later, despairing reiteration of the real message of the earlier 'Excelsior'. Though the flames seem to say 'Aspire!' they are mocked by the night wind: 'Hollow/ Are the visions that you follow.' The works of poets are but 'flying sparks' from God's forges; and since 'The dead laurels of the dead/ Rustle for a moment only', the only reward is in 'the doing'. The structures of 'Fata Morgana', 'The Haunted Chamber' and 'The Meeting' omit Longfellow's customary applications, concluding in citations of loss, premonitions of death and the bitter-sweet reunion of old friends for whom no other friends remain. The visionary structure of 'The Hanging of the Crane', putatively a hymn to domesticity, traces not only the growth of the table of a newly married couple but also its cruel shrinking in old age. And 'Morituri Salutamus' is a predictable reminder to Longfellow's Bowdoin classmates fifty years later that the 'gulf stream of our youth may flow/ Into the arctic regions of our lives', but the most stirring passage has a tonic sincerity rarely so nakedly expressed in his work:

> Whatever poet, orator, or sage
> May say of it, old age is still old age.
> It is the waning, not the crescent moon;
> The dusk of evening, not the blaze of noon;
> It is not strength, but weakness; not desire,
> But its surcease; not the fierce heat of fire,
> The burning and consuming element,
> But that of ashes and of embers spent,
> In which some living sparks we still discern,
> Enough to warm, but not enough to burn.

The truth is that Longfellow holds out few rewards for 'days well spent' and nothing but failure for those who aspire to more extraordinary accomplishment. His vision grimly acknowledges the depressing actualities of routine human activities, inevitable decline and decay. His stoic message is the overt sign that he saw little to be optimistic about; his repetitive diction, tonal balance and poetic structures are its formal equivalents. Longfellow may be more languid than the other Fireside Poets in his melodic catalogues of 'drooping

161

souls' (as he calls them in 'Endymion') whose destinies are 'fraught with fear and pain', but his poetic mission was both proffered and accepted in that spirit. That he was so widely read indicates that his was no dourly unique vision. 'The Singers', an 1849 parable of three different kinds of poets—the youthful, mature and old singers whose respective gifts 'To charm, to strengthen, and to teach' are in reality one and the same gift—is a fair statement of how Longfellow viewed that mission. Its aesthetic and its moral basis are the same, one that is consonant with his belief as early as 1832 that poetry 'should' be made 'an instrument for improving the condition of society, and advancing the great purpose of human happiness'. Those terms establish the ground for most of this generation of poets, but the recurring language of care is a reminder of how difficultly, not how effortlessly, that sanative task was undertaken.

His contemporaries tended to regard the poet of Craigie House as the very model of human sweetness, generosity and congenial companionship, an image that has by and large shaped our own image of the successful public poet whose serenity is almost indistinguishable from complacency. The poetry itself, however, suggests that Longfellow was neither serene nor complacent. To assume that the recurring concern with care in his verse betrays a human complexity undreamt by his contemporaries, that his seeming placidity was achieved by masking inner tensions, is necessary for any accurate revaluation of the most popular of the Fireside Poets. But Longfellow is only the most conspicuous of that hierarchy whose works should be re-read for what they reveal of an era too easily designated as optimistic.[8] Their response to their harshly progressive, competitive society may finally be more escapist than realistic, but the fact that their consolations were so minimal—holding out the general moral and social good that might come despite inauspicious conditions—indicates the inadequacy of one theory: that the Fireside Poets were minor because 'they failed to respond, except superficially, to the new experience of being American in the middle of the nineteenth century.'[9]

Friends as well as peers, each of this group honoured the others as the sequence of deaths began, until Holmes's in

1894, when none was left to mourn the falling of 'The Last Leaf'. Between 1878, Bryant's death-date, and Holmes's sixteen years later, the pessimism of Mark Twain that became increasingly suggestive of his darkening final years would come to seem more modernly congenial than the kind of idealism represented by the Fireside Poets. If all these men died in an age apparently inimical to their temperaments and teachings, it may be that the new age was no longer able to read their works except as sacred texts. All of these poets were buried as national institutions, revered and honoured more as icons than as men or writers, and as icons they were invested with the same spiritual configurations as an earlier nation that had both sanctioned and sanctified them. But the real configurations are in the lines they wrote, which record an impressive struggle with the demons of fear, failure and loss, and a realistic appraisal not only coexisted with the public rôles these men assumed—moral guardian, teacher, uplifter, spokesman for national values—but also significantly ratified those rôles.

One of the reasons that Emerson's optimism was so iterative is that it ran across, not with, so much of the American grain. Many Americans who intellectually believed that they should and could be hopeful giants emotionally still clung to a view of the human enterprise that the Enlightenment and a liberal religion of humanism failed fully to displace. If we prefer to remember the idealistic Yankee spirit that could generate and maintain so many reforms in that period once called 'The Flowering', we should not forget the Yankee scepticism that resisted or bemusingly tolerated them. But despite their obsession with the strife and cares of day-to-day life, the Fireside Poets were finally conservators, commited more to society than to man, a bias that shows up in the reason behind not only their support of the Civil War—not to free southern slaves but to preserve the union—but also their resolute cultivation of the domestic affections—to preserve and strengthen the family, the basic unit of a civilized society, and the close-knit circle of like-minded friends, the most dependable carriers of culture.

What Holmes, that quintessential Brahmin, offered his non-Brahmin readers—tolerance, decency, compassion, moderation, faith in both scientific and moral progress, and the rational belief that common sense was available and operable in men of all ranks—was what in varying degrees all the Fireside Poets offered their public, even the often fiery Whittier and the often testy Lowell. Readers obviously agreed that such values were normative and good despite all the widespread lapses in the moral and political structure of American society. They, like the authors they loved, were aware of discrepancies, dislocations, injustices and failures, and were perfectly attuned to the shortcomings of American life as well as human life generally. Theirs, like the poets', was a chastened hopefulness, not naïveté.

NOTES

1. *Mark Twain Speaking*, ed. Paul Fatout (Iowa City: University of Iowa Press, 1976), pp. 135–36.
2. Quotations from the Fireside Poets are drawn from the following texts: *William Cullen Bryant: Representative Selections*, with Introduction, Bibliography and Notes by Tremaine McDowell (New York: American Book Company, 1935) and these Cambridge Editions—*The Poetical Works of Longfellow* (Boston: Houghton Mifflin, 1975); *The Poetical Works of James Russell Lowell* (Boston: Houghton Mifflin, 1978); *The Poetical Works of Whittier* (Boston: Houghton Mifflin, 1975); and *The Poetical Works of Oliver Wendell Holmes* (Boston: Houghton Mifflin, 1975).
3. Leon Howard, *Victorian Knight-Errant: A Study of the Early Literary Career of James Russell Lowell* (Berkeley: University of California Press, 1952), p. 355. Martin Duberman, in *James Russell Lowell* (Boston: Houghton Mifflin, 1966), emphasizes the man of affairs rather than the poet.
4. Robert Penn Warren, *John Greenleaf Whittier's Poetry: An Appraisal and a Selection* (Minneapolis: University of Minnesota Press, 1971), p. 25. See also Samuel T. Pickard, *Life and Letters of John Greenleaf Whittier* (Boston: Houghton Mifflin, 1895), p. 573.
5. Warren, p. 35.
6. See particularly Clarence Gohdes, *American Literature in Nineteenth-Century England* (New York: Columbia University Press, 1944), especially the chapter 'Longfellow'.
7. See Edward Wagenknecht, *Henry Wadsworth Longfellow: Portrait of an American Humanist* (New York: Oxford, 1966), pp. 21–8, and Hyatt H. Waggoner, *American Poets from the Puritans to the Present* (Boston: Houghton Mifflin, 1968), pp. 42–4.

8. For a recent recapitulation of this old view see Chapter 3 of Everett Carter's *The American Idea: The Literary Response to American Optimism* (Chapel Hill: University of North Carolina Press, 1977).
9. Waggoner, p. 84. In an otherwise admirable treatment, George Arms is also unduly apologetic about the achievement of the Fireside Poets in his *The Fields Were Green: A New View of Bryant, Whittier, Holmes, Lowell, and Longfellow* (Stanford, Calif.: Stanford University Press, 1953).

8

Alone with God and Nature: The Poetry of Jones Very and Frederick Goddard Tuckerman

by DAVID SEED

1

Despite biographical connections between Jones Very and Frederick Goddard Tuckerman, the work of the one seems at times a throw-back to the seventeenth century, while the other's can sound surprisingly modern. Very shared with his New England contemporaries certain habits of mind traceable to the Puritans. His sonnets are the clear products of intro-spection, but an introspection which he channels into con-ventional Christian patterns which he can then exploit dramatically. Unlike Emerson Very takes few spiritual risks in his poetry. Its strength rather lies in its disciplined texture, its capacity to rearticulate traditional Christian *topoi* and in Very's notion of poetic voice. The latter springs from his astonishingly (and to the other Transcendentalists, embar-rassingly) literal belief in inspiration. Where Emerson exploited metaphors of inspiration and Thoreau looked into the hidden principles of nature, Very quite simply believed that he was communicating directly with the deity. Hence nature is usually a means for him, a source of analogies and parables

166

which give the reader relief from a constant plainness of expression.

Whereas for Very isolation defines man's relation to God, for Tuckerman it becomes a liability since his poems are all the more secular. He draws—at times rather dilettantishly—on his personal interests in botany, astronomy and the classics in order to articulate states of anxiety and uncertainty. Since God has, as it were, receded out of sight, Tuckerman is denied Very's sense of clear goals. Nature becomes more important, but not to offer an alternative inspiration as in Emerson's '*Waldeinsamkeit*' so much as for self-expression. Because the transcendental realm seems too much out of reach in Tuckerman's poetry he lacks the confidence of say Emerson or Thoreau. Characteristically he produces limited, low-key poems whose hesitancy resembles that found in William Ellery Channing perhaps, or much more importantly in Tennyson. This hesitancy can become mannered but it can also produce unpredictably powerful lyrics when Tuckerman turns his sense of isolation to good advantage.

2

Although of recent years interest has grown in the poetry of Jones Very (1813–80), there is still considerable disagreement about how to place his work. He has been described as a Calvinist and a Unitarian; it has even been denied that he was a Transcendentalist although his poems have appeared in Perry Miller's anthology of the movement.[1] Certainly Very had strong contacts, both personal and literary, with the Transcendentalists. In his own time Elizabeth Peabody discovered him in 1837 and the following year he met Emerson, who at first welcomed him warmly but grew more and more uneasy about Very's mysticism. Very took the general Transcendentalist belief in inspiration to a literal extreme where he believed that the Holy Ghost was speaking through him. This disturbed Emerson and Hawthorne but prompted the more benign Bronson Alcott to say of him: 'He is a mystic of the most ideal class; a pietist of the transcendental order.'[2] Very shared Emerson's scepticism about institutionalized religion—he stated in an essay that 'religion at the present day is almost lost in forms'—but withdrew into a puritan mysticism where there was no place for self-reliance.[3] Although he produced several anti-slavery poems Very had little interest in reform and spent the last forty years of his life in virtual retirement.

Very's treatment of Nature will help to clarify that he had some beliefs in common with the Transcendentalists but ultimately diverged from them. Once again we encounter disagreement among the critics. We are told that Very held two contradictory attitudes to Nature; he saw it as inert and external on the one hand, and on the other infinite and perfect. It is also asserted that Very took over Emerson's theory of correspondences, or that Very saw Nature as a spiritual guide but not a means of conversion.[4] It is difficult to attribute a consistent attitude to Very because his earliest nature poems are rather stilted exercises in the late Augustan style. His more mature productions drop the stylized diction but are constantly vitiated by a tendency to moralize. 'The Wind-Flower' centres on an emblem of trusting faith and the conclusion to 'The Snow-Drop' extracts a lesson of hope. A different group ('To the Humming-Bird', 'To the Fossil Flower', etc.) presents a series of meditations on time. It is very rare to find Very relaxing enough to allow his feelings to be projected on to a natural object; usually his poetry impresses through its sheer self-control. He manages this in the sonnet 'The Columbine' where a loss of self-consciousness leads the poet to merge with nature. Similarly in 'The Song' ('When I would sing of crooked streams and fields') the expanse of nature undermines Very's original design ('my song all powerless yields') and enables him to recapture the undirected delight of a child. Such yieldings of the self are only intermittent because ultimately Very did not trust nature. On a visit to Emerson in 1838 the latter noted that 'during a walk through Walden Woods, Very said he was so overwhelmed by the beauty of the autumn there he almost forgot "that the world was des[e]rt and empty, all the people wicked".'[5] Very was content to regard Nature doctrinally as a secondary means of revelation but only if it did not rival God's primacy or remind him of the profane world he had left behind. Hence his wary, defensive attitude to nature. Tuckerman had far fewer qualms about indulging his delight in nature because it took him temporarily out of his melancholy. For him nature can have a positive therapeutic value.

At least three poems and Very's essay on Shakespeare demonstrate the probable influence of Emerson on Very's formulation of a doctrine of Nature. A hymn entitled 'The Forms of Nature and that Unity of Their Origin' posits a 'One Eternal Mind' (a kind of Over-soul) from which emanate all natural phenomena. The poem celebrated the design not the details of nature, locating man within an ascending series:

> In Nature's primal plan
> Prophetic types are seen;
> Which lead us onward up to Man,
> Their end, and destiny;
> A unity of mind and thought
> Through every form and being wrought.[6]

This all-embracing unity is alternatively expressed in the sonnet 'The flowers I pass have eyes that look at me' as a reciprocity between the self and different aspects of nature strikingly similar to that described in Emerson's *Nature*; the flora nod to Emerson, and he nods back to them. Very possessed a copy of *Nature* and quoted from it in his essay on Shakespeare, so the similarity is unlikely to be coincidental. In the three-stanza poem 'Nature' Very's spirit rises from the body and flies across the landscape with a speed that anticipates Whitman. As the tempo of the poem rises Very moves beyond the immediately physical to transcendentally 'purer streams of bliss', which again resembles a similar movement in Emerson's 'Two Rivers' where the poet breaks the bounds of the Concord River to adumbrate 'sweeter rivers' pulsing through nature itself.

Currents also flow through the essay on Shakespeare where they connote the forces of nature to which man should yield. Drawing variously on Wordsworth, Emerson and Carlyle, Very puts forward Shakespeare as an ideal individual because he possessed the power of 'harmonizing' with nature. This is a prelapsarian gift of childhood which only a privileged few can revive. As Gittleman points out, the key terms in this essay are 'love', which indicates a merging of the self in nature, and 'sin', which connotes a retention of selfhood.[7] Although ostensibly discussing a literary subject Very broadens the issues by using a heavily spiritual idiom. The essay touches on many issues relevant to Very's writings—the divine origins of poetry, the relation of the self to nature, and above all the prime necessity of obliterating the will. It concludes with the following exhortation:

> Let us labor then, knowing that the more we can erase from the tablets of our hearts the false fashions and devices which our own perverse wills have written over them, the more will shine forth, with all their original brightness, those ancient primeval characters traced there by the finger of God, until our whole being is full of light.[8]

Very's main proposition in this essay is that man should take up an adjacent and equivalent rôle to that of Nature in that both are emanations from God. He can only do this by deliberately (and paradoxically) giving up his will. Very actually experienced this process during a prolonged rebirth from 1835 to 1838. These were the pivotal years of his life and decisively swung his poetry away from nature to religion. Idleness and passivity do not have the Romantic value of freeing the imagination in his poetry, but rather suggest a stance of receptivity towards the divine. As Very's life became more religious, so his sense of the writer's rôle shifted away from his early ambition to revive the epic. His earliest formulations assert independence. Thus 'the true poet will look without for no rules drawn from others.'[9] As a result of his enthusiastic reading of *The Excursion* Very also conceived an exalted rôle for the poet: 'a higher motive, a something within him . . . prompts him to awaken in màn a consciousness of his high destiny. . . .'[10] Very's grandiose ambitions could lead to spiritual arrogance, but after his conversion he adopts the far humbler rôle of spiritual guide in his poems. In 1839 he sent a series of sonnets to the *Western Messenger* in the hope that 'they may help those in affliction', and when planning the selection of his poems which was published that same year he wanted them to be arranged thematically to give a clear spiritual cycle. He also wanted to include as a preface three inspirational epistles 'To the Unborn'. Emerson refused both suggestions.[11] It seems clear that Very saw his religious poems as vehicles and this is why he regularly addresses the reader. 'The Narrow Way' is typical in that the poet's rôle suddenly becomes evident as a means of helping the reader out of spiritual difficulties: 'For I will words of comfort to thee speak,/ And onward with thee to my home I'll go.'

Although Very rejected Calvinism and stated that 'we are all free agents and have the power of overcoming the world if we choose', his religious poetry reverts in several ways to the style of the Puritans.[12] Since he believes that his poems are spiritual vehicles, he keeps a spare and sinewy style, and only uses rhetorical figures to elaborate on points of religion. He repeatedly contrasts things of this world with those of the world to come and even experiments with a dialogue between the soul and the body. He draws on traditional Puritan imagery such as the journey towards salvation and the battle between good and evil. Although he does not retain the Devil as such, neither does he go to Emerson's extreme in rejecting evil. Instead he retains a personification of evil called 'the king of terrors' or 'the foe'. Very also retains doomsday imagery as in 'The Flood' where fire will fall on the ungodly, but the poet's attitude is pitying rather than the smugly sanctimonious God's-eye view which Michael Wigglesworth adopts in *The Day of Doom* (1662).

A unique sequence of sonnets entitled 'The Puritans' dealing with the foundation of Salem (Very's home town) demonstrates Very's attempts to take his bearings from his Puritan ancestors. The narrative sets up a rhythmic alternation between danger and security, danger being viewed as a test of faith. Thus storms at sea give way to an idealized description of the virgin land where they anchor; the joys of summer lead into the tribulations of winter, and so on. Clearly modelled on Old Testament precedents, Very's story demonstrates the guiding providential hand of God on his faithful remnant, and leaves his reader in no doubt about this lesson. During the voyage a minister preaches a sermon 'of trust in God' ('The Sabbath') which stands as a synecdoche for the series, just as Very's narrative takes the example of Salem to describe the whole Puritan enterprise. The series in short celebrates the spiritual courage of the settlers and commemorates such saints as Roger Conant, John Endicott and Francis Higginson. There is little point in objecting that Very irons out internal tensions such as that between Conant (the first settler of Salem) and Endecott (its first governor), or that he oversimplifies the process of settlement, since his commitment to the Puritans is evident from the very first. He idealizes their quest both as a search for freedom and as an attempt to establish a Christian commonwealth (as if they were the same thing) and glosses euphemistically over the conquest of the 'red men': 'before a wiser race they melt away!' In this series we witness Very naïvely accepting the Puritans' actions within their own accounts—his sense of a guiding providence is virtually identical with Increase Mather's—but also setting up a continuity between his own period and the seventeenth century. The concluding sonnet raises a paean of praise for the Puritans' heritage. Very wags his finger at his contemporaries: 'Descendants of the Puritans . . . See that ye tarnish not their honest name'; and lifts the poem to a climax of millennarian hope.

The sequence frankly idealizes the Salem settlers into saints and extends a procedure which Very follows in many of his poems, namely the depiction of moral exempla. Details and description in 'The Puritans' are selected carefully with one view in mind: to highlight the tribulations and eventual triumph of those who believe in God's providence. The exemplary status of each episode frequently detracts from its dramatic immediacy giving a wooden effect, and Very's jump from moralizing to a crescendo of exhortation glosses over the historical distance between himself and the Puritans. Tuckerman by contrast can lament the passing of a wilderness which has to a certain extent happened during his own lifetime.

In 'The Puritans' Very puts forward the saints of Salem as exemplars to be emulated, but his main exemplar is Christ. Many of the religious poems re-enact particular events from Christ's life, his passion in 'The Meek', his calming of the waters in 'The Priest', and so on. Very regularly develops an event or passage in the Bible, filling it out imaginatively and in effect giving the reader a poetical gloss on scripture. A sonnet from 1839 will exemplify this procedure. Its title ('Behold He Is at Hand That Doth Betray Me') consists of Christ's prediction of his betrayal by Judas. The poem begins with a half-quotation of Christ's accusation of the multitude that come to arrest him. It uses phrases such as 'clubs and staves' (Matthew XXVI.55) as signals to the reader that the speaker is imitating, but not *mimicking*, Christ's passion. Recognizing these signals plays an important part in reading such poems. In this particular sonnet an allusion to Christ's scourging intensifies the accusations which play on the reader's sense of shame. Very's use of biblical allusion can at times become very complex as in the sonnet 'The Weary and Heavy Laden' where the title is played off against the burst of joy in the first line at the rest which Christ offers (Matthew XI.28). Images of spiritual absence lead into a hinge-line which introduces the dawn of hope in the sestet:

> It comes! bid every harp and timbrel sound;
> Bring forth the fatted calf; make merry all;
> For this the son was lost, and he is found;
> Was dead, and yet has heard his Saviour's call.

The instruments for this exuberant celebration are taken from the Old Testament, although music does play a part in the parable of the prodigal son. Just as the short phrases suggest merriment, so recognition of the biblical parable helps to draw the reader into a dramatically evoked situation, and suggests a superimposed layering of voices (Very, the father, Christ) which recedes towards God.

The notion of voice is crucial to understanding Very's religious poetry and has been discussed interestingly by Lawrence Buell in a comparison with Whitman. Buell relates voice to the adoption of a dramatic rôle by the poet and says of Emerson: 'There is no identity in nature or history which the inspired soul may not assume.'[13] Emerson feels equally free to speak as Alphonso of Castile or as a maenad, just as Whitman devises an expanded 'I' which can include a whole range of American identities. Their difference from Very revolves partly around what repertoire he feels licensed to use. Very limits his rôles within the confines of Christianity so that, even when he speaks as Nature, it is as a carefully sanctified Nature. Buell is certainly right that Very is practising an imaginative self-projection, but to approach this aspect of his work in a purely literary way only tells part of the story. As we shall see, Very's notion of voice grows directly out of his belief in man's individual responsibility to open himself to the word of God. Once he achieves sanctification he becomes the efficient receptor of the voices of the spirit.

The root of Very's adoption of different voices is his belief in the Word, in a primal *Logos* which he considers in two sonnets. The first of these ('There is no voice but that which speaks in Thee') indicates the Word's independence of time by accumulating a variety of verb-tenses. The second ('The voice that speaks when thou art in thy tomb') sees the Word as the matrix of all things ('the womb'). Very can only articulate his subject through paradox ('speechless yet ever speaking') and by moving to and fro between the senses of sight and hearing; the Word is both a light and a voice, as if to show its independence of earthly classification. Similarly in 'The Voice of God' Very sets up a contrast between a childish (and perhaps Old Testament) belief that God's voice is one of thunderous threat and a mature realization that it spreads through everything.

One of the most obvious consequences of Very's belief that the Word is all-encompassing and eternal, is the prominence of voices in his poetry. The voices might summon or plead, but always suggest the possibility of spiritual communication. Thus the sonnet 'Enoch' contrasts the behaviour of 'gladdened millions' towards God with the 'sweet converse' of the patriarch. The fifth and sixth lines swing away to the wind of the spirit (the *ruach* or breath of God), as much ignored as the Word itself: 'I heard the wind in low complaint go by/ That none its melodies like him could hear'; the central part of the poem presents three versions of the Word—dialogue, music and teaching—to underline the gap between humanity and an ideal figure like Enoch. Here the main impression is of opportunities lost. Elsewhere the urgency of regeneration might be emphasized, hence the general importance in Very of verbs of utterance: 'speak', 'bid' and above all 'call'.

174

In 'The Voice of God' Very suggests that, although the call is constant, it will not be heard if man is 'heedless'. The process of salvation can thus only begin when the self opens its ears and takes up a stance of receptivity. One of Very's sonnets predictably glosses Christ's words in Matthew XIII.9: 'Who hath ears to hear, let him hear.' In a letter to H. W. Bellows of 1838 describing his conversion Very explained that his 'former change . . . was but the hearing of the voice of John in the wilderness of my heart'.[14] William James and others have pointed out how frequently conversion narratives present the incursion of the Other into the self via alien voices.[15] Very seems to have seen rebirth as a two-stage process: first the convert hears John the Baptist's voice and second the voice of Christ. The obvious precedent here is the general outline of the gospel-narratives, but Very's notion of conversion has a curious consequence for his poetry. In effect the self becomes destabilized. As the individual submits his will to God, he loses his singular identity and becomes the locus of different voices. This is why Very can speak as one of the saved, or as Rachel, John the Baptist or even God, without any sense of arrogance. All these voices emanate from the Word and by virtue of his conversion Very has become a passive vessel of that Word, a personified means of communication with the unregenerate reader. Hence in the covering letter which Very sent to Emerson in 1838 with his essay on Shakespeare he explained: 'you hear not mine own words but the teachings of the Holy Spirit.'[16] The very simplicity of his poetical voice together with his belief that the Word is potentially available to everyone usually enables him to avoid a tone of spiritual élitism. In 'The Journey' he explains to the reader 'these words thou hear'st me use were given me.' In 'The Old Road', on the other hand, the transmission takes place within the poem which begins with a speaker asking God why his way is neglected. The answer from 'a still, low voice' shifts the tone of the poem towards direct exhortation but again without a suggestion of arrogance. Indeed the frequency with which God's voice is heard in Very's poems suggests that God is near and accessible. This suggestion is highly strategic since Very tries to encourage the reader towards salvation rather than threaten him with the opposite.

175

Despite its grammatical errors, the 'Epistle on Miracles' sheds light on Very's notion of voice. In the epistle he grapples with the changes in identity which take place during rebirth and warns the reader as follows: 'He who who [*sic*] speaks is external to you; he speaks you [*sic*] from without; but it is outward from within. . . .' Having thus complicated origin and location he continues: 'I was *once* as you *now* are; but I am changed *and as* such exert the power of raising you from the dead; I, this *new I*, stand without *you* that is the old *you* which I was, and knock' [Very's emphases].[17] It should be evident from these passages that Very's notion of rebirth has a direct effect on his pronouns both in the epistles and in his religious poems. He struggles here to express different relations between self and voice. Since he has been reborn the old Very is radically different from the new, so different that the pronoun 'I' becomes a misnomer: 'who this I is which speaks; you, the dead, or unraised cannot know. . . .' The situation is further complicated by the fact that, as David Robinson has pointed out, Very uses the 'I' as an exemplary speaker.[18] Since rebirth for Very means the willed abandonment of the self to God, we cannot then expect the first person pronoun to indicate confessional poetry. Rather the 'I', and for that matter Very's other voices, represent the temporary dramatizations of different spiritual forces or human exempla.

It now becomes possible to see in a rather different light a phenomenon which bewildered Buell, namely Very's repeated habit of shifting voices within individual poems. Buell found the jerk from the divine to the human disorienting and complained that it was sometimes impossible to resolve the speaker into a single voice. In fact this difficulty grows directly out of Very's literal application of the doctrine of inspiration. Since he has given up his individuality he can only be *spoken through*, and hence the adoption of different voices from poem to poem and the shift of voice within a poem shows Very taking on a little of the privilege of God. However, for us lesser mortals rather more prosaic questions now arise, particularly whether the shifts in voice have any tighter logic than the vagaries of the spirit. 'The Holy of Holies' opens with an address from one of the reborn to one

of the unsanctified. In the sestet Very suddenly capitalizes
the adjective 'My' as if the speaker has become God. The
final couplet, however, draws back from this extreme
identification as if suggesting that it is only an analogy, that
the saint will be God just as the convert will be a form of
Christ: 'And thou shalt be My son, and I thy God/ To lead
thee in the way thy Master trod.' Here the shift from the
human to the divine suggests the process of sanctification,
while the resolving couplet indicates the pattern which the
relation of speaker to listener will follow. 'The Guest' is
rather a more complex example. It begins with an allusion to
the Sermon on the Mount (Matthew VII.7: 'knock, and it
shall be opened unto you'), except that the status of the
petitioner has shifted. Partly because Very alludes to Christ's
words and partly because the 'selfish owner' stays within his
dwelling, it is as if *God* has become the petitioner. Even
though Very avoids capitalization, an assertion like 'Blessed
is the man that doth my call attend', which formally resembles
the anaphora at the opening of the Sermon on the Mount,
suggests the divine rather than the human. When in line 10
Very explicitly refers to Christ's visitation (his 'call' as he
punningly puts it) this shift seems to confirm retrospectively
the divine identity of the opening voice. In fact we need not
decide between the divine and human because, especially in
the first four lines, Very gives a local exemplum of inhospitality
which he can then expand to include the more weighty topic of
Christ's calling. By shifting the initiative for the call from man
to Christ he renders sanctification all the easier. The sanctified
man's voice is assimilated by the divine, just as in 'The
Branch' Very presents himself as living 'in Christ'. Voices in
Very's poems then shift according to the particular didactic
emphasis he is putting, and we should not expect what is after
all a rather secular requirement of consistency.

I have been suggesting that an awareness of the beliefs
underlying Very's mysticism is crucial to an understanding of
the formal peculiarities of his poetry. However, as early as
1936 Yvor Winters argued that it was not necessary to adopt
Very's beliefs to appreciate his poems.[19] Very has to adopt
secular means towards the spiritual end of conversion and
hence appeals to quite a broad range of emotions. His voices

exhort, cajole, urge but rarely threaten, and as such can be appreciated dramatically as renderings of spiritual states. Very is usually careful to make these states as accessible as possible by drawing on traditional images or familiar objects for his raw materials. A possible precedent can be found in George Herbert's devotional series *The Temple*. Very never captures Herbert's sense of personal struggle since his poetical voices are of the sanctified, but he uses similar and at times identical titles to Herbert's and also incorporates domestic situations into his poems (as in 'The Removal', for instance).

Very's religious poems revolve around such oppositions as the sacred against the profane or the saint against the unregenerate. Many of the sonnets begin abruptly with an arresting phrase or paradox. The octave then develops the worldly implications of the opening; the sestet shifts to the spiritual and works towards an affirmation of hope in the final couplet. These poems work towards the transcendental and make manifest a particular aspect of the Word. The following sonnet ('The Son') uses a simpler structure of analogies and is useful to demonstrate Very's sense of form:

> Father I wait Thy word. The sun doth stand
> Beneath the mingling line of night and day,
> A listening servant, waiting Thy command
> To roll rejoicing on its silent way;
> The tongue of times abides the appointed hour,
> Till on our ear its solemn warnings fall;
> The heavy cloud withholds the pelting shower,
> Then every drop speeds onward at Thy call;
> The bird reposes on the yielding bough,
> With breast unswollen by the tide of song,
> So does my spirit wait Thy presence now
> To pour Thy praise in quickening life along,
> Chiding with voice divine man's lengthened sleep,
> While round the Unuttered Word and Love their vigils keep.[20]

The opening lines suggest suspension through participles like 'listening' and 'waiting', or more precisely a tension between motion and immobility. Very articulates this tension through two counterpointed motifs of waiting ('abides', 'withholds', etc.) and uttering; God's 'word', 'command', etc. will as it were set things in motion. Analogies expand the speaker of the first line outwards to include all of nature; 'a listening servant' could be in apposition to 'sun' or 'I'. Within fixed bounds the poem enacts surges of movement (the rolling of the sun, the falling of the rain, etc.) which are all predicated on the utterance of God's word. But since Very holds movement in firm check by the rhyme-scheme of the sonnet, its very pattern becomes an analogue of God's power. Undoubtedly the sonnet appealed to Very because it offered a concise highly disciplined poetical form. As we shall see, Tuckerman took the opposite attitude to the sonnet. He revels in run-on lines and in blurring the distinction between sections, whereas Very constantly exploits the sonnet's capacity to restrict and compress.

Very's strengths as a poet lie in creating an internal tension within his sonnets, in playing one part off against another, and in densening the texture of his poems with biblical allusion, punning (as in 'quickening' in the sonnet quoted above) and metaphors. Because his poetical range is limited he does not avoid repetitiveness, and metrical discipline can often collapse into woodenness. Nevertheless his artistry decidedly contradicts Emerson's supercilious comment in his review of Very's poems that they made 'no pretense to literary merit'.[21]

3

The poetry of Frederick Goddard Tuckerman (1821–73), like that of Very, takes as its starting point the isolation of the individual. Whereas Very spent his last years in seclusion, so Tuckerman lived as a virtual recluse in Greenfield. Both pursued their poetic vocation with characteristic New England earnestness, Very seeing most of his poetry as an extension of his religious life, Tuckerman as a means of self-exploration. In fact there are enormous differences between the two writers. Very directs his poems at an individual reader and attempts to catch him up in the drama of salvation, while Tuckerman uses the sonnet form for quiet self-examination. Very refers his religious poems to a future point of sanctification when the oppositions within his sonnets will lapse. Tuckerman takes his bearings either from his immediate natural surroundings or from the past, particularly in coping with the loss of his wife.

Very often seems a throw-back to seventeenth-century Puritan poetry, while Tuckerman's anxious introspection and use of natural settings to embody psychic states at times looks forward to modernism.[22]

Even the biographical connection between the two writers only helps to emphasize their literary differences. For a brief period Very was Tuckerman's tutor at Harvard and when in 1860 Tuckerman had a volume of poems printed he sent a copy to his former mentor for comments. With a slight air of embarrassment Very admitted that he could not assess the poems as literature but nevertheless praised Tuckerman's natural descriptions and his spiritual control of feeling: 'Your sonnets tell of grief but purified and consoled by faith, which alone can sustain us in life's trials and give us peace'.[23] Very is mistaken in this account because Tuckerman uses God in his first sonnet-sequence as a focus for a desired relief from feeling. God is a much more remote and intermittent presence throughout Tuckerman's poetry and Sonnet I.28, which Very cites as particularly pious, gestures towards God, but across a daunting 'barren azure' expanse. Tuckerman repeatedly yearns for 'reconcilement', i.e. a harmonious balance between feeling, thought and nature, and yet this is figured, perhaps in divine terms, as an end-point—an ultimate goal rather than a state he can actually achieve.

The most striking single characteristic of Tuckerman's poetry is his repeated preference for melancholy themes. Two crucial biographical factors here were probably the death of his wife in 1857 and his lack of purpose in life. Although trained as a lawyer, Tuckerman soon abandoned his practice and concentrated his activities in amateur naturalism. This streak of melancholy has a direct bearing on Tuckerman's sense of literary vocation. In the poem 'Inspiration' allusions to Milton and Shakespeare as exemplars of genius turn out to be ironic because the poet can manage so little. The cherished sources of Romantic optimism—the privileged origin of poetry, the virtue of solitude, the joy at 'reading' Nature and a faith in Love—all collapse as Tuckerman plaintively admits 'All these, to music deep, for me unfold,/ Yet vaguely die: their sense I cannot hold.'[24] In spite of its title, 'Inspiration' is a poem about uncertainty. Tuckerman inches tentatively forward in a search for firm value, and it is his capacity to question his own impulses which underlies the movement of many of his poems. 'A Soul that out of Nature's Deep' sketches out a poet-figure rather similar to that in say Emerson's 'Wood-Notes'. He has privileged access to wisdom; his 'secret eye' looks into the ultimate depths of Nature. In short he is a kind of seer, the personification of insight. But suddenly he falls prey to a mysterious and irresistible sorrow which jaundices his vision and replaces primal unity with strife:

> Yet sometimes, doubting, discord-tost,
> Came voices to his side:
> Echoes of youth, and friendships lost,
> Or lost, or left aside. (269–72)

The confident flow of the quatrains now slows down to jerky, hesitant phrases. Nature proves to be deceitful and misleading, but the roots of this betrayal lie in the self. This poem presents a narrative of moods which shift in a disconcertingly unpredictable manner and which imply, as his sonnet sequences confirm, that for Tuckerman selfhood was a problem.

For Tuckerman the privileges of Romantic faith are undermined by a crucial lack of confidence in his literary enterprise. He sent a copy of his 1860 volume to Hawthorne with a covering letter which explained that his book 'was not written to please anybody, and is addressed to those only who understood it'.[25] The extreme diffidence which he shows about his own abilities suggests an anxiety which is incorporated into several poems. Sonnet II.12 hinges on a crucial contrast between desire and capacity—'the high desire, the faint accomplished deed'. Sonnets V.14–16 display a weary tone as if the poet has prematurely aged and contain the desperate refrain 'Let me give something!' Characteristically tentative, the best that Tuckerman can hope for here is 'some faint fruition'. Since the achievements of the self are so problematic, the reader is thrown back on to sheer temperament, just as Tuckerman keeps returning to himself. Sonnet III.10 opens with the poet walking broodily along the sea-shore and then verges on solipsism as the natural scene collapses inwards:

... still but myself I find
And restless phantoms of my restless mind:
Only the moaning of my wandering words. ...

The sonnet form is particularly congenial to Tuckerman
because it enables him to circle around psychic states, par-
ticularly those of lassitude, pathos, indecision, doubt and
sorrow. This tendency helps to explain why his longer poems
are comparatively unsuccessful. 'Rhotruda', a narrative of the
days of Charlemagne, replaces a sequence of actions with two
pictures. 'Mark Atherton', a narrative of colonial New
England, is clogged with unnecessary verbiage and poeticisms,
and Tuckerman's occasional foray into monologue is vitiated
by his incapacity to establish a dramatic situation. His only
successful long poem, 'A Sample of Coffee Beans', is a pastiche
Yankee tale of a local poet being tricked by an itinerant
peddler.

Although Tuckerman knew Emerson the most important
literary friendship he formed was with Tennyson. In 1850 he
acquired a copy of the latter's 1842 volume of poems and made
extensive marginal annotations. In 1851 and 1854 he made two
trips to Britain, meeting Tennyson on both occasions and
discussing the latter's poems with him. Tuckerman even
suggested ways of improving 'Maud' and 'The Charge of the
Light Brigade' which Tennyson so respected that he presented
his friend with the manuscript of 'Locksley Hall'.[26] It comes as
no surprise then that Bryant and Emerson both found strong
signs of Tennyson's influence in Tuckerman's own poems.[27]
This influence emerges in various ways. Tuckerman uses
landscape to articulate psychological states, as Hallam noted in
his famous review of Tennyson. Tuckerman produces at least
one Tennysonian poem about a high-born lady ('Elidore'), and
his Sonnet I.11 comes so close to 'Ulysses' that it amounts to
virtual pastiche. This sonnet follows Tennyson's monologue in
contrasting motion with lassitude; both poets figure this motion
in terms of the sea—a voyage in 'Ulysses', an analogy in the
sonnet—and both attach positive value to motion (as against
the *goals* of the motion) because it brings relief from inertia. As
we shall see, however, there is a still more important influence
from Tennyson to be noted.

Before going any further we should examine how Tuckerman makes a virtue of his own states of uncertainty by using the sonnet form in an astonishingly flexible way. The following example, II.23, enacts a search for spiritual enlightenment which draws on a traditional association between light and transcendental vision:

> Some truths indeed may pierce the spirit's gloom,
> Yet shine unapprehended: grand, remote;
> We bow before their strength, yet feel them not—
> When some low promise of the life to come,
> Blessing the mourner, holds the heart indeed,
> A leading lamp that all may reach and read—
> Nor reck those lights, so distant over us,
> Sublime, yet helpless to the spirit's need
> As the night stars in heaven's vault: yet thus
> While the great asterisms mount and burn
> Unheeded for their glory, this its height
> Has reached, but lingers on till light return,
> Low in the sky, like frosty Sirius,
> To snap and sparkle through the winter's night.

One formal difference from Very which emerges immediately is that Tuckerman carefully blurs the distinctions between octave and sestet, and between rhyming lines. Golden has noted that in one of his workbooks Tuckerman wrote out lists of exact and dissonant rhymes. The former were for moods of certainty, the latter for agitated states.[28] In other words rhymes were to be psychologically mimetic, whereas for Very they were to hold together spiritual and profane contrasts or to give epigrammatic crispness. Tuckerman here enacts the ruminations of a mind brooding on its spiritual predicament. The lines move tentatively and go back on themselves in the repeated 'yet'. Tuckerman thus sets up an oscillating progression as if he sets up a reason for faith and then knocks it down. As the poem develops the possible significances of the stars shift from moral emblem ('leading lamp') to neutral physical phenomena—mere 'asterisms'. Tuckerman's repeated use of half-rhymes, in-rhymes and sound-repetition disguises the metrical pattern and allows the syntax to flow according to local emphasis. Characteristically Tuckerman does not over-resolve the poem which suggests a psychological process is taking place beyond the end of this poem. The contrast he has drawn between the lofty but inaccessible stars and one in particular which is low (therefore more accessible and therefore more suggestive of spiritual hope) does not leave ambiguity behind. Sirius is both the brightest single star *and* associated with the Dog-days, i.e. with a seasonal period of depression which resembles that state from which the poet is trying to escape. Tuckerman had a constant interest in astronomy and his use of the stars is always precise.

This sonnet shows many of the general characteristics of Tuckerman's poetry. His close attention to sound, rhyme and nuance suggest the quiet meditative flow of some of Coleridge's poems ('Frost at Midnight', for example). A drawback with Very's poetry is that a pattern becomes discernible whereas Tuckerman often places the reader within a predicament which began before the poem and which will continue afterwards. Sequence and process are thus crucial to his sonnets.

The open-endedness of the sonnet just discussed suggests that Tuckerman was making use of sequences, which is confirmed by the fact that, however many textual alterations he made to his poems, the order of the sonnets remained constant in his manuscripts.[29] While by no means the best sonnet sequence, the Fourth Series (1860–72) is compact enough to be examined as a whole to see how effective a sequence Tuckerman creates. The opening sonnet depicts an internal allegory of the soul's conflict with doubt, fear and other negative forces. Figured as a hill-top city, the soul is passive, its only movement being inwards away from the oncoming armies. Sonnet 2 continues the same image but shifts into positive action by depicting a different part of the self—thought—as a mailed archer who sends his arrows so swiftly they catch fire. The initiative has thus switched to the self from its enemies, and it now remains for Sonnet 3 to perform the task of explanation and commentary. The second line takes up the flashing fire of the preceding poem to play on the meanings of 'lightning' and the rather awkward 'enlighteneth' in order to underline the mind's strength; it 'may cleave the shades of sin', a clause which skilfully combines the physical vigour of the gesture, the insubstantiality of the self's enemies and their moral nature. The sixth line of the sonnet startlingly shifts our attention on to the source of light, i.e. to God, and the poem concludes with examples of the wonderment that God's enlightenment brings. What began as a deep impulse has now become a quality of profundity.

One of the simplest devices Tuckerman uses to create sequence is to begin sonnets with connectives like 'and', 'yet' or 'but'. Needless to say, these must be supported by a more substantial continuity of thought and image. Thus the 'yes' at the beginning of Sonnet 4 takes up the preceding sonnet's affirmation of God and, through exhortation, insists on the moral value of striving, perhaps a sign of Tennyson's influence. Tuckerman sets up a contrast between concentrated thought and directionless introspection, the latter a guilty and frivolous pleasure which might be shattered by a sudden summons to war, hence the reference to Antigenidas, the flautist teacher of Alcibiades.

The variations on the initial military metaphor of the series are now left behind in Sonnet 5 by cautionary advice to lukewarm believers. Tuckerman softens his earlier insistence on effort to affirm the value of patience and the mutual love that patient faith can bring. Then follows a pair of sonnets which demonstrate two phases in a particular case of such love. The first stage presents the Wordsworthian idyll of the two bark-collectors: a man and his son who are 'alternate helpers'. The boy, from his father's instruction, comes to love astronomy and wood-lore. Suddenly in Sonnet 7 comes a summons to war like that threatened in Sonnet 4. Tuckerman skilfully avoids any closer reference to the war than allusion, and the war's entire violence is concentrated in breaking the two apart: 'the knot was rent.' The poem slows down into the pathetic image of the father reading the last letter from his now dead son.

Sonnet 7 both extends this story and begins the resolution of the series. The immobility of the old man in his grief is taken up into a contrast between authentic virtue and the false allurements of guile. The latter has glitter, the former a lethargic and weary movement like sargasso weeds. Whereas the series began by exploring the possibilities of the self to find equilibrium (the military metaphors express, of course, its *lack*), Tuckerman has gradually shifted on to nature and this supplies the series' conclusion. The ocean deeps of Sonnet 8 become the depths of the New England woodland of Sonnet 9 which frames industrial progress with images from the wilderness of the past and with the poet's gesture of rejection ('I heed them not') in searching out wild plants. The last sonnet draws together the many references to nature in the form of an invitation to the reader to join the poet-naturalist in searching out the miraculous secrets of the landscape. The looked for harmony between reader and poet, an easy companionship, as it were, revives the relationship between the two bark-gatherers and supplies a satisfying final note of promise in nature's fullness.

It is quite likely that the model for Tuckerman's sonnet-sequences was 'In Memoriam'. He had acquired his first volume of Tennyson's poems in 1850, and had first met the poet in 1851. The earliest date for Tuckerman's first sequence is 1854. Timing and biographical connections make it almost certain that Tuckerman knew of 'In Memoriam' and indeed the similarities between the works are very close indeed. Both poets are writing their way out of loss through a serial sequence of short lyrics which examine particular stages in the process. Both set up a dialectical relation of self to setting which might mirror mood or agonizingly remind the poet of the lost friend or wife. Both writers broaden their individual sense of loss outwards to include religious doubt, and both unify their sequences by local connections or by recurrent images. Finally both poets experience, and then immediately question, a fleeting contact with the dead subject of their sequences (Tennyson in lyric 95, Tuckerman in I.23). The list could be extended, to include the alternation between hope and despair for instance, but enough has been said to show a similar approach to self-examination.

Tuckerman's repeated uncertainty and his lack of faith in, for instance, literary inspiration indicate that he had little in common with the Transcendentalists. N. Scott Momaday has argued convincingly that 'The Cricket' follows a completely different line of approach to that of Emerson or Bryant's 'Thanatopsis' in concentrating on nature's particulars rather than its unity, and in its willingness to accept uncertainty.[30]

Momaday discusses only one poem but his argument applies to Tuckerman's general treatment of nature. His sonnet 'And so, as this sphere now turning slow' is quite uncharacteristic in affirming a cosmic unity through 'deep analogy'. Its Emersonian celebration of the whole is in fact the exception that proves the rule, since Tuckerman usually confines himself to accurate description of particulars. He was a trained botanist and compiled a herbarium of flowers gathered on his visit to Britain in 1851.[31] Many of Tuckerman's textual revisions tighten up the precision of his descriptions, and several of his poems demonstrate wonderment at nature's miracles. In Sonnet IV.10 Tuckerman invites the reader to come into the countryside for a dawn ramble so that he can witness 'nature's secrecies', the unobtrusive but nonetheless fascinating flora and fauna to be found in the Massachusetts hills. At times this fascination can result in a poetry of names as in 'A Soul that Out of Nature's Deep' where the poet-figure celebrates plants by an enumeration which produces lines such as 'yew, garget, dogwood of the pools'. This rather ornate, tessellated surface is only one of a whole range of effects which Tuckerman manages in his treatment of nature. The sonnet 'April' resembles Emily Dickinson's 'A something in a summer's day' in rendering an elusive seasonal character, but Tuckerman manages his poem through a finely delicate rendering of haze, light and stillness to suggest an expectancy ('What holds this brooding rest?') of seasonal change.

One crucial factor in Tuckerman's attitude to nature is nostalgia for the disappearing wilderness. Sonnets II.18–19 articulate his sad recognition of change ('The woods have fallen, across the meadow-lot/ The hunter's trail and trap-path is forgot'), made all the more poignant by the fact that it has taken place so recently. Through a temporary indulgence of fancy Tuckerman recaptures this lost past, partly through natural images, partly through images of pioneer life, but the latter recede into 'dark shadings of the past' (II.20). Hand in hand with this nostalgia goes a hostility towards industrialization and rural clearance which Tuckerman presents as violence to the landscape itself. And, as we might expect from a poet of private means, he expresses hostility to the very notion of use, sighing over the desecration of a landscape which should be preserved for delighted contemplation.

Although commentators on Tuckerman's poems from Very onwards have praised the concrete rendering of nature, it also needs to be stated that for Tuckerman nature represented a problem. Its status constantly shifts in his poetry and its meaning eludes him. In I.9 he sadly recognizes that 'we . . . tease the sunbreak and the cloud/ For import'. Nature tantalizes Tuckerman in hinting at hidden truths and then blocking access to these truths when he recognizes the non-human autonomy of natural things. We have already seen an example of this difficulty in the sonnet 'Some truths indeed' where the stars waver ontologically between signifiers (leading the poet towards transcendental truth) and physical light-sources. In II.24 Tuckerman explores the frustrations of grief in terms of the *resistance* exerted by the poet's surroundings. This sonnet contrasts markedly with other poems where Tuckerman relies too heavily on conventional associations between feeling and scene (loss with sunset, anger with storm, etc.). The sonnet opens with an emphasis on things, divorced from their previous significance by grief and reduced to mere objects:

> Each common object too, the house, the grove,
> The street, the face, the ware in the window, seems
> Alien and sad, the wreck of perished dreams:

The flat listing of things captures their physical presence which oppresses the poet and begins a series of slightly self-dramatizing actions ('I leave the town', 'I climb', 'I rave', etc.). He turns to the countryside for emotional relief, but nature's intractability mocks him constantly and refuses to respond to or reflect his mood ('I roar to the unmoved skies'). Tennyson catches exactly the same tone of alienation in lyric 7 of 'In Memoriam' where the poet's sense of loss is expressed through a bleak image of dawn: 'On the bald street breaks the blank day.' Tuckerman's sonnet shows the poet trying futilely to get emotional bearings from his immediate surroundings and depends for its effect partly on not converting any object or scene within the poem into metaphor.

The one poem which embodies Tuckerman's different attitudes to Nature and which makes a fitting conclusion to a

discussion of his poetry is his fine ode 'The Cricket'. This work
has attracted considerable critical attention but most accounts
do not do justice to its variety. Golden describes the poem as a
'dream piece in which the poet, adrift in time and place,
reviews his life'; Mordecai Marcus and Momaday broadly
agree that the ode engages with the attractions of death, but
Marcus decides too categorically that the cricket 'functions as
a symbol of death' throughout the poem.[32] Only Yvor Winters
has fully recognized how the significance of the cricket shifts as
the poem progresses.

The opening section humorously rescues the cricket from
literary obscurity, and in place of a grandiose invocation to a
muse Tuckerman turns to the cricket for lyrical assistance:
'Shall I not take to help me in my song/ A little cooing cricket?'
(10–11). In the second section Tuckerman develops the fact
that the cricket can only be perceived through its sound by
expanding it outwards to become the very voice of nature. Now
the lines move more slowly as Tuckerman evokes a Keatsian
state of glutted drowsiness. Drawing on the ode 'To Autumn' he
figures himself and a companion half-asleep beside a brook,
while the surrounding heat, light, smells and sounds are
'stunning the sense to slumber'. Tuckerman alters the pace of
the poem here by varying the stressing and by shifting weight
from verbs to adjectives like 'trellised' and 'trammeled'. But at
no point in the ode is sound forgotten for long, and as the section
closes the cricket's song reasserts ubiquity through a more
lyrical rhythm and through spatial metaphors:

> At hand, around, illimitably
> Rising and falling like the sea,
>   Acres of cricks! (36–8)

Up to this point, Marcus notwithstanding, the cricket has
embodied the sheer vitality of nature. In Section III, as Yvor
Winters notes, Tuckerman moves away from celebration and
enjoyment to the more sombre, non-human aspects of
nature.[33] As the tone becomes more solemn the metre shifts
into pentameter with varying rhyme-patterns. The references
to childhood and sunshine (keeping a continuity with the
preceding section) soon give way to nocturnal associations and
barren landscapes:

Night lover too; bringer of all things dark
And rest and silence; yet thou bringest to me
Always that burthen of the unresisting Sea,
The moaning cliffs, the low rocks blackly stark; (43–6)

The cricket has now been internalized to focus related associations of darkness, death and pain, and has pulled the poet into the past of his memory.

Section IV contains this process by moving into the distant past of mythology. Momaday has argued that here the unity of the poem is damaged, but the worst charge that can be levelled against Tuckerman is that his classical allusions are so obscure. In fact this section makes explicit the bucolic undertones of the poem's very subject. The cricket figures prominently in Classical Greek literature and participates in the shady brookside *topos* found on Theocritus's fifth idyll and in Plato's *Phaedrus*. The twin theme of song and music unifies this whole section from the singing swans of the River Cayster, through the reeds used for Pan-pipes and the cricket-brooch of Psamathe to the Arcadian horns of the last line.[34] The classical references are both nostalgic and mournful (Psamathe bewailing her dead son Linos, for example), and yet the cricket is a constant presence, affecting god and hero alike.

Tuckerman's nostalgia both lifts the tone and triggers off a Shelleyan impulse in Section V to penetrate into nature 'like the Enchanter old' in order to gain access to its 'articulate voices', of which the cricket's call is one. This privileged insight with its associated seer-like status is sketched out as a hypothesis, but the turning-point in this section comes in line 115 where Tuckerman falls back on the acceptance of provisional and limited knowledge. Before this can cause any self-pity he puts his acceptance within the context of a transience which undermines human capacity:

It matters not. Behold! the autumn goes,
   The shadow grows,
The moments take hold of eternity. (122–24)

Tuckerman now accepts his own mortality. A recognition of his own limitations had anyway grown out of his failure to grasp nature's secrets, and this recognition helps to explain his general preference for close, small-scale renderings of nature.

Since the whole system is inaccessible, Tuckerman predictably tends to concentrate on particular settings and particular objects.

In their different ways Tuckerman and Very have been the victims of unjustifiable critical neglect. Even now there is no reliable edition of their poetry in print. Yvor Winters' over-enthusiastic assertion that 'the three most remarkable American poets of the nineteenth century' are Very, Tuckerman and Emily Dickinson does the former poets a disservice in exaggerating their good qualities.[35] Very's sonnets show the egotism latent in Transcendentalism turning itself inside out; by a sheer effort of individual will he submits himself to the inspirational voices of God. Tuckerman, writing after the first surge of Transcendentalist enthusiasm had run its course, no longer feels confident in referring his predicaments to the divine and produces some astonishingly fine and precise pieces of self-analysis as a consequence. Both poets have their besetting faults—Very his doctrinal rigidity, Tuckerman his hesitancy and melancholy—but they do embody important directions taken by the New England poetic mind in the period 1830 to 1870.

NOTES

1. Yvor Winters, *In Defense of Reason* (London: Routledge & Kegan Paul, 1960), p. 264; David Robinson, 'Jones Very, the Transcendentalists, and the Unitarian Tradition', *Harvard Theological Review* 68 (1975), 105; Nathan Lyons, 'Introduction', *Jones Very: Selected Poems* (New Brunswick: Rutgers University Press, 1966), p. 10; J. A. Levernier tries to strike a middle position in his 'Calvinism and Transcendence in the Poetry of Jones Very', *E.S.Q.* 24 (1978), 30–41.
2. Edwin Gittleman, *Jones Very: The Effective Years 1833–1840* (New York: Columbia University Press, 1967), p. 271.
3. MS essay 'The Soul', John Hay Library, Brown University [p. 28].
4. Anthony Herbold, 'Nature as Concept and Technique in the Poems of Jones Very', *New England Quarterly* 40 (1967), 244–59; Carl Dennis, 'Correspondence in Very's Nature Poetry', *New England Quarterly* 43 (1970), 250–73; Robinson, 'Jones Very, the Transcendentalists . . .', p. 120.
5. *The Journals and Miscellaneous Notebooks of Ralph Waldo Emerson*, Vol. 7, ed.

A. W. Plumstead and Harrison Hayford (Cambridge, Mass.: Belknap Press, 1969), p. 154.

6. W. I. Bartlett, *Jones Very: Emerson's 'Brave Saint'* (Durham, N.C.: Duke University Press, 1942), p. 143. There is no standard edition of Very's poems. James Freeman Clarke's 1886 edition of *Poems and Essays by Jones Very* is neither complete nor textually reliable. It has been reissued by Transcendental Books (1965) and as a number of the *American Transcendental Quarterly* (Winter, 1974). Nathan Lyons' 1966 selection confines itself to Very's religious poems but is textually reliable.

7. Gittleman, p. 205.

8. *Poems and Essays by Jones Very* (Boston: Houghton Mifflin, 1883), p. 52.

9. Very, 'Influence of Christianity and of the Progress of Civilization on Epic Poetry', *Christian Examiner* (Boston) 24 (May 1838), 208.

10. Gittleman, p. 78.

11. Bartlett, p. 195; Gittleman, p. 336.

12. 'The Soul' [p. 4].

13. Lawrence Buell, *Literary Transcendentalism: Style and Vision in the American Renaissance* (Ithaca, N.Y.: Cornell University Press, 1973), p. 313.

14. Harry L. Jones, 'The Very Madness: A New Manuscript', *C.L.A. Journal* 10 (1967), 199.

15. William James, *The Varieties of Religious Experience* (New York: Collier Books, 1961), p. 192; A. C. Underwood, *Conversion: Christian and Non-Christian* (London: George Allen & Unwin, 1925), pp. 164–65.

16. Gittleman, p. 194.

17. MS 'Epistle on Miracles', Wellesley College Library [pp. 1–2].

18. Robinson, 'The Exemplary Self and the Transcendent Self in the Poetry of Jones Very', *E.S.Q.* 24 (1978), 207–14.

19. Winters, p. 272.

20. Lyons, p. 47.

21. Bartlett, p. 106. The review appeared in the *Dial* of July 1841.

22. The most extreme case for Tuckerman's modernity is put by Eugene England in his article 'Tuckerman's Sonnet I:10: The First Post-Symbolist Poem', *Southern Review* 12 (1976) 323–47.

23. MS. letter of 24 April 1861 in Houghton Library, Harvard University.

24. *The Complete Poems of Frederick Goddard Tuckerman*, ed. N. Scott Momaday (New York: Oxford University Press, 1965), p. 81. The textual validity of this edition has been questioned by T. P. Lynch in his article 'Still Needed: A Tuckerman Text', *Papers of the Bibliographical Society of America* 69 (1975), 255–65.

25. Samuel A. Golden, *Frederick Goddard Tuckerman: An American Sonneteer*, University of Maine Studies, 2nd series, No. 66 (Orono: University of Maine Press, 1952), p. 27.

26. Golden, *Frederick Goddard Tuckerman* (New York: Twayne, 1966), pp. 35–8.

27. Golden, *An American Sonneteer*, pp. 33, 29.

28. Golden, *Frederick Goddard Tuckerman*, p. 77.

29. *Frederick Goddard Tuckerman*, p. 57.

30. N. Scott Momaday, 'The Heretical Cricket', *Southern Review* 3 (1967), 43–50.

31. In the Houghton Library.
32. Golden, *Frederick Goddard Tuckerman*, p. 108; Mordecai Marcus, 'The Poetry of Frederick Goddard Tuckerman: A Reconsideration', *Discourse* 5 (Winter, 1961–62), 79.
33. Winters, *Forms of Discovery* (Chicago: Alan Swallow, 1967), p. 260.
34. The second meaning of 'tettix' in Classical Greek is a gold brooch with the head of a cicada which was used by the Athenians to pin up their hair. The scope of Tuckerman's classical allusions in this poem is a subject in itself.
35. Winters, *Forms of Discovery*, p. 253.

9

Imaging America: Paintings, Pictures and the Poetics of Nineteenth-century American Landscape

by GRAHAM CLARKE

1

The Rising Glory of America (1771), the collaborative would-be national epic by Hugh Henry Brackenbridge and Philip Freneau, is a characteristic American poem in the way it declares an assumed mythic status for the continent. As in Walt Whitman's 'Song of Myself' (1855) its visionary rhetoric envisages a land—a new found American land—freed, as it were, from history as it shines forth the presence of God. To look upon the land thus is to inscribe with the eye those energies which underpin the special value of America. The land—the prospect ahead—is at once to be seen and imagined as a composite image of the continent's destiny. For Brackenbridge and Freneau, and a line which follows them, this is both the literal glory of America and its power as myth—a power and glory which the poem must define, must image, in the land itself.

We are, of course, to meet such compulsive rhetoric time

and again throughout nineteenth-century American literature. In relation to the landscape, however, such mythicizing has a central significance. For one of the most recurrent concerns of both the American poet and painter is to view the continent through an aesthetic and a language equal to its mythic and literal status. Just as *The Rising Glory of America* announces that a 'newer world now opens to . . . view',[1] so the insistence on the novelty of the terrain and its distinctiveness for (and to) the eye underlines its difference from Europe and the terms by which America must give meaning to its land. Thus, in part, the poem's determination to establish a native tradition appropriate to the prospect of the continent. In its 'rising glory' the 'happy land' is celebrated as ideal fact and, as it is, so the Potomac will 'vie with Thames' as a river of equal national importance. As it does so 'A Homer and a Milton [will] rise' to meet and sing its independent status and with them will come 'A second Pope' and 'Another Denham'.

Milton, Pope, Denham: English poets whose landscape poems suggest models[2] for their native equivalents. As Thoreau and Whitman were to insist, however, such poems could impose a way of seeing the land which entraps rather than enraptures the eye. Indeed the distinctions between the native claims of the home terrain and the conventions and values of an alien landscape tradition create a continuing conflict for the American who would view his new lands in a new way—with an American eye appropriate to their implicit meaning.

It is easy, of course, to see this conflict in relation to the more extreme of American landscapes—the plains, prairies, deserts and mountain ranges of the West. These become distinctive geographies which, in their specific topographical features, question in fundamental ways the forms and assumptions of a foreign landscape tradition. As Howard Mumford Jones argues, to 'become imaginatively potent' America had

> indeed to be realized Westward—[had], that is, [to] be expressed in words and pictures. A convention of values had to be set up derived from it . . . concerning [America's] westward terrain. To articulate this concept, modes of expression . . . had to be discovered or invented.[3]

Webb, Turner and Merk have all insisted on such distinctiveness, just as Cooper, Twain, Whitman, Bierstadt, Church and Moran offer literary and pictorial examples of the Western aesthetic alluded to by Jones.[4] And yet to insist on the West in this context is to recognize the conflict at its most basic level. We have to remember that for the poet, in particular, the West had an essentially symbolic meaning; there was little specific descriptive or topographical poetry concerned with the Western areas. It is, indeed, Whitman's 'Passage to India' rather than William Cullen Bryant's 'The Prairies' which defines for us a characteristic sense of the West's significance in nineteenth-century American culture.[5]

Thus we can easily give too much weight to the West in the development of an American landscape art and, in turn, forget how crucial the more traditional *Eastern* terrains were to the debate. Indeed, we must keep in mind how many quintessentially 'American' texts and paintings take for their habitats Eastern settings which, by the nineteenth century certainly, were settled, cultivated and, in many cases, obvious tourist attractions. Poets and painters shared similar landscapes—a scenery of farm and field, of orchard and forest, of mountain, lake and river: a green land—the Hudson River Valley, the Adirondacks, Catskills and White Mountains, the Merrimac River, Lake George, Niagara, Long Island and, to be sure, Walden Pond.

Much of the 'glory' of this scenery was the way it seemingly exemplified God's presence on the continent and confirmed America's status as a text of absolute and ultimate meaning.[6] As God's 'text' it was at once complete and ideal, a literal prospect which signified an implicit mythic dimension. The American poet and painter who would speak to this 'true' meaning, this original image, had to establish an aesthetic freed from entrapping conventions and traditions which stood between the eye and its divine object. The response to Eastern American sceneries is basic to this effort to create a native imaging of the continent's significance and, in its difference from the West, reveals important aspects of the way the land was seen and pictured. As Barbara Novak, for example, has suggested, 'The large paintings dealing with the West were not more and more American, but often more and more baroque in their rhetoric and ambition.'[7] Thus, she argues, there emerges two distinctive responses, Eastern and Western, where each 'gathers to itself a definition of sublimity—one reconfirming a traditional interpretation, the other departing from and restructuring it'.[8] Luminism fulfils that radical restructuring of the sublime and, in its *Eastern* locales, finds an aesthetic, an image, equal to the divine status of America. It is, indeed, an image which underlies the basic difference, in the nineteenth century, between a painting and a picturing of the continent. It is what I want to term the imaging of America.

2

The West, then, immediately inspires—by its scale if nothing else—a rhetoric insistent on grand perspectives. As with 'Song of Myself' it 'inhale[s] great draughts of space'. By comparison the East is essentially small-scale—local, particular, and quietly ambitious with an art that signifies America's spiritual meaning in the ordinary, the found and the domestic. An Eastern sublime thus effaces art, as it does the artist, for the land is, itself, the art—is, that is, the picture made by God. To 'paint' it is to draw away from the original, to make false the purity of a meaning held *in* the land. Thus in the words 'picture' and 'painting' we have two significant counters each holding within them elements of the distinction between East and West, between Europe and America, between a foreign and native 'eye'. As Eastern locales assert their presence in the painting and poem, so they rework the meaning of landscape into a native picturing as painting becomes increasingly associated with all that is false, foreign and artificial. The new lands offer, that is, a prose-picture as the absolute image of the continent's rising glory: its imminent transcendent state.

In part such a distinction, between the traditional and radical, the alien and native, the natural and artificial, is suggested by the novelist and critic John Neal who, in the *Yankee* (1829), bemoaned the poor condition of American landscape painting:

> We may as well acknowledge the truth. Painting is poetry now. People have done with nature—life is insipid, prose flat. The

standard for landscape is no longer what we see outstretched before us, and on every side of us, with such amazing prodigality of shape and color. We have done with the trees of the forest and the wilderness, the broken-up and richly-dyed earth, overrun with wild-flowers and bravely handled herbage; weary of what we see on our right hand and on our left, whenever we go abroad with our hearts for a sketch-book; of the blue deep and the blue-sky—and of all that painting of that master who used to be looked up to as an authority in landscape—God.[9]

The differences between 'prose' and 'poetry' recall Constable's intention to establish a 'natural painture'[10] and, like Constable, there is a commitment to a *plein-air* approach: an open encounter with the land itself. But Neal's insistence on the landscapes 'outstretched' before the eye lays stress upon the native aspects of his terrain and, in turn, of seeing it correctly. America is, thus, an image of prodigal shape and colour, a picture by the 'master' and 'authority': God. To look upon the land is to see it as both America and as God's domain—as its image is given ultimate credence and absolute sanctity as an ideal real habitat. The American scene is, thus, God's art: a prose of which there can be no higher (i.e. truthful) account.

Neal's distinction, however, is more than a call to an independent native style. Just as his insistence on an all surrounding perspective ('every side of us') questions the fixed point of view and the frame in favour of the panorama, so the difference between poetry and prose suggests the way an appropriate *poetics* of landscape is related to a fundamental (and radical) reworking of their meanings—meanings which, in turn, owed their assumed values to their association with painting. It is thus that he relates them to distinct pictorial traditions connoting the respective values which each implies. Significantly, then, the 'standards of landscape' are the eighteenth-century English artists Richard Wilson and Philip de Loutherbourg who,[11] as such, are seen as representative of a false and foreign poetic. In contrast to both their art and influence 'the landscape of Ruysdael was true, theirs untrue' or, as it were, 'his plain prose, theirs poetry'.

In opposing Ruysdael and Wilson as examples of different traditions, Neal follows Sir Joshua Reynolds's distinction in the *Discourses*—although Neal inverts the assumptions behind Reynolds's argument and radically rewrites the values by which landscape is given meaning. As he places Ruysdael above Wilson (the 'English Claude'), so Reynolds places Claude, Nicholas Poussin and Gaspar Dughet above the work of the Flemish and Dutch schools.[12] Theirs was a local, common, realistic (i.e. prosaic) art, whereas Claude and his seventeenth-century contemporaries sought a general, ideal nature: a *beau ideal* which embodied poetic principles. Thus 'That the practice of Claud Lorrain . . . is to be adopted by Landschape Painters, in opposition to that of the Flemish and Dutch schools, there can be no doubt.'[13] No doubt because Claude offered a poetic truth intent on 'perfect form': a harmony consistently figured in relation to a classical arcadia and Virglian pastoral. Indeed Claude, and the Claudian frame, has a central position in the landscape aesthetics of English landscape. Not only is he a constant presence in Wilson and Gainsborough, his ideal pictorial unity is implicit in the picturesque which, in William Gilpin's definition, is directly related to painting—that is 'capable of being *illustrated in* painting', or, as it were, in relation to Claudian poetic principles.[14]

Poetry and prose, the Claudian and the Dutch traditions, thus establish themselves as extreme alternatives in the attempt to *image* America. Indeed Claude is as central to the poetry of Pope and Thomson as he is to eighteenth-century English landscape painting—further evidence of how his influence was inimical to a native aesthetic where the 'environment was new; democratic, and undisciplined: the tradition aristocratic, moralistic, and orderly'.[15] The prosaic and poetic accounts of the Continent's meaning, of an America correctly *seen*, relates directly to the insistence on an individual native form appropriate to the land itself. As late as 1872, for example, William Cullen Bryant in *Picturesque America* insists on the especial significance of America for 'art'. 'It will be admitted', says Bryant, 'that our country abounds with scenery new to the artist's pencil', an endless progression of 'mountains and valleys, gorges and rivers, and tracts of sea-coast, which the foot of the artist has never trod' or, as it were, marked and measured.[16]

And yet the debate between a land 'new' to art and an art appropriate to the land remains constant throughout the nineteenth century. Neal's insistence on a prose account suggests a realistic image—an art open to the individual nature of the continent. Such prose risked what Coleridge called being merely 'dutchified'—a dull impression which, once again, lacked the symbolic dimension of a land alive with sacred meaning: God's picture. The poetics of American landscape, however, close that gap between the real and ideal—to infer from the land itself, as *the* text, an ideal notation of the real which, in turn, frees the image from the frame; from, in short, the artistic and the conventional. What Leo Marx described as an ideal 'middle ground' so central to Crèvecoeur's new world, 'a rural landscape, a well-ordered green garden magnified to continental size',[17] becomes part of a 'poetic' account—a pastoral world which still frames the 'seen' in relation to Claudian principles. A 'prosaic' America emerges in the insistence on America as the picture: alive, new, fresh; in short, God's locale. It is, thus, a denotative text which merely requires its equivalent image on the page or canvas. As distinct from Europe America had 'no abbeys in picturesque ruins, no stately cathedrals . . . no aristocratic mansions . . . no ancestral homes', but instead 'a fresh, vigorous, broad continent for its field in the natural world, grand, wild, and inspiriting . . .'.[18] What for Henry James and T. S. Eliot were aspects of the thinness of the American scene were the ideal counters of a radical prose picture wherein lay the revised vision of a poetic account and picturing of the continent.

3

Just as, however, Neal's insistence on the differences between a poetic and prose account inferred the values implicit in each term, so we find in 'painting' and 'picture' (as nouns and verbs) equal extremes and radical alternatives. That poetry and painting are seen as synonymous and equal aesthetic categories is, for example, clearly stated by Asher B. Durand (1766-1886) in his almost archetypal 'portrait' of America at mid-century: *Kindred Spirits* (1849). Barbara Novak has called the painting 'the perfect exemplar of the American negotiation between the

real and the ideal'[19] and appropriately suggests one significant
pair of 'kindred spirits' in a perfect balance. The scene is that of
a natural region (the Catskills) untouched by settlement or
agriculture. It thus connotes a sense of America as, once again,
prodigal and inspiriting—grand and wild—as stream, trees,
sky and rock exhibit a found unity. There is no mark of the
human and yet neither is this a wilderness inimical to human
needs. Durand, of course, completes the scene in relation to the
two figures who, from an extruding ledge, look out and over the
'natural' American scene. Thus the second 'pair' of kindred
spirits—of man and nature within a transcendent unity (an
Emersonian 'synthesis'). As the figures stand there so we see the
scene through their presence. Indeed they, more than the
formal composition, frame the prospect and the point of view.
The figures are Thomas Cole the *painter* (1801–48) and William
Cullen Bryant the *poet* (1794–1878): the third pair of kindred
spirits. They share the same outlook, the same view on their
common (American) subject. Durand's portrait becomes a
celebration of the kindred arts and the reciprocal relationship
between them—emphasized in the painting in the way Cole
speaks to Bryant and Bryant views the scene. The painter has
indeed become the poet.

And if we look at Bryant's 'The Poet' (1863) so one sense of
how he will 'frame' his poem, his 'lay', is given directly in
relation to painting:

> Seek'st thou, in living lays,
>   To limn the beauty of the earth and sky?
> Before thine inner gaze
>   Let all that beauty in clear vision lie;
> Look on it with exceeding love, and write
> The words inspired by wonder and delight.[20]

Bryant's choice of 'limn' here is significant. Why, we might
ask, does he not use 'to paint' instead? Although 'to limn'
implies a reference to the earlier American limners, by the
mid-nineteenth century it would certainly have been some-
thing of an anachronism. Its use here focuses our attention
upon it, especially if we recall its earlier meaning in relation to
illumination. To limn is, thus, both to paint and to illuminate
the 'beauty' of the scene, or, as it were, to reveal rather than

201

copy what the eye sees. Painting is not copying, not once agaiⁿ a prose response but a poetic: an 'inner gaze' which (like Wordsworth's 'inner eye') will 'see into the life of things'. This is, then, the act of vision: what Wordsworth called 'an aspect more sublime' which, here, is part of an Emersonian transcendence in the midst of wonder, delight, and love. 'Clear vision' which at first suggests clarity, outline and vividness (that immediate prose response) is now rather a directness associated with the poetic relationship implied in this act of limning: spiritual, sublime, visionary. The gaze penetrates its world into a higher, general and more poetic truth.

There are here, then, two levels of meaning which relate both to Neal's distinction between prose and poetry and to Reynolds' notion of contrasting Dutch and Italianate traditions. Although Bryant seemingly speaks to sight (to vision), the act seeks an ideal poetic world rather than the literal 'prose' world stretched out before the eye. And as with the poem so with the act of painting and 'art'. Where on the surface the poet looks on nature he does so with the eye of the painter—a painter who does not 'copy' but, intent on an America sublime, consistently seeks an ideal symbolic image. Indeed, if we want a more painterly parallel, Bryant's sonnet, 'To Cole, the Painter Departing for Europe' (1829), offers similar 'poetic' advice to the painter:

> Thine eyes shall see the light of distant skies:
>> Yet, Cole! thy heart shall bear to Europe's strand
>> A living image of thy native land,
> Such as on thy own glorious canvass lies.
> Lone lakes—savannahs where the bison roves—
>> Rocks rich with summer garlands—solemn streams—
>> Skies, where the desert eagle wheels and screams—
> Spring bloom and autumn blaze of boundless groves.
> Fair scenes shall greet thee where thou goest—fair,
>> But different—everywhere the trace of men,
>> Paths, homes, graves, ruins, from the lowest glen
> To where life shrinks from the fierce Alpine air.
>> Gaze on them, till the tears shall dim thy sight,
>> But keep that earlier, wilder image bright.[21]

Bryant wrote this the same year as Neal's essay for the *Yankee*. The distinctions suggested between Europe and America are fundamental integers to extreme forms of landscape. Bryant's native scene is untainted, evincing from the artist what the poet called (in his funeral oration to Cole) 'acts of religion'. In contrast Europe is viewed as a landscape of history and association—old at once to 'art' and the 'eye' in its signifying complexity. Indeed the sonnet evinces a remarkable sense of the specific qualities of American scenery. It notes basic geographical features—lakes, savannahs, deserts, for example—and the presence of the land as, once again, inspiriting. The 'atmosphere' is at once fresh, vivid, wild and novel, and America is a 'bright' land as it shines forth God's (not man's) image: a sublime and living image of the land's prophetic and sacred status.

When we refer the poem to Cole, however, Bryant's response is more problematic. His use, for example, of 'solemn', 'garlands', 'groves' and 'fair' is immediately recognizable as part of a stock eighteenth-century English poetic vocabulary rather than as a language capable of limning the bright, clear land of America. In turn, we must remember that Bryant's image of clarity, that 'earlier, wilder image', that 'living image of our own bright land', is precisely that which 'upon thy glorious canvass lies' (and how suggestive 'lies' is here). Bryant identifies his ideal (living) America with Cole's painting—that 'beauty' which in 'The Poet' is part of the 'clear vision' (the 'gaze' of Cole and, in *Kindred Spirits*, of Bryant also). Cole's art is seen as a poetic equivalent: a pictorial parallel to the poetic language Bryant wants. Why, however, the insistence on 'bright' and 'clear', for without seeing a Cole painting we might think that his art is an image of the prose account Neal sought. Cole's painting, however, has nothing of the prosaic about it, and nothing of the clear or bright. His painting, certainly (like the essay 'American Scenery')[22] is a testament to his adopted native land and a celebration of a divine America, but it has nothing independent about it—nothing, that is, which offers a distinctive American gaze into the real *seen*. Cole's art, rather, is consistently structured in relation to quite specific and predetermined aesthetic principles. Thus, a painting 'is not like a scene in nature, where the eye can embrace the whole circle of the horizon, but is bounded like a view taken through a window'.[23] The words 'bounded', 'view' and 'window' form the basis of Cole's frame to his 'lay' of America and split themselves away from a natural (and native) base: 'circle', 'horizon' and 'whole' which, with their central significance for Emerson and Thoreau, stand as silent tokens of the continent's totality and of an aesthetic which seeks the 'scene in nature'.[24]

And just as Cole imposes his distinct frame around the scene, so the clear image is antipathetic to his sense of the sublime: to the poetry of painting. Like Burke, Cole insists that 'poetry with all its obscurity, has a more general as well as a more powerful dominion over the other art [painting]'; and he agrees that 'there are reasons in nature why the obscure idea, when properly conveyed, should be more affecting than the clear.'[25] The connotative status given to 'poetic' language is, then, fundamentally distinguished from a denotative (and prosaic) language. Louis Noble, Cole's biographer, underscores such a distinction when he tells us that Cole was 'always the poet, when he was the painter'[26] and emphasizes the general over the particular, the suggestive over the specific, and the vague and obscure over the clear and bright. His view returns the painterly to a poetic conception of the kind defined by Reynolds who (in the *Discourses*) warned, via Claude, that 'nature' is 'not to be too closely copied' and that 'There are excellencies in the art of painting beyond what is commonly called the imitation of nature.'[27] Cole, like Reynolds, insisted that painting is a 'creative, as well as an imitative act',[28] directing his animus against the prosaic and denotative in favour of the 'poetic' and symbolic. The painter's 'vision' is held within an associative poetic vocabulary. Thus it is not the 'detail' that should 'attract the eye, but the whole' and therefore, Cole admits,

> I never succeed in painting scenes, however beautiful,
> immediately on returning from them. I must wait
> for a time to draw a veil over the common details,
> the unessential parts, which shall leave the great
> features, whether the beautiful or the sublime dominant
> in the mind.[29]

It should not surprise us that his 'favourites' in landscape 'are Claude and Gaspar Poussin' or that, in 1841, he is critical of developments in English landscape painting because 'design is forgotten.' Consistently, Cole's 'vision' is offered in relation to a Claudian harmony as proscribed by Reynolds. The 'living image' is structured 'according to an *a priori* sense of composition'[30]—a design and frame which shows how 'his art was based upon the seventeenth-century European tradition to a degree from which no love of New World Scenery could completely free him.'[31] Thus, for Cole, 'To walk with nature as a poet, is the necessary condition of a perfect artist.'[32]

4

Cole's dependence upon Claudian schema and his 'poetic' assumptions concerning the nature of painting and painterly truth or vision reveal an aesthetic principle close to the Reynoldsian *beau ideal* of eighteenth-century English landscape painting—precisely the kind of poetic standards to which Neal objected. Such a poetic ideal clearly cuts across the call for an independent native art capable of imaging the local on its own terms. The 'gaze' so crucial to Bryant and his view of 'limning' has nothing of the vernacular about it. The Claudian preferences denigrate Dutch and Flemish 'naturalism' to the level of common detail and do so at a time when, as Neal insisted, it was precisely in the lavish prose of America, its common detail, that an American eye and ideal figuring was required. As Whitman was to look upon a *democratic vista* so Thoreau would map and sound Walden Pond: a flattening and particularizing process which shunned the hierarchical, the conventional and the formulaic—in short, everything upon which the Claudian and the picturesque depended. In opposition to the 'frame' of painterly values Whitman stressed the open road and, like Emerson and Thoreau, allowed the eye to move outwards to the horizon—detailing a world which, in the completed image of America, was seen as 'The Rounded Catalogue Divine Complete': what has been called pantheistic or transcendental *realism*, an ideal American prose account of the scene as seen.

The gap between this 'ideal realism', for example, and an ideal painting, is suggested by Frederick Church's *New England Scenery* (1851) which, while it offers a vision of the land as an ideal construct, does so in relation to easily identifiable traditions. In its literary context this is Crèvecoeur's pastoral

America—a Virgilian Arcadia spreading beyond the canvas into the continent's Western terrain. But as a New England scene it is by no means local or specific. It is, rather, a painting 'composed of paraphrasings of vignettes of the north-eastern United States' or, as it were, 'several pictures in one composition'.[33] Its unity lies in the degree to which Church has composed an ideal landscape: a general image which figures the prospect *of* a glorious America. Thus 'what Church imagines is a pristine Yankee Arcadia: a thriving agrarian paradise'.[34] He does so, however, through declared painterly principles, for the scene is Claudian to a high degree—its setting, point of view and repose reminiscent of that general harmony so praised by Reynolds and Cole. The iconography might be Yankee, but its use of an idealizing vocabulary allows little, if any, direct contact with the land 'outstretching' before the native eye. It is once again a poetic not a prosaic ideal.

In an ideal prosaic account meaning is never imposed. The land is thus a picture in its own right. More and more as the 'poetic' response to the American scene is revised throughout the nineteenth century, so 'painting' gives way to 'picture' as the 'gap' is closed between ideal and real, poetic and prosaic. The contours of the land are in themselves part of a privileged outline as its particular make-up is seen as a sanctified iconography. The picture is 'alive'—an art which need only be imaged and named to infer the presence of its spiritual and mythical 'being'. Look, for example, at the first Part of Whittier's 'Pictures':

> Light, warmth, and sprouting greenness, and o'er all
> Blue, stainless, steel-bright ether, raining down
> Tranquility upon the deep-hushed town,
> The freshening meadows, and the hill-sides brown;
> Voices of the west-wind from the hills of pine,
> And the brimmed river from its distant fall,
> Low hum of bees, and joyous interlude
> Of bird-songs in the streamlet-skirting wood,—
> Heralds and prophecies of sound and sight,
> Blessed forerunners of the warmth and light,
> Attendant angles to the house of prayer,
> With reverent footsteps keeping pace with mine—
> One more, through God's great love, with you I share

A morn of resurrection sweet and fair
   As that which saw, of old, in Palestine,
   Immortal Love uprising in fresh bloom
   From the dark night and winter of the tomb![35]

Written in 1852 this is an equivalent in poetry of Church's *New England Scenery*. Unlike the painting, however, the scene is given a reverend status by the way in which the poem views the external world *as* itself the picture. There is, for example, no obvious formula by which the scene is constructed. The eye celebrates a unity while, equally, allowing for caught particulars. Indeed the use of 'and' allows the eye to spread out over the land, joining and connecting the elements rather than enclosing and framing them. As it does, so there is no limning for the scene is already 'limned'—glazed (as a painting) with the 'ether', pure and all-encompassing, which literally bathes it in a spiritual light. This is a sanctified world of untouched energies—suggested by the pristine colours (green, blue, steel-bright) and the stilled image of a providential America: 'a morn of resurrection sweet and fair'. Indeed there is a remarkable sense of *plein-airism* about the response: a freshness and openness which survives despite the somewhat obvious metre and, as the poem develops, the heavily intended religious significance. It stands as a mix between the painterly and pictured, not wholly content, in the end, to offer the image without its symbolic inference. At its best, however, it is close to Emerson's 'Fragments on Nature and Life', seeing the 'fragments' as found pictures which lack the formal qualities of made art, but are, indeed, suggestive of nature itself as the artist who 'paints with white and red the moors/ To draw the nations out of doors' and allows the hardened brilliance of a suddenly seen glazed (and 'glassed') natural picture in which 'A score of airy miles will smooth Rough Monadnoc to a gem.'[36]

5

As distinct from Cole's and Bryant's general idea, the focus of a *pictured* America was on the given particular—the found scene. Thus, like Ruskin in *Modern Painters*, Asher B. Durand wanted to 'draw with scrupulous fidelity' and referred the artist 'to nature early'.[37] To draw as such is to trace the outline of an image sufficient in itself, for 'the Great Designer of these glorious pictures has placed them before us as types of the Divine attributes.' Pictures, not paintings. 'Painting' gathers about it values dependent upon traditions outside a land figured by God for a privileged American eye. If 'Cole and others' had begun, in The Hudson River School, the beginnings of an American line, Durand still insisted upon a 'natural landscape painter'—that is, one who would inscribe the sacred meanings through a transference of the living image to the page and canvas. As Whitman wanted a poetry 'not marshalled in rhyme and meter', so, for Durand, the 'virgin charms' of his 'native land' become the single compulsive subject—a continuous picture which speaks to a divine prose. As European painterly conventions failed to signify this divine picture, so Durand's call for an indigenous style parallels Whitman's rhetoric in the 'Preface' to *Leaves of Grass*. 'Why should not the American landscape painter', asks Durand, 'in accordance with the principles of self-government, boldly originate a high and independent style, based on his native resources?'[38] The fidelity he seeks gives to the continent's prose its 'high style'— the native equivalent of the *beau ideal*—but, in so doing, *perihypsous* moves down to the road and, like Whitman's *Leaves*, is to be found by the roadside 'under your boot-soles'.

If Bryant was Cole's 'Kindred Spirit', so Whitman was Emerson's, evidence 'of an American bard at last', and 'The Poet' (1844) shows how distinct are the two pairings. Painting remains Bryant's term and roots his viewpoint firmly in its European base. 'Picturing' becomes Emerson's, splitting itself away from tradition, just as his essay looks towards an American metre for the continent. To Emerson 'America is a poem in our eyes; its ample geography dazzles the imagination, and it will not wait long for metres.'[39] As Durand saw the land as a picture, so here it is a poem: the subject alive with its overriding brilliance and prodigality. In 1844 Emerson looked 'in vain' for the poet he sought but his poetics, and their significance *to* the land, are clear: an ideal prose account of the poem in the eye. Thus 'the world is not painted, or adorned, but is from the beginning beautiful.' As art returns to that beauty, unadorned and unpainted, so the poem will return, also, to its radiant base in nature, in America. The land is, once again, a sublime presence which is framed, not by the painter, but by its own boundary: the horizon. Consistently Emerson insists upon the implicit tranquillity and unity of the land as a pristine and dynamic picture: a radiant image of God's divine energy. It is, thus, this picture which has a central meaning to any language truly 'poetic' and adequate to a picturing of the poem in the eye of the American. As Durand sought 'nature', so Emerson advocates a language close to things—to the prose of the land. He wants, as will Pound and William Carlos Williams, contact between word and thing, so that the image exists as the stilled presence of the continent's meaning: an ideal-real account. A healthy poetic language is that which keeps close to the land. Nature in America is a picture and 'offers all her creatures to [the poet] as a picture-language'.[40] Such is its significance that 'the world is a temple, whose walls are covered with emblems, pictures, and commandments of the Deity. . . .' Words, to retain contact with the picture, must return to their original and highest function: not as general or abstract terms but as vivid counters linked directly to facts, to things. Thus 'the poet is the Namer, or language-maker' because 'The etymologist finds the deadest word to have been once a brilliant picture.' Language is here both object and light—once again the radiant image of a sacred America. It is, paradoxically, the clear and bright image for which Bryant looked, but now the prose *is* the poetry. 'Every word was once a poem', that is every fragment and detail, every named object complete as 'art'. A picturesque language 'reattaches things to nature and the whole'. And just as America is a poem in the eye, so 'objects paint their images on the retina of the eye.' Art resigns itself to the real, for the 'condition of true naming, on the poet's part, is his resigning himself to the divine *aura* which breathes through forms . . .'.

Emerson's ideal account is of a language of things seen as stilled energies: a shimmering luminous world where America is both picture and poem. Art, so to speak, becomes artless. In a pictorial sense the Claudian schema gives way to a *plein-air* account which seeks the 'fidelity' of the Dutch school while assenting to the myth of an ideal-real scene. Emerson is critical, for example, of Pope, Johnson and Addison because 'they write as if they had never seen the face of the country but had only read of trees and rivers in books'[41] and, we might add, in paintings. As distinct from such eighteenth-century view-points Carlyle is praised because he is 'a painter in the Dutch style than we have had in literature before. It is terrible—his closeness and fidelity: he copies that which was never seen before.'[42] This celebrates a common but sacred prose, and the land is viewed as a single and continuous picture which art must image. In 'The Adirondacks' (1858), for example, so significantly subtitled 'a *journal*', the 'real' is an endless and all-encompassing stream of pictures. Emerson is literally immersed in a divine typology as 'the sacred mountains drew around' him and he looked upon 'skies of benediction'. As he continues his journey, 'so lofty pictures came and went' in a continuing oneness for 'O world!/ What pictures and what harmonies are thine.'[43]

6

The picture, not the painting, becomes the ideal: a prose-poetic antagonistic at once to aesthetic convention and hierarchies. Thoreau's judgement on the picturesque is symptomatic, for example, of a general rejection of eighteenth-century landscape principles which, in themselves, remained part of a popular aesthetic relationship to the land. Indeed the 'picturesque' is basic to Bryant and Cole, as it is to one aspect of a tourist's eye-view of the continent—witness, say, *The Home Book of the Picturesque* (published in 1852).[44] Thoreau's criticism, in the *Journals*, is aimed primarily at William Gilpin. Thus the 'elegant Gilpin', as he calls him, is 'superficial' and 'goes not below the surface' of things.[45] The degree to which the picturesque depended upon seventeenth- and eighteenth-century landscape painting is thus part of its surface response. Like Ruskin, Thoreau insists on a 'deeper' significance—a penetration into the land held within a factual accounting of its there-ness.

This 'transcendent hyper-realism'[46] is thus rooted in the object, the fact as a luminous detail. The 'essential facts' of *Walden* are all integers within the wider *picture*. Whereas in Church's *New England Scenery* we find a composed (Claudian) *beau ideal*, so in Thoreau's picture the scene is, simply, the seen:

> What is a New England landscape this sunny August day?
> A weather-painted house and barn, with an orchard
> by its side, in the midst of a sandy field surrounded
> by green woods, with a small blue lake on one side. A
> sympathy between the color of the weather-painted
> house and that of the lake and sky.[47]

And he adds that 'The weather-painted house. This is the New England color, homely but fit as that of a toad-stool' (1856). We could not be further from Claude and the picturesque. The landscape is a 'natural' American scene—'homely but fit'. All blends into a single unity, a general 'sympathy' which is further suggested by a natural artistry, for even the house is 'weather-painted' with the purest of New England colours. And just as there is a stress on a 'natural' palette, so there is no obvious frame within which the scene is structured. Indeed, the stress is upon the accurate 'seeing' of clear and particular objects. As Thoreau resists an 'aesthetic' vocabulary, so the elements spread out into a field of meaning—'by', 'in', 'surrounded', 'on' and 'between' connect the particulars into a single dynamic relationship. As this is a found unity, a natural composition, so the basic colours (green, blue, sandy) complete the natural and native picture. If anything, one is reminded here of American folk and naïve art in the way the images exist as both clean pigments and are free of any controlling perspective.[48] Crucially, however, Thoreau is absent—he does not seek to possess the picture but rather to inscribe it onto the page as a found presence. New England is alive—a luminist text which is itself the picture.

And just as Thoreau offers his 'picture', so Whitman too catches his characteristic native scene:

> Through the ample door of the peaceful country barn,
> A sunlit pasture field with cattle and horses feeding,
> And haze and vista, and the far horizon fading away.[49]

This is 'A Farm Picture', as Thoreau's was *a* 'New England landscape'. Amy Lowell called this imagist (and indeed it looks forward to Ezra Pound and William Carlos Williams in its compression and objectivity).[50] We might more correctly insist on how basic to American poetics is the image, the picture. Matthiessen comes close to it (in relation to Whitman) when he suggests that it 'is not fanciful or arbitrary to think of Whitman's poems in relation to the development of open-air painting.'[51] Whitman's open road, and his journeyings intent on the notation—and celebration—of native *stuff* is on a par with *plein-airism* and, for example, the influences of the Dusseldorf and Barbizan schools. Such 'naturalism' is echoed by Millet when he insisted that he 'would paint nothing that was not the result of an impression directly received from Nature, whether in landscape or in figures'[52]; a viewpoint echoed by Whitman when he said that *Leaves of Grass* was 'really only Millet in another form'.[53] But a distinction must be made between landscapes such as 'A Farm Picture' and those reminiscent of Millet which include figures (for example, 'A Paumanok Picture'). Matthiessen's comparison between Whitman ˙and the work of W. S. Mount (1807–68) thus suggests that figures play a central rôle in such genre-like excursions in search of an American vernacular. What we might more properly suggest is that the essence of such picturing seeks the presence of an American ideality: the land as a spiritual condition in which the figure is essentially absent from the scene. Such sublime images exclude human activity and such evidence as there is of human energies (buildings, for example) is given its 'natural' status in the scene. Thus 'A Farm Picture', like Thoreau's 'New England Landscape', is bereft of figures in a way that the work of Mount or George Bingham (1811–79) could never be.

Whitman's poem speaks to calm and silence: to a stillness which is, once again, a picture—the caught image of a native and pure America. The barn offers itself as an exemplary motif of recovered identity—a natural artifact: what Constance Rourke, in discussing Charles Sheeler, called *ur-formen*.[54] The poem is, then, a picture which seeks nothing other than the scene itself. Indeed the extent to which it displaces a painterly or poetic account is further suggested by the way that the 'frame' to the 'picture' is the 'ample' door through which we see the found landscape. As in *Song of Myself* so 'The big doors of the country barn stand open and ready.' Open in both their suggestion of native formal procedures (*pleinairism* and a 'free' poetic line) and their invitation to a 'true' American scene, just as 'ready' infers the potential implicit in the land for there

Whitman will 'behold God in every object'. Thus Whitman's picture-prose account of an ideal America. Nothing is to be 'painted' or made 'poetic' for all is at once picture and poem. In the (uncollected) 'Pictures' each image becomes a picture amidst the picture-poem of America. Thus he sees 'hundred and thousands' of pictures, for, as he moves over the surface of his sacred land, so 'every rod of land or sea affords me, as long as I live, inimitable pictures.'[55]

In Whitman's poetry the insistence is on a radical version of a picturesque language in which 'America' is the constant and compulsive subject. The conventions and values of, for example, Gilpin's picturesque dissolve in favour of a prosaic (but ideal) imaging which is itself the lifting of the 'actual' into the text. The *beau ideal* of a native American art is, thus, the literal configuration of the land made vital by the myth of its sacred presence. In 'spontaneous me' the immediate response ('without check', with 'original energy') is given credence in relation to a world vivid, alive, and magical:

> The hillsides whiten'd with blossoms of the mountain ash,
> The same late in autumn, the hues of red, yellow, drab,
>   purple, and light and dark green,
> The rich coverlet of the grass, animals and birds, the private
>   untrimm'd bank, the primitive apples, the
>   pebble-stones,
> Beautiful dripping fragments, the negligent list of one after
>   another as I happen to call them to me or think of
>   them,
> The real poems, (what we call poems being merely
>   pictures,)[56]

The 'real poems' are, then, 'beautiful dripping fragments'— images, particles of Whitman's divine world to which his words will (re)attach themselves. Thus so the United States remains 'essentially the greatest poem' with its 'veins' full of 'poetic stuff'. Here there is no imposed principle of order and meaning. As in 'Song of the Open Road' what we have is 'The earth expanding right hand and left hand,/ The picture alive, every part in its best light'. Part of the richness of the 'scene' is the intensity and range of colour. Indeed, there is a sense in which Whitman is so insistent on reaching the 'real poems' that he is, literally, squeezing the words onto the page in the

213

way he would with tubes of oil paint—a celebration of colour and the this-ness of the artist's medium. Such 'picturing', however, is a clue to the way in which this world of 'beautiful dripping fragments' is seen, for, as Richardson tells us, 'The year 1856 is a landmark in the history of the painter's medium.'[57] A landmark because at that point intense colours were made available to the landscape painter: crimson, deep yellows and blues, for example. Here Whitman adopts such a range with its sheer visual presence: hues of red, yellow, purple and green. This, indeed, like Thoreau's 'New England landscape', is precisely the clear and bright image for which Bryant looked. But whereas the first Hudson River School painters 'limited their palette to dull greens and browns within a fairly restricted range',[58] the 1850s in particular, and most obviously the *luminists*, saw a vivid and fresh America placed upon the canvas. That is *limned*: illuminated. The colour difference underlines the radical revision in the movement from painting to picture. Whereas, in *The Home Book of the Picturesque* Cooper spoke of his preference for 'sober and sombre colors in landscape'[59] as 'aids' to the picturesque (and his own allegiance to Cole and Bryant), so luminism, as one central native art, broke into America as the live picture. The soft and diffused light of Claude gives way to the clean light of an America where 'atmosphere was as metaphysical as it was physical'.[60]

And indeed it is to luminism we should look for the pictorial equivalent of a sacred 'prose' account of the kind Neal wanted. Luminism pictures rather than paints American landscapes. The quietism so characteristic of its viewpoint is at once an attempt to 'trace' the colour silence of a sublime American space and condition: a poetry of the divine fact and fragment. In Fitz Hugh Lane (1804–65), Martin Johnson Heade (1819–1904) and John Frederick Kensett (1816–72), for example, there is a determined absence of literary and pictorial reference. Whether it is marsh, beach, barn, or rock, there is a consistent concern to establish as direct a relationship between 'reader' and the original 'picture' as possible. The art, as such, transcends itself in favour of the object. Luminism seeks to be 'a powerful penetration of the real. It is not a poetry imposed, through certain conventions of the picturesque, *upon* nature.'[61]

Significantly, too, these artists achieve this ideal American presence in Eastern, not Western, locales. While their sacred typologies gather credence from Western myth, they avoid any movement into such rhetoric (as we find, for example, in the grandiose scenes of Albert Bierstadt) in favour of the less obviously dramatic and extreme Eastern landscapes. As with Thoreau and Whittier (and Whitman) the authentic locales are in the East—lake, coast, mountain, river and farm. Their pictures redefine and refine the meaning of the continent by returning to its first recorded scenes. Thus, despite the enormous symbolic presence of the West in the nineteenth century, the East remains an ideal habitat for the authentic picture of America. We should not be surprised then that, in *Specimen Days*,[62] after writing on the death and funeral of William Cullen Bryant, Whitman enters upon a 'Jaunt up the Hudson'. He does so as a tourist (with the Hudson as a tourist spot) and as a viewer and picturer of the scene. Thus he renews and rewrites its meaning—returning to an almost too obvious scenery to suggest the distinctiveness of his eye-view. For if the Hudson suggests (and recalls) Thomas Cole, so it also suggests Bryant. Indeed Bryant's 'A Scene on the Banks of the Hudson'[63] is a poetic equivalent of Cole's paintings. As distinct from such precursors Whitman will 'make up the scene' through the endless objects (and vista) before him. He celebrates 'the constantly changing but ever beautiful panorama' a (pan—all, horama—sight); Whitman, as it were, bids 'to see all' and, in so doing, to complete the picture of America.

Picture, then, effaces painting and, in the poem, reveals how the term suggests part of a radical and insistent revision of a landscape poetic basic to the American vision. Indeed its efficacy as an aspect of an American aesthetic is further underlined by the continuing relationship between poetry and the visual arts in the twentieth century and how, especially, photography was identified as both a modern and American medium. The photograph was seen as the extreme of painting and, in its similarities to the picture, expressed a further dimension of an aesthetic appropriate to the image of the land. Just as in 'Song of the Exposition' Whitman declared how 'The photograph . . . shall be created before you',[64] so Samuel Morse insisted how the daguerrotype was 'undoubtedly destined to produce a great *revolution* in art . . .'.[65]: a revolution which was extended by the poetry of Ezra Pound and William Carlos Williams who in their concern with the visual continued the attempt of the American poet to find a language that would make contact with a divine and objective world. It is what, significantly, Williams applauded in the work of Alfred Stieglitz. Stieglitz, says Williams, saw that 'The photographic camera and what it could do were peculiarly well-suited to a place where the immediate and the actual were under official neglect.'[66] As Waldo Frank suggested, Stieglitz achieved what the American poet wanted—an image of America in which 'vision and reality are one'.[67]

NOTES

1. See *A Hugh Henry Brackenbridge Reader*, ed. Daniel Marder (Pittsburgh, 1970), pp. 56–60.
2. I am thinking, for example, of the most obvious: *Paradise Lost, L'Allegro*, 'Windsor Forest', and *Cooper's Hill*.
3. Howard Mumford Jones, *O Strange New World!* (New York, 1952), p. 353.
4. The literature, of course, is massive and varied. In relation to this essay the most obvious critical texts would be: Tony Tanner, *The Reign of Wonder* (Cambridge, 1965); Henry Savage, Jr., *Discovering America* (New York, 1979); Roderick Nash, *Wilderness and the American Mind* (New Haven & London, 1967); Henry Nash Smith, *Virgin Land* (New York, 1950); Edwin Fussel, *Frontier: American Literature and the American* (Princetown, 1965); and Leo Marx, *The Machine in the Garden* (New York, 1964).
5. The West, so to speak, as a *direction* rather than a place, although, clearly, prose accounts and journals are central. One is, however, reminded of Twain's jibe in *Roughing It* where, as his narrator moves further and further west, so 'The poetry was all in the anticipation—there is none in the reality' (Ch. XVIII).
6. See Sacvan Bercovitch, *The Puritan Origins of the American Self* (New Haven and London, 1975).
7. Barbara Novak, *Nature and Culture, American Landscape and Painting 1825–1875* (New York, 1980), p. 31. This, along with her earlier *American Painting in the Nineteenth Century* (New York, 1969), remain basic and excellent texts for the period.

8. Ibid., p. 33.

9. *American Art 1700–1900: Sources and Documents*, ed. John W. McCourbrey (Englewood Cliffs, N.J., 1965), p. 145.

10. See C. R. Leslie, *Memoirs of the Life of John Constable* (London, 1951 edition), p. 15.

11. *American Art*, p. 146. For a detailed discussion of Wilson and Claude see David Solkin's *Richard Wilson* (Tate Gallery, 1982).

12. Barbara Novak has discussed the Claudian and Dutch influences on American art in the nineteenth century in her 'Influences and Affinities: The Interplay between America and Europe in Landscape Painting before 1860' in *The Shaping of Art and Architecture in Nineteenth-century America* (Metropolitan Museum of Art, 1972), pp. 27–35.

13. Sir Joshua Reynolds, *Discourses on Art* (New Haven & London, 1959), ed. Robert R. Wark, p. 70. 'Discourse IV'. Claude's pictures 'are a composition of the various draughts which he had previously made from various beautiful scenes and prospects' (p. 70).

14. William Gilpin, *On Picturesque Beauty* (1792).

15. G. L. Huddleston, 'Topographical Poetry in the Early National Period', *American Literature* 38 (1966–67), 321.

16. *Picturesque America or The Land We Live In*, ed. William Cullen Bryant (New York, 1872, two volumes), Vol. 1, preface.

17. Leo Marx, *The Machine in the Garden*, p. 141.

18. *American Art*, pp. 133 and 135.

19. *Nature and Culture*, p. 185.

20. *The Poetical Works of William Cullan Bryant*, ed. Parke Godwin (New York, 1883; 1967 edition), Vol. 2, p. 136.

21. Ibid., Vol. 1, p. 219.

22. See *American Art*, pp. 98–109.

23. Louis L. Noble, *The Life and Works of Thomas Cole*, ed. Elliot S. Vesell (Cambridge, Mass., 1964), p. 212.

24. The circle, like the horizon, is a basic figure for both Thoreau and Emerson.

25. See Edmund Burke, *A Philosophical Enquiry . . . Into the Sublime and the Beautiful* (1757), especially Part II, Section IV (Obscurity) and Part V, Sections I–VII (on Words).

26. Noble, p. 52.

27. See the *Discourses*, pp. 44, 45.

28. Noble, p. 210.

29. Ibid., p. 185.

30. Novak, *American Painting*, p. 33.

31. J. T. Solby and D. C. Miller, *Romantic Painting in America* (New York, 1943), p. 16.

32. Cooper said of Cole's 'The Course of Empire' that it was 'a great epic poem' and commented on his 'Poetic feeling'. See Noble, p. 166–67. For detailed discussions of the relationship between Cole and Bryant and painting and poetry see Donald A. Ringe, *The Pictorial Mode* (Lexington, 1971) as well as his 'Painting as Poem in the Hudson River Aesthetic', *American Quarterly* 12 (Spring 1960), 71–83. James T. Callow, *Kindred*

Spirits, Knickerbocker Writers and Artists, 1807–1855 (Chapel Hill, 1967), and C. L. Sanford, 'The Concept of the Sublime in the Works of Thomas Cole and William Cullen Bryant' in *American Literature*, XXVIII (1957), 434–48, are of related interest.

33. David C. Huntingdon, *The Landscapes of Frederick Edwin Church: Vision of an American Era* (New York, 1966), p. 35.

34. Ibid., p. 36.

35. *The Poetical Works of John Greenleaf Whittier* (Oxford, 1919), p. 160.

36. Emerson, *Poems* (New York, 1884), p. 282.

37. *American Art*, p. 110.

38. Ibid., p. 113.

39. See Emerson's essay *The Poet*.

40. See *The Poet* and the quintessential *Nature*.

41. 29 July 1837. *Selected Writings* (New York, 1965), p. 69.

42. 11 August 1851. Ibid., p. 152.

43. *Poems*, pp. 159–70.

44. *The Home Book of the Picturesque or American Scenery, Art, and Literature*, with introduction by Motley F. Deakin (Gainesville, 1967 edition).

45. *The Journal of Henry D. Thoreau*, ed. B. Torrey and F. H. Allen (New York, 1906), Vol. VI, pp. 57, 59.

46. The phrase is Novak's.

47. *The Journal*, Vol. IX, p. 24.

48. Similar, in one sense, to the response of William Carlos Williams to the exhibition of American primitives in 1954. *See* 'Painting in the American Grain' in *A Recognizable Image*, ed. Bram Dijkstra (New York, 1978), pp. 238–45.

49. *Leaves of Grass* (Reader's Edition, New York, 1965), p. 274.

50. *Walt Whitman* (Penguin Critical Anthology), ed. Francis Murphy (Harmondsworth, 1969), p. 220. 'And this is the very essence of that type of poetry which we have learnt to call Imagistic.'

51. F. O. Matthiessen, *American Renaissance* (New York, 1941; 1968 edition), p. 599. Matthiessen makes an important argument for the *Dutch* influence on American art.

52. Jean Francois Millet, letter to Alfred Sensier (1850). See *A Documentary History of Art*, Vol. III, selected and edited by E. G. Holt (Garden City, 1966), p. 355.

53. Quoted by Matthiessen, p. 602.

54. See Constance Rourke, *Charles Sheeler: Artist in the American Tradition* (New York, 1938).

55. See 'Pictures' in the *Reader's Edition* of *Leaves*, pp. 642–43, and the notes on this uncollected poem.

56. *Leaves of Grass*, p. 103.

57. E. P. Richardson, *Painting in America* (New York, 1965), p. 219.

58. John I. H. Baur, 'Trends in American Painting, 1815–1865' in *M. and M. Karolik: Collection of American Paintings, 1815–1865* (Cambridge, Mass. 1949), p. lii.

59. *The Home Book of the Picturesque*, p. 58.

60. *American Painting of the Nineteenth Century*, p. 91.

61. *American Light, The Luminist Movement 1850–1875*, ed. John Wilmerding (Washington, 1980), p. 25.
62. See 'Death of William Cullan Bryant' and 'Jaunt Up the Hudson' in *Specimen Days*.
63. *Poetical Works*, Vol. 1, p. 193.
64. *Leaves of Grass* (Reader's Edition), p. 200.
65. Quoted in John Wilmerding *American Art* (Harmondsworth, 1976), p. 71.
66. 'The American Background', see in William Carlos Williams, *Selected Essays* (New York, 1969), p. 160. See also *A Recognisable Image: William Carlos Williams on Art and Artists*, edited and introduction by Brian Dijkstra (New York, 1978). See also Albert Gelpi's essay in *American Light*: 'White Light in the Wilderness', pp. 291–311.
67. *America and Alfred Stieglitz: A Collective Portrait*, ed. Frank, Mumford, Norman, Rosenfeld and Rigg (New York, 1934), p. 109. The whole volume is, of course, central to the continuing debate of an American aesthetic.

Notes on Contributors

GRAHAM CLARKE teaches English and American literature at the University of Kent at Canterbury. He is the author of recent articles on Victorian fiction, Hawthorne and Charles Olson.

ROBERT VON HALLBERG teaches at the University of Chicago and is the author of *Charles Olson: The Scholar's Art* and *American Poetry and Culture, 1945–1980*.

BRIAN HARDING teaches American literature at the University of Birmingham and is the author of *American Literature in Context, 11, 1830–1865* (1982).

JAMES H. JUSTUS, Professor of English at Indiana University, has written on such American authors as Charles Brockden Brown, Hawthorne, Hemingway, Faulkner and other twentieth-century writers of the American South. His most recent book is *The Achievement of Robert Penn Warren* (1981).

MARK KINKEAD-WEEKES is Professor of English at the University of Kent at Canterbury. He is the author (with Ian Gregor) of *William Golding: A Critical Study* (1967, rev. edn., 1983), *Samuel Richardson, Dramatic Novelist* (1973) and has written extensively on African literature and aspects of the English novel.

A. ROBERT LEE teaches American literature at the University of Kent at Canterbury. He is editor of the Everyman *Moby-Dick* (1975) and four previous collections in the Critical Studies series. Among other recent publications is his B.A.A.S. pamphlet *Black American Fiction Since Richard Wright* (1983) and essays on Chester Himes, Richard Wright, Mark Twain, Emily Dickinson and Robert Penn Warren.

ERIC MOTTRAM is Professor of English and American Literature at King's College in the University of London. He has published books on Kenneth Rexroth, Paul Bowles, Allen Ginsberg, William Burroughs and others, and, with Malcolm Bradbury, edited and contributed to the *Penguin Companion to American Literature*. His last three books of poetry were *Elegies*, *A Book of Herne* and *Interrogation Rooms*.

JIM PHILIP was educated at Cambridge and Sussex Universities. He has also been a Visiting Fellow at the University of Pennsylvania. He lectures at Essex University on modern English and American literature, and has published extensively in both these fields.

DAVID SEED teaches American literature at the University of Liverpool. Among his recent publications are articles on Henry James, Thomas Pynchon, I. B. Singer, James Fenimore Cooper, Henry Roth and Ernest Hemingway.

Index

Index

Index

Moore, Thomas, 90
Morse, Samuel, 215
Mumford, Lewis, 119

Neale, John, 197, 202
Niebuhr, Barthold, 137
North American Review, 87

Odyssey, The, 120
Olson, Charles, 10, 98, 135; 'Maximus, at Tyre and at Boston', 19; 'The Kingfishers', 14
Owen, Wilfred, 134

Peabody, Elizabeth, 167
Perse, Saint-Jean, 28
Plath, Sylvia, 10
Poe, Edgar Allan, 9, 10, 11, 16, 80–99, 146, 151; *Eureka*, 11, 85; *Politian*, 87, 96–7; 'The Philosophy of Composition', 11, 85, 94, 135; 'The Poetic Principle', 11; 'The Raven', 94; *Tamerlane and Other Poems*, 82
Pope, Alexander, 195, 209
Pound, Ezra, 8, 9, 98, 135, 209, 211, 216; *Guide to Kulchur*, 83
Poussin, Nicholas, 199, 204
Proclus: *On the Theology of Plato*, 105

Quixote, Don, 120

Reynolds, Sir Joshua, 198, 202, 205, 206; *Discourses*, 199, 204
Richards, I. A., 89
Rosenberg, Isaac, 134
Ruskin, John: *Modern Painters*, 207

Sandburg, Carl, 10, 135, 146
Sartre, Jean-Paul, 14; *Critique de la Raison Dialectique*, 14; *L'Etre et le Néant*, 14
Santayana, George, 115
Sexton, Anne, 10
Shakespeare, William, 86, 169; *Coriolanus*, 20
Southern Literary Messenger, 83
Spenser, Edmund, 86; *The Faerie Queen*, 135
Stevens, Wallace, 9, 32, 135; 'Asides on an Oboe', 32
Stieglitz, Alfred, 216

Taylor, Edward, 65
Taylor, Thomas: translations, 104–5, 107
Tennyson, Alfred Lord, 9, 182; 'In Memoriam', 135, 186, 188; 'Locksley Hall', 182; 'Maud', 182; 'The Charge of the Light Brigade', 182; 'Ulysses', 182
Thoreau, Henry David, 9, 13, 35, 119, 166, 205, 210–11, 215; 'New England Landscape', 211, 212, 214; *Walden*, 20, 33, 210
Transcendentalism, 8, 11, 65, 152, 166, 167, 168, 186
Traubel, Horace, 39
Trilling, Lionel, 34
Tuckerman, Frederick Goddard, 11, 12, 166, 167, 168, 179–91; 'A Sample of Coffee Beans', 182; 'A Soul that out of Nature's Deep', 187; 'Elidore', 182; 'Mark Atherton', 182; 'Rhotruda', 182; *Sonnets, First, Second, Third and Fourth Series*, 180–91; 'The Cricket', 186

Very, Jones, 11, 12, 166, 167–79, 180, 183; 'Behold He Is at Hand That Doth Betray Me', 173; 'Enoch', 174; 'Epistle on Miracles', 176; 'Nature', 169; 'The Branch', 177; 'The Columbine', 168; 'The Flood', 171; 'The Guest', 177; 'The Holy of Holies', 176; 'The Journey', 175; 'The Narrow Way', 171; 'The Old Road', 175; 'The Priest', 172; 'The Puritans', 171–72; 'The Sabbath', 171; 'The Snow-Drop', 168; 'The Song', 168; 'The Wind-Flower', 168; 'The Voice of God', 174–75; 'The Voice that speaks when thou art in thy tomb', 174; 'There is no voice but that which speaks in Thee', 174; 'To the Fossil Flower', 168; 'To the Humming-Bird', 168; 'To the Unborn', 171

Weaver, Raymond, 119
Whitehead, Alfred: *Process and Reality*, 34
Whitman, Walt, 8, 9, 10, 11, 13–42, 43–60, 119, 147, 173, 196, 205, 208, 212–13; 'A Backward Glance O'er Travel'd Roads', 32; 'A Broadway Pageant', 39; 'A Farm Picture', 210; 'Crossing Brooklyn Ferry', 11, 31, 44, 56–9; *Death-Bed Edition*, 9; *Drum-Taps*, 37, 125, 134; 'Great Are the Myths', 19; 'Hours Continuing Long. . . .', 37; 'I Sing the Body Electric', 29; 'Jaunt up the Hudson', 215; *Leaves of Grass*, 9, 21, 29, 32, 33, 44, 135, 207; 'Long, Too Long America', 38; 'Me Imperturbe', 36; 'Out of the Cradle endlessly rocking', 11, 36, 51–6; 'Passage to India', 25; 'Pioneers! O Pioneers', 38; 'Poem of the Child that went Forth. . . .', 34; 'Reply! Reply!', 23; 'Song of Myself', 9, 28, 29, 44, 194, 197, 212; 'Song of the Exposition', 215; 'Song of the Open Road', 213; 'The Sleepers', 28; 'Visages', 21; 'When Lilacs last in the dooryard bloom'd', 11, 44–51; 'Years of the Unperform'd', 38; 'Years of the Modern', 38
Whittier, James Greenleaf, 10, 12, 29, 148, 157–58, 215; 'Anniversary Poem', 134; 'Barbara Frietchie', 134; 'Ichabod', 157; 'Massachusetts to Virginia', 157; 'Maud Muller', 157; 'My Playmate', 157; 'Snow-Bound', 158; 'Telling the Bees', 157, 158; 'The Barefoot Boy', 157; 'The Homestead', 157; 'To My Sister', 158
Wigglesworth, Michael: *The Day of Doom*, 171
Wilbur, Richard, 81
Wilson, Edmund, 88
Wimsatt, William K., 88
Winters, Yvor, 85, 88, 98, 177, 189, 191
Wittgenstein, Ludwig, 20
Wordsworth, William, 86, 169, 202; *The Excursion*, 170; *The Prelude*, 135

Yeats, William Butler, 134

Zukovsky, Louis, 135